IMAGES
of America

DORMONT

On the cover: Those standing at the intersection at the 2900 block of West Liberty and Mississippi Avenues in the 1930s would have seen this sight while looking toward Pittsburgh. The dome, center left, was on Heinrich's Pharmacy at the corner of West Liberty and Potomac Avenues, the borough's main business intersection. (Courtesy of Dormont Historical Society.)

IMAGES
of America

DORMONT

Dormont Historical Society

ARCADIA
PUBLISHING

ISBN 978-0-7385-6301-5

Published by Arcadia Publishing
Charleston, South Carolina

Printed in the United States of America

Library of Congress Catalog Card Number: 2008924459

For all general information contact Arcadia Publishing at:
Telephone 843-853-2070
Fax 843-853-0044
E-mail sales@arcadiapublishing.com
For customer service and orders:
Toll-Free 1-888-313-2665

Visit us on the Internet at www.arcadiapublishing.com

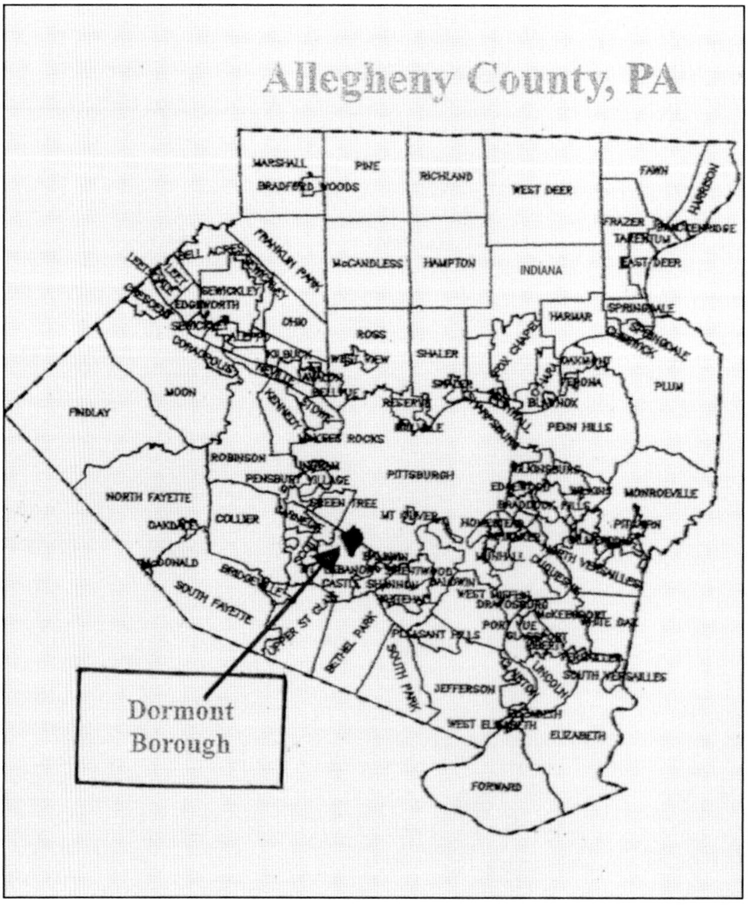

The location of Dormont, an independent borough only 0.77 of a mile square, is shown in relation to its neighbors and to its place in Allegheny County, western Pennsylvania.

CONTENTS

ACKNOWLEDGMENTS

This book is dedicated to all who have supported the Dormont Historical Society since its incorporation in 1999 through memberships and donations of memorabilia, memories, monetary gifts, and countless hours of volunteering. Without you, we would not be able to preserve the history of our borough.

Special thanks is extended to those borough officials who could see that, by providing a home for our large collections, they were helping to preserve Dormont's history in such a way as to have it be accessible to all interested persons now and in the years to come.

We of the Dormont Historical Society hope that the pages of this book will show how each aspect of life here has been enhanced by the contributions of those who have given of their time, talents, and energy to make Dormont a place where we have been happy and proud to live. Unless otherwise noted, the information and pictures in this book have been taken from our collections. Where there were discrepancies, the most reliable sources were used.

INTRODUCTION

The area that is now Dormont borough was originally claimed by the Delaware and Shawnee Indians until the Six Nations, or Iroquois Confederation, assumed jurisdiction of the area. In 1768, the territory was part of the transaction in which Fort Stanwix was purchased from the Six Nations and parcels, or patents, of land could be bought by the early settlers.

After being part of Cumberland County, in 1771 the area became part of Pitt Township, Bedford County. Two years later, Pitt Township was made part of Westmoreland County, and in 1781, at the settlement of the Pennsylvania-Virginia boundary dispute, the area was designated to be part of Penn Township in Washington County. It was 1788 before the area was declared to be in St. Clair Township, Allegheny County.

The borough was formed from parts of Scott, Union, and Mount Lebanon Townships in 1909, 1915, and 1921. The resulting area covered eight plans of lots carved out of Espy, Anderson, and Fetterman farms. Residents wanted to use the name Mount Lebanon for their new area. However, settlers to the south, forming their own township, had rights to that name because a post office known as Mount Lebanon had been established in 1855. The South Hills Board of Trade accepted a coined name derived from the French *mont d'or*, or "mountain of gold," for the new borough.

Although the area was designated as a borough in March 1909, it was not officially organized until May 3, 1909, when Hugh M. Stilley was elected president of council and other officials were selected and committees appointed. Final letters of incorporation were granted by the courts in October 1909. Dormont was the first outlying municipality in the South Hills of Pittsburgh to be incorporated by that year.

The intention had been to join the City of Pittsburgh later, as neighboring territories known as West Liberty, Beechview, and Brookline had done. The leaders of the borough movement, 150 freeholders, contended that they were not opposed to annexation to the City of Pittsburgh, but they wished to see the community have the benefits of certain improvements instead of turning all their tax collections over to the city to be spent elsewhere. They wanted that tax money used locally for boardwalks, the paving of a few streets, and the erection of streetlights. After many heated discussions, that group prevailed, keeping the borough independent. As early as July 1909, a program for the grading, paving, and curbing of all streets was begun. At the first election, F. G. Brown was elected burgess by a majority of the 165 votes cast.

For several years after the organization, the building of homes was the most active in the history of any newly formed municipality in western Pennsylvania. Within a few years, available vacant property within the limits of the borough was substantially used for residential dwellings.

When Potomac Avenue was widened and paved in 1912, its name was changed from Banksville Road. Early on, names of most of the other streets were changed also. As of now, no record has been found telling exactly why most of the new names were chosen.

Pittsburgh Railways extending its trolley service to Potomac Avenue in 1913, and adding regular service in 1914 made the borough attractive to those looking for homes. When access to the city of Pittsburgh became easy with the opening of the Liberty Tunnels in 1924 and the building of the Liberty Bridge in 1928, the population of the borough experienced a 478 percent growth within the next decade.

Through the years, Dormont's schools advanced from the wooden Snyder Avenue one built in 1905 to the modern Dormont Elementary School, which opened at the intersection of Annapolis and Grandin Avenues in 1996. Between those years, Hillsdale School, Kelton Grade School, and Dormont High School had been built to meet the needs of the growing population. A high school was built in 1922 where the new elementary school would be erected. In 1964, the school districts of Dormont, Castle Shannon, and Green Tree were consolidated to form Keystone Oaks School District. After a high school was built, Dormont High School was used as a middle school before it was closed and razed in 1996.

Some history has come from memories and thus could not be included in the following pages. Those memories, too, are part of the borough's history, as the following examples show. Chief Albert Ruehling used to ride his horse in local parades. Hamburgers used to cost 5¢ at the Brass Rail on West Liberty Avenue. A house was moved from the corner of Potomac and Broadway Avenues to the corner of Potomac and Voelkel Avenues so that the land between those blocks could be developed commercially. There were tennis courts where the Hollywood Theater is. For a dime, a person could go to the Delton Theater and sit through two screenings. Hopscotch, hide-and-seek, and Run, Sheep, Run were some of the games children played outside. People went to the pool for hours—swimming, playing cards, or just talking. An A&P store used to be where George the Tailor has been, and a confectionery where Fibber McKee's was. In the 1920s, men would go to the news store on Potomac Avenue to watch the baseball scores being posted on a bulletin board as they were received by telegraph. Firemen used to have water battles at the intersection of Broadway and Potomac Avenues. An early July 4 celebration was held on a vacant lot at the corner of Potomac and Glenmore Avenues.

Like other communities, Dormont has changed during the years. However, its residents and amenities have kept it a fine place to live and, hopefully, will continue to do so through another 100 years.

One

Scenes

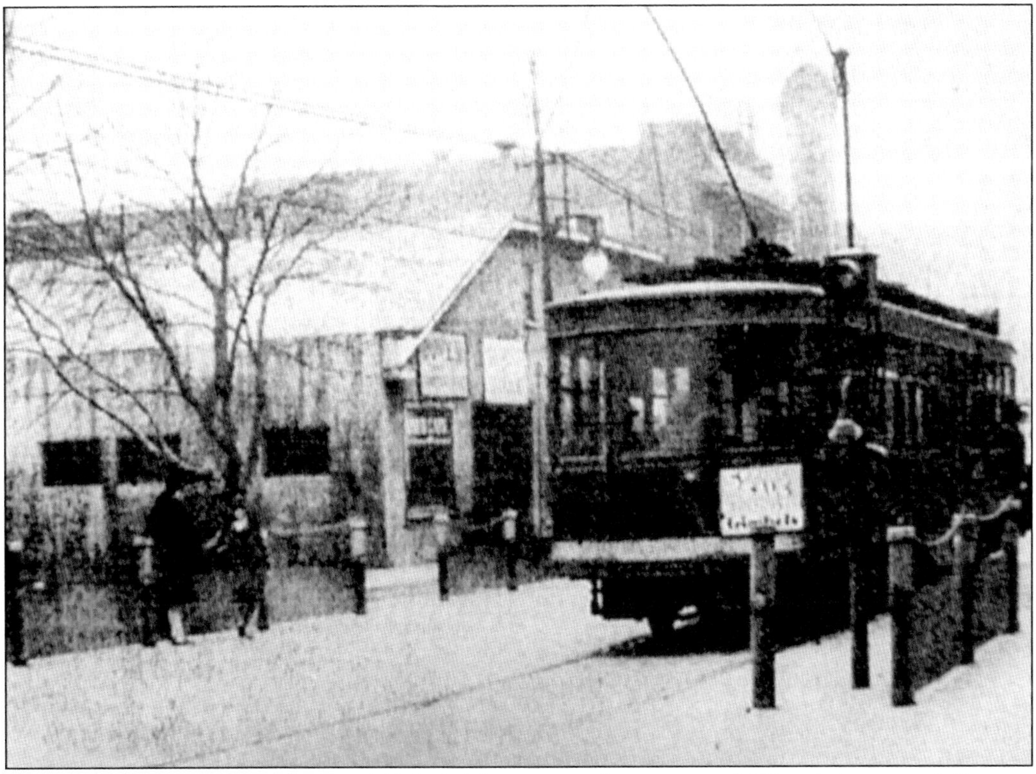

Early trolleys stopped in front of Hahn's Nursery at the corner of West Liberty and Pioneer Avenues. Next to the streetcar tracks, one of the safety zones is evident. These were places for riders to stand while waiting to get onto the trolleys or until it was safe to cross to the sidewalk after having gotten off. Sometimes they were concrete platforms.

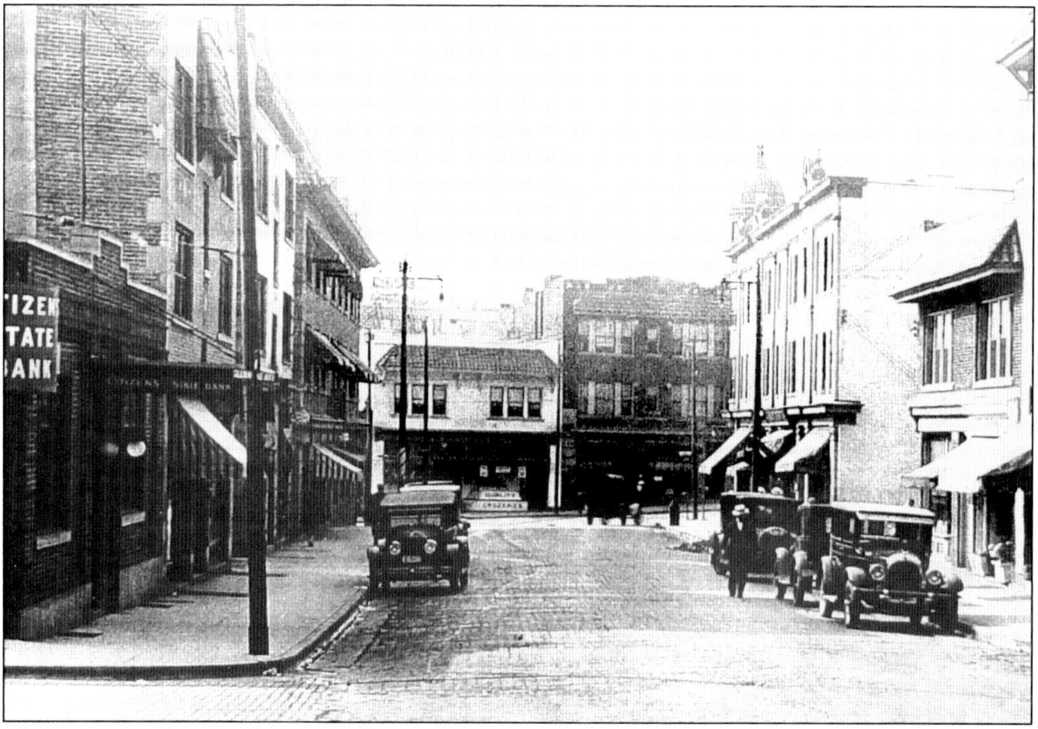

This picture, taken in the 1930s, shows the same intersection as the picture on the cover of this book. It was taken looking down Potomac Avenue toward West Liberty Avenue from Glenmore Avenue. Many of the borough's earliest businesses were located in the block.

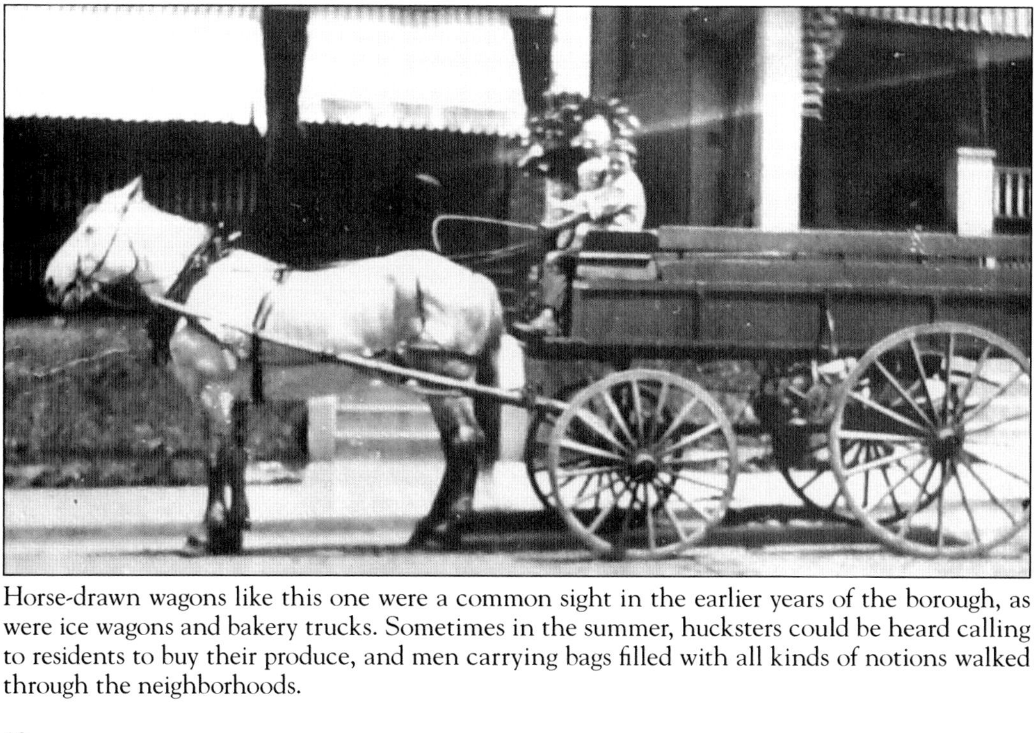

Horse-drawn wagons like this one were a common sight in the earlier years of the borough, as were ice wagons and bakery trucks. Sometimes in the summer, hucksters could be heard calling to residents to buy their produce, and men carrying bags filled with all kinds of notions walked through the neighborhoods.

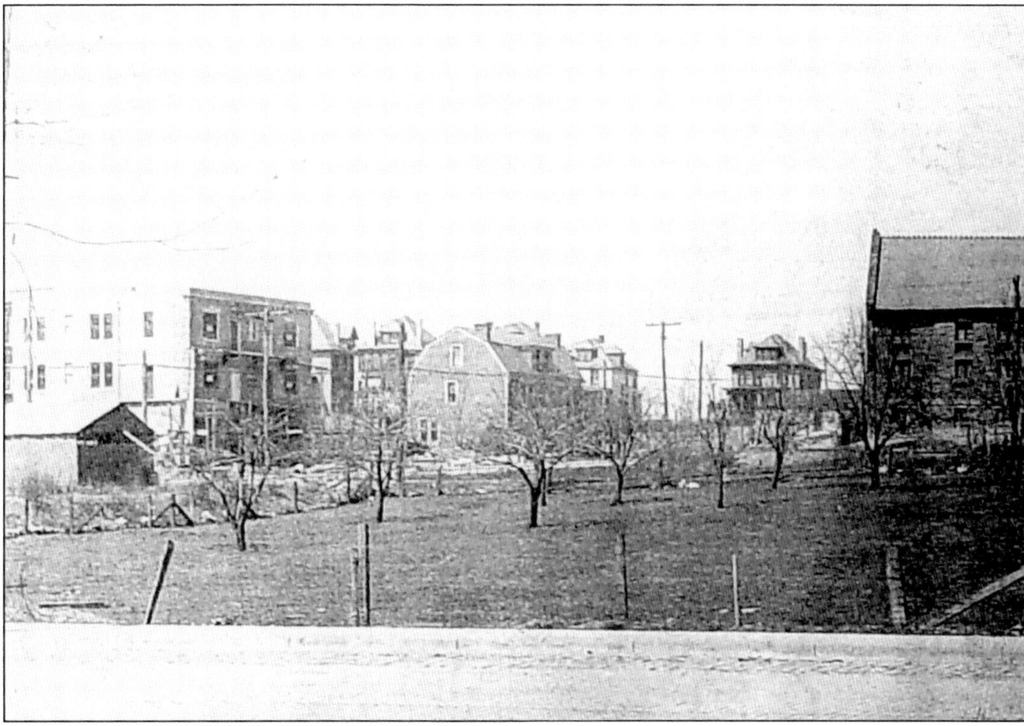

The Dormont Masonic Hall would soon be erected early in the second decade of the 20th century on this vacant lot near the intersection of West Liberty and Potomac Avenues, which is to the left. The structure in the distant right is the original brownstone Dormont Presbyterian Church built in 1909.

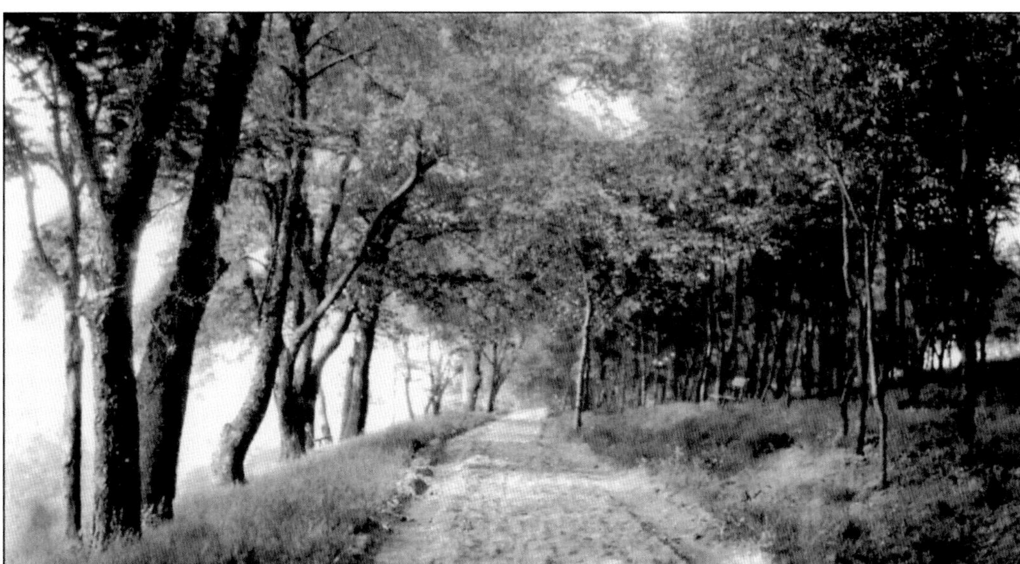

Pittsburgh Southern, a narrow-gauge railroad, operated between the West End and Washington, Pennsylvania, from 1877 until 1884. According to records, it crossed this tip of Dormont Park near Memorial Drive.

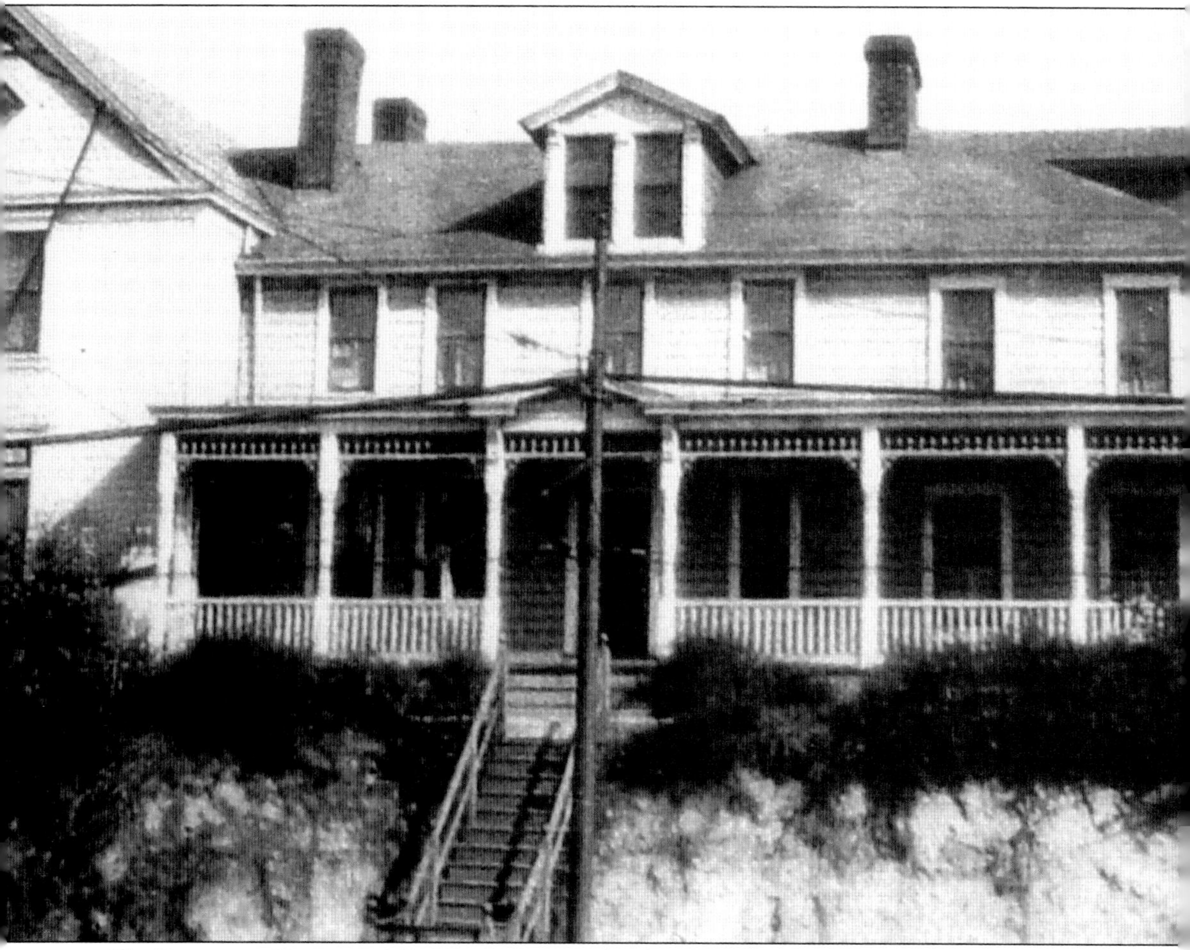

The Fetterman Homestead, Dormont's pioneer landmark, which sat back on West Liberty Avenue, was bounded by Wisconsin and Mississippi Avenues. Built by George and Hannah Fetterman, on land her father bought for 23¢ an acre in 1788, the original house had but two rooms. As generations of the family resided there through the years, they added to the house until there were 30 rooms, as shown here. In the 1900s, the house and 76 acres were sold and the acreage laid out in lots. The house was demolished in 1940 for the building of Dormont Village.

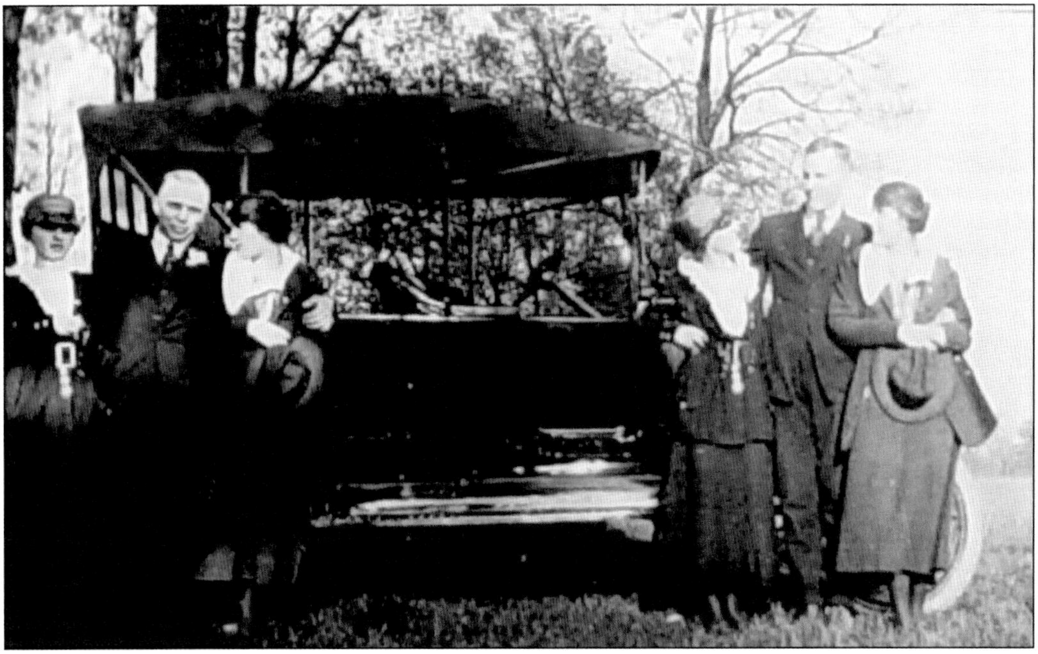

Members of the Fetterman family are standing by their new touring car.

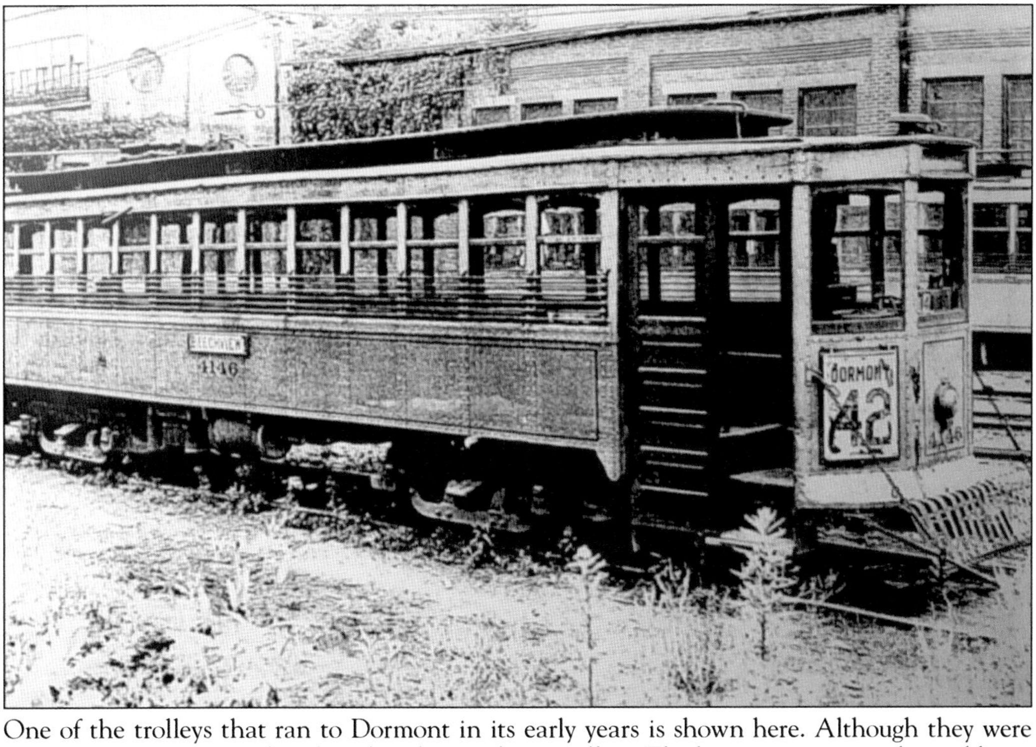

One of the trolleys that ran to Dormont in its early years is shown here. Although they were really orange, most people referred to them as being yellow. The heating system in these old cars was beneath the seats, which could mean very hot legs for those who were lucky enough to get seats in the winter.

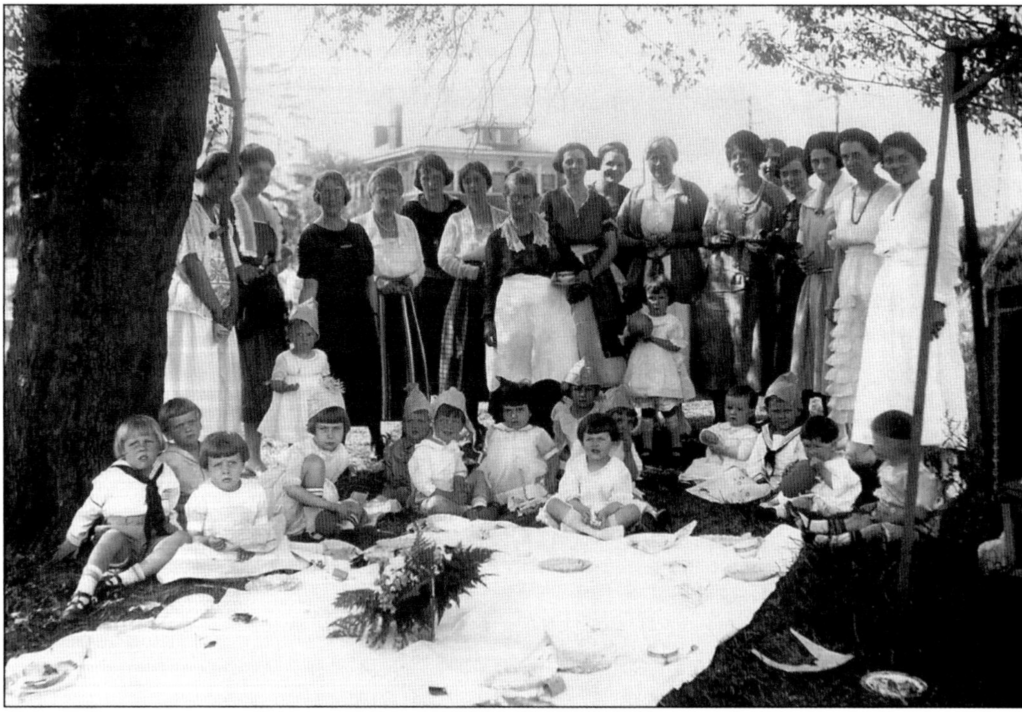

Grace Best, wife of burgess William Best, attended a picnic at the corner of West Liberty and Pioneer Avenues in the early 1920s. She is the sixth person from the left in the back row.

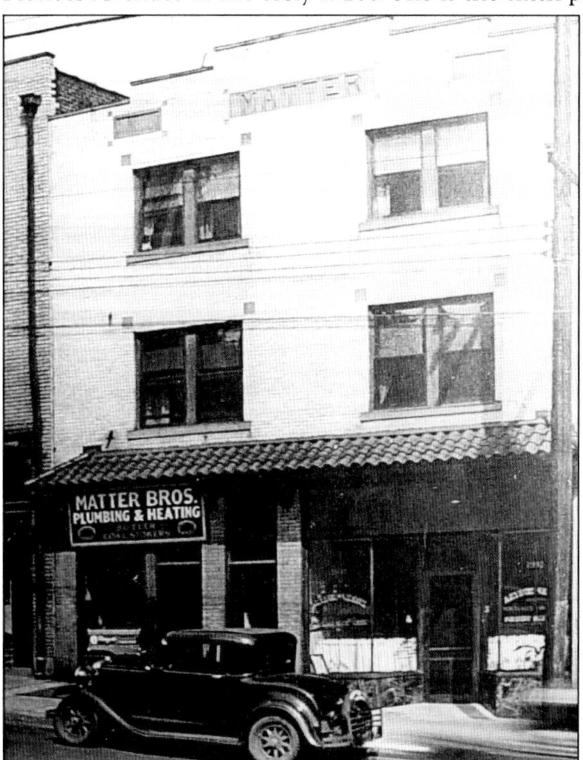

No. 2932–2934 West Liberty Avenue was the location of Matter Brothers Plumbing and Heating from 1926 to 1961.

This handsome World War I memorial stood in front of the borough building on West Liberty Avenue.

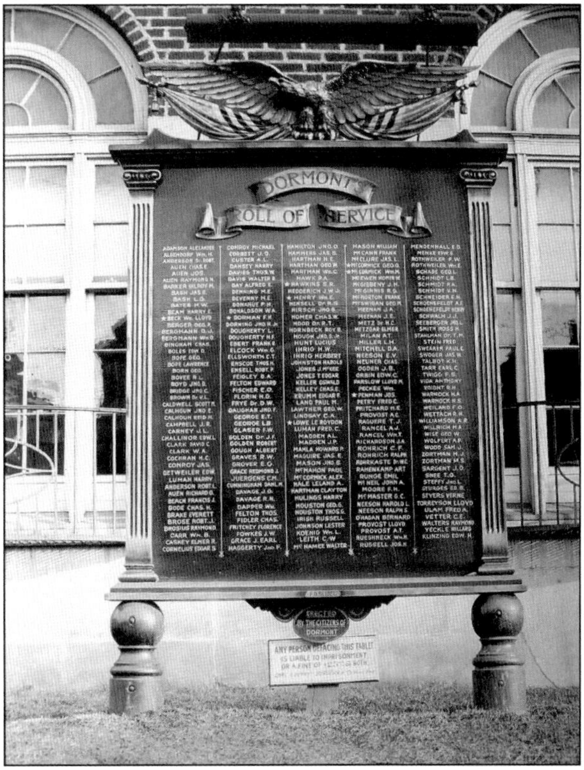

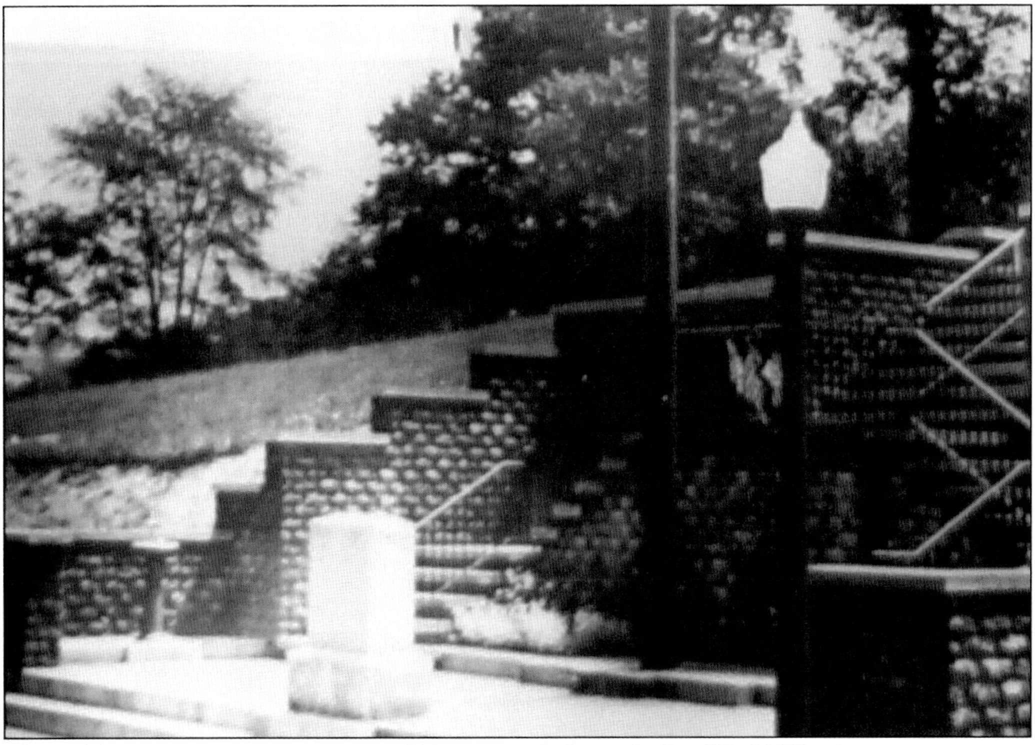

The Soldiers Monument on Memorial Drive was dedicated after World War I.

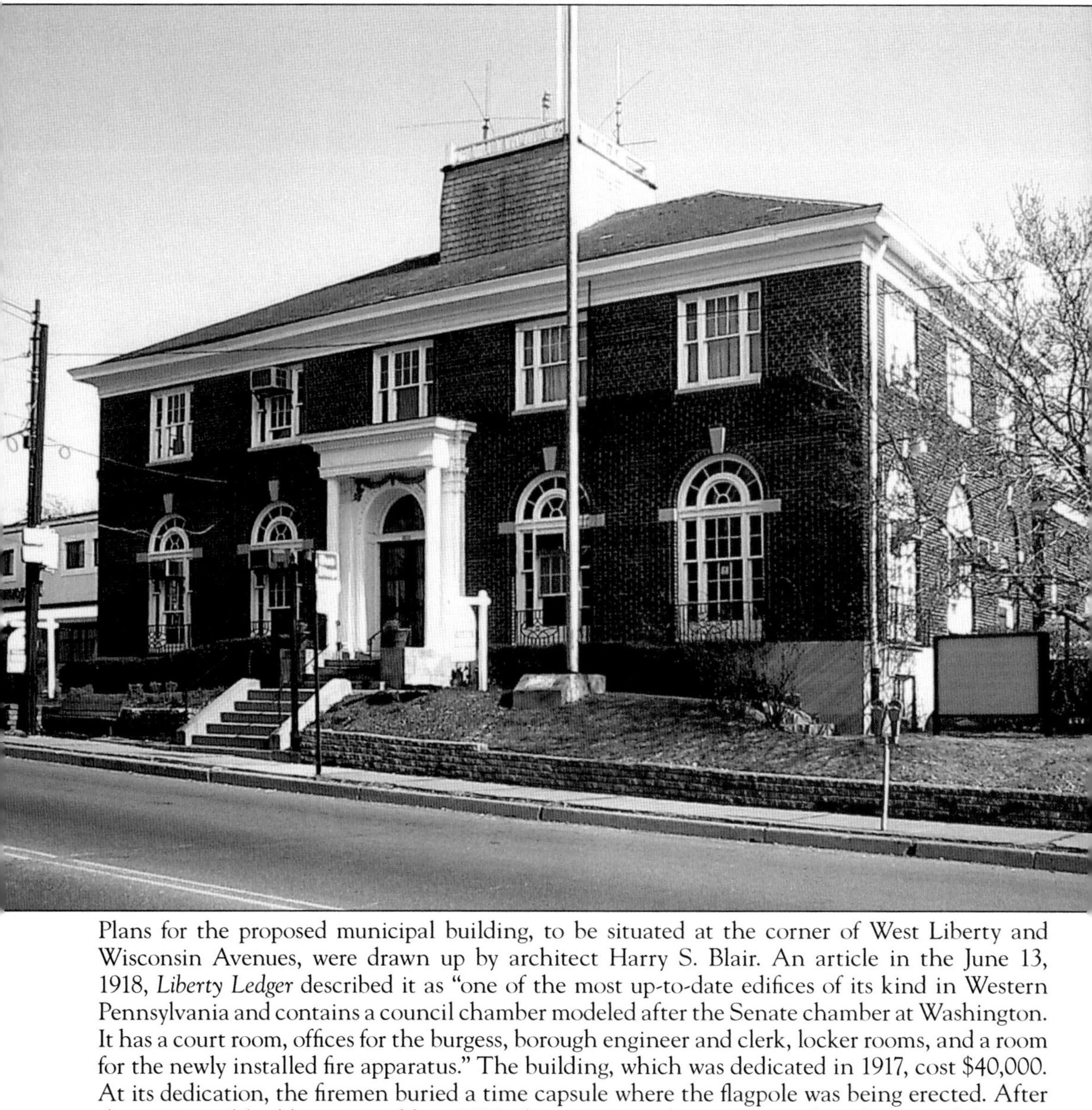

Plans for the proposed municipal building, to be situated at the corner of West Liberty and Wisconsin Avenues, were drawn up by architect Harry S. Blair. An article in the June 13, 1918, *Liberty Ledger* described it as "one of the most up-to-date edifices of its kind in Western Pennsylvania and contains a council chamber modeled after the Senate chamber at Washington. It has a court room, offices for the burgess, borough engineer and clerk, locker rooms, and a room for the newly installed fire apparatus." The building, which was dedicated in 1917, cost $40,000. At its dedication, the firemen buried a time capsule where the flagpole was being erected. After the municipal building was sold in 1999, the time capsule was reburied at the site of the new fire station.

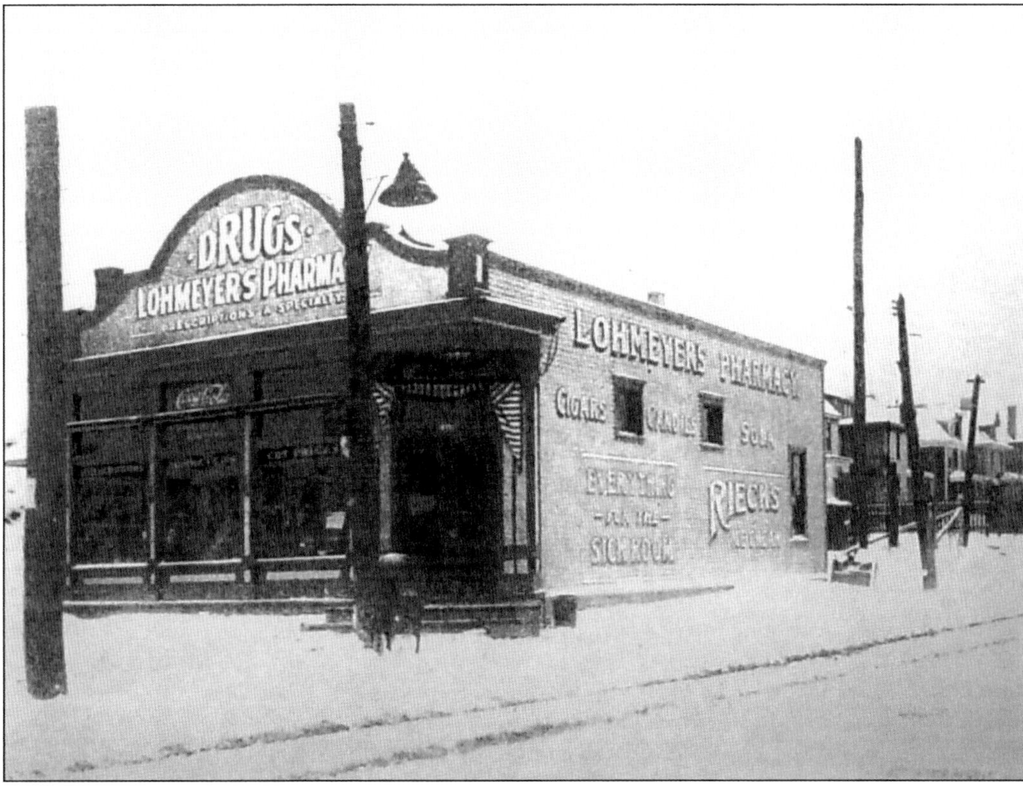

Pittsburgh Railways extended trolley service as far as Lohmeyer's Pharmacy, at the intersection of Potomac and Broadway Avenues, in 1903. From there, the trolley went to the turnaround near McFarland Road and then returned to the city on its single track. Regularly scheduled service was initiated the next year.

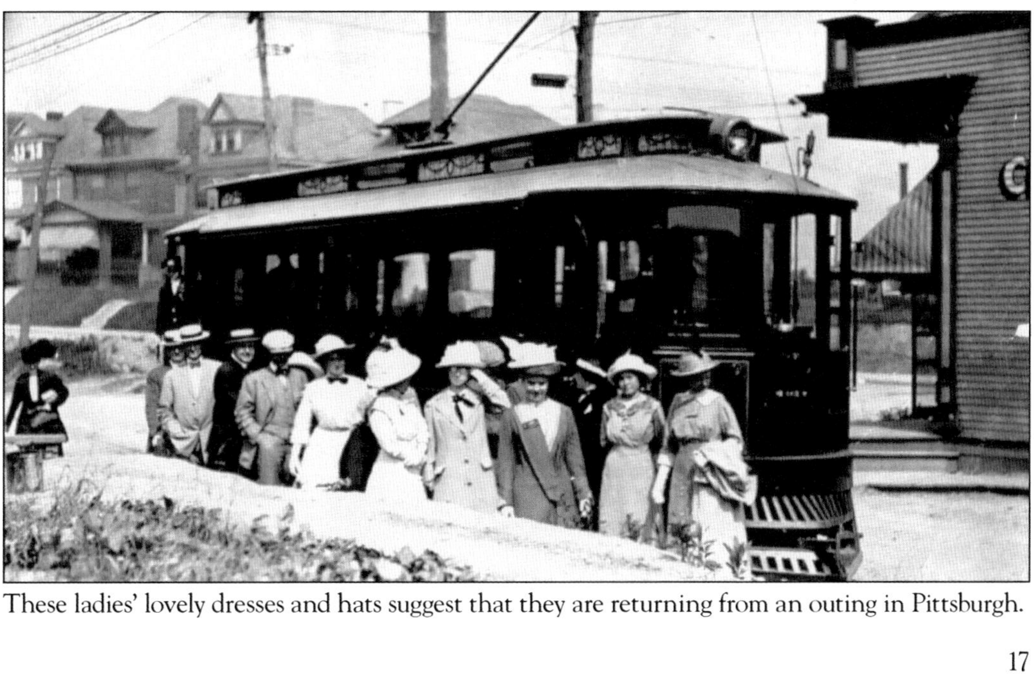

These ladies' lovely dresses and hats suggest that they are returning from an outing in Pittsburgh.

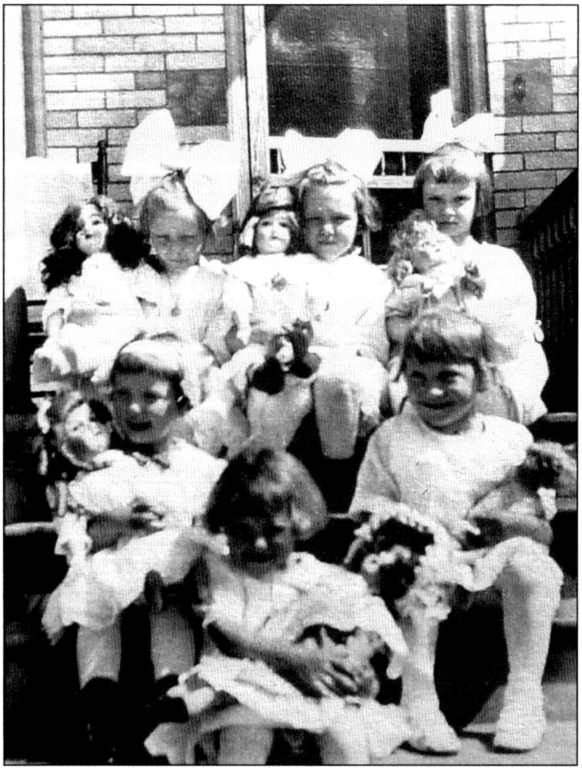

Thilda Barton and her friends wait to have their picture taken with their dolls on the front steps of her home at 2973 Glenmore Avenue.

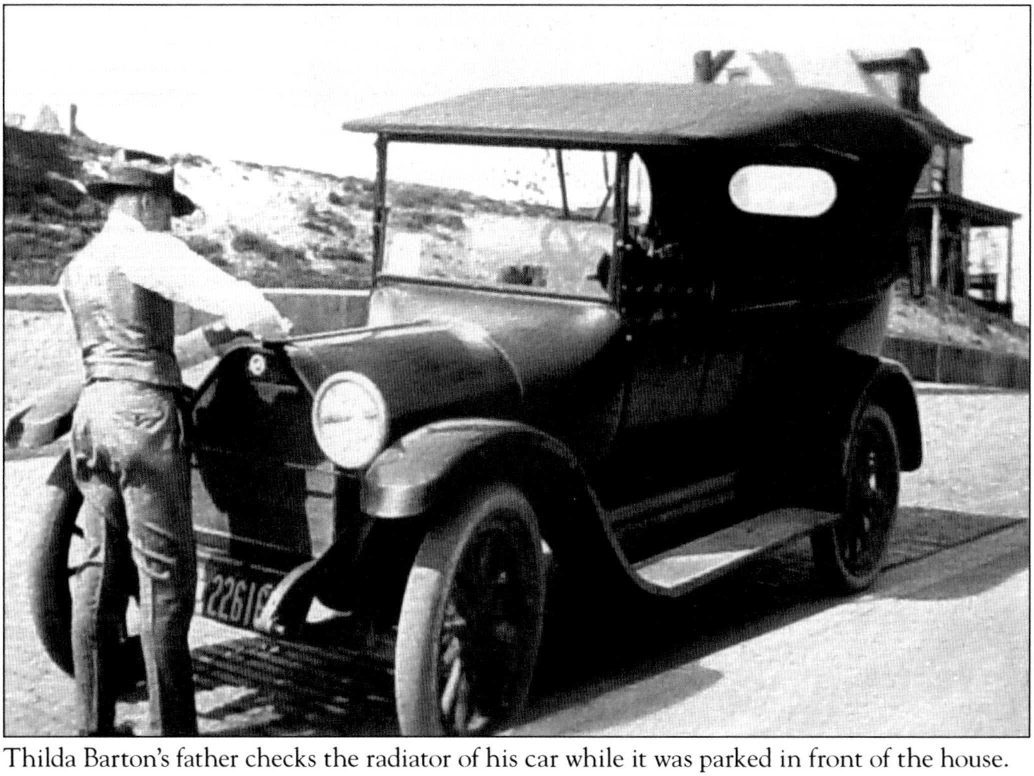

Thilda Barton's father checks the radiator of his car while it was parked in front of the house.

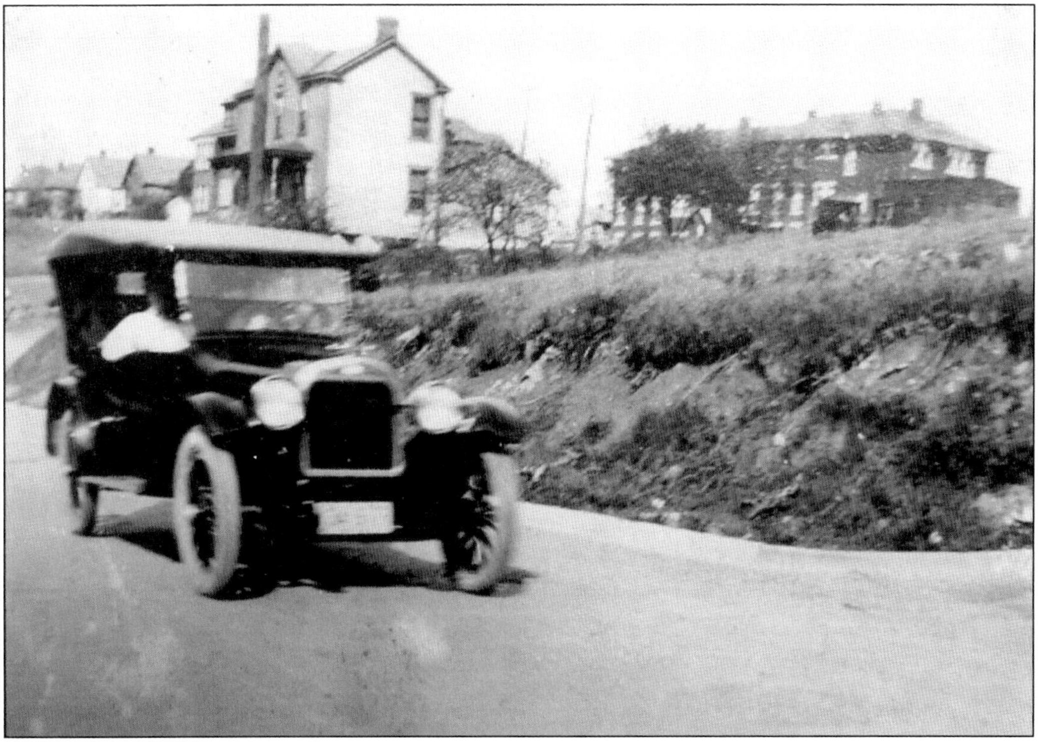

Few houses had been built in the 2900 block of Crosby Avenue by the mid-1930s.

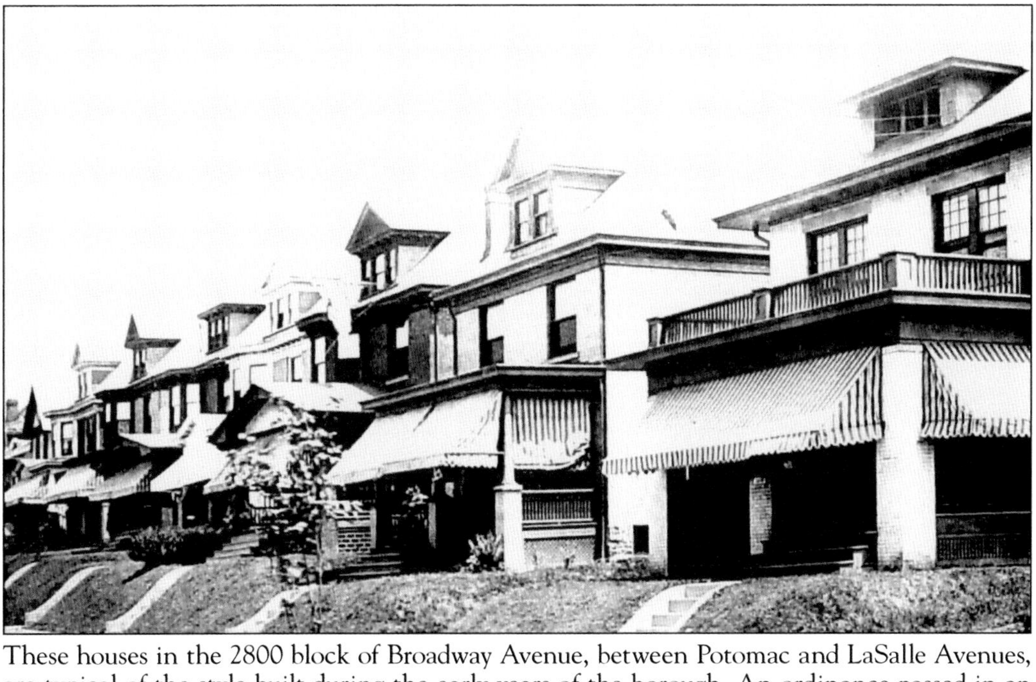

These houses in the 2800 block of Broadway Avenue, between Potomac and LaSalle Avenues, are typical of the style built during the early years of the borough. An ordinance passed in an early year of the borough dictates that all buildings in the borough must be of brick, brick veneer, or stone.

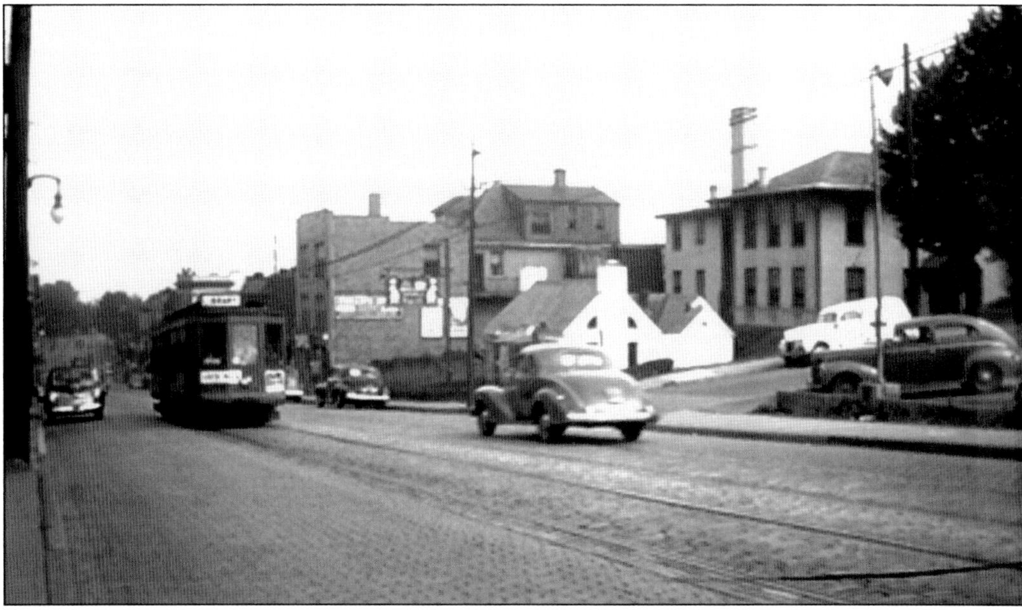

An old streetcar works its way up the 2900 block of West Liberty Avenue. Sometimes the trolleys on these streetcars would come off the wires. The motormen would have to get out and put them back on before the streetcars could continue on their way. On sleety days, the trolley wires would spark and the lights inside the cars would flicker.

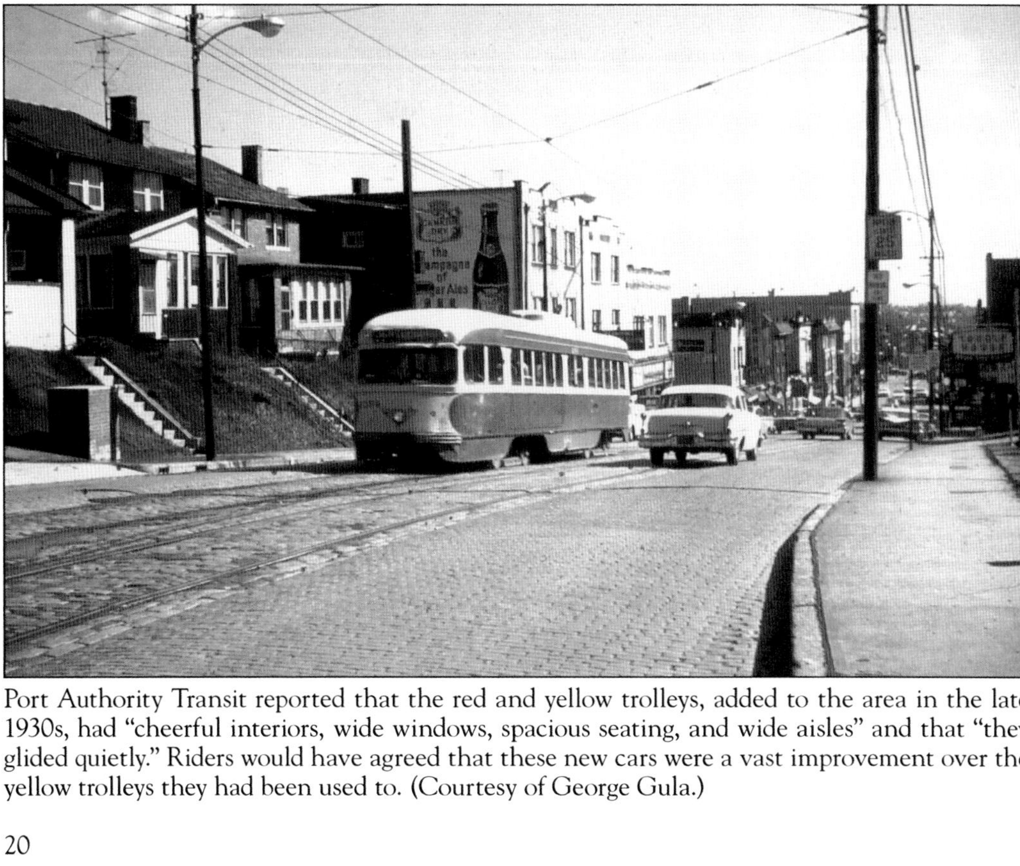

Port Authority Transit reported that the red and yellow trolleys, added to the area in the late 1930s, had "cheerful interiors, wide windows, spacious seating, and wide aisles" and that "they glided quietly." Riders would have agreed that these new cars were a vast improvement over the yellow trolleys they had been used to. (Courtesy of George Gula.)

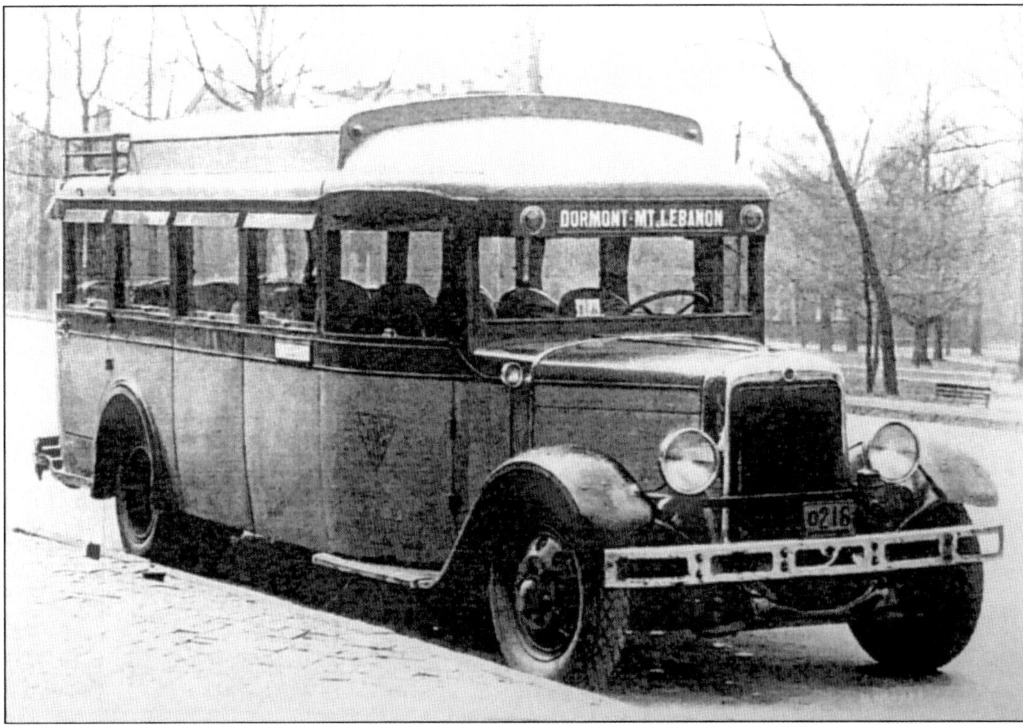

For just a few years, buses like this one were used in neighboring communities.

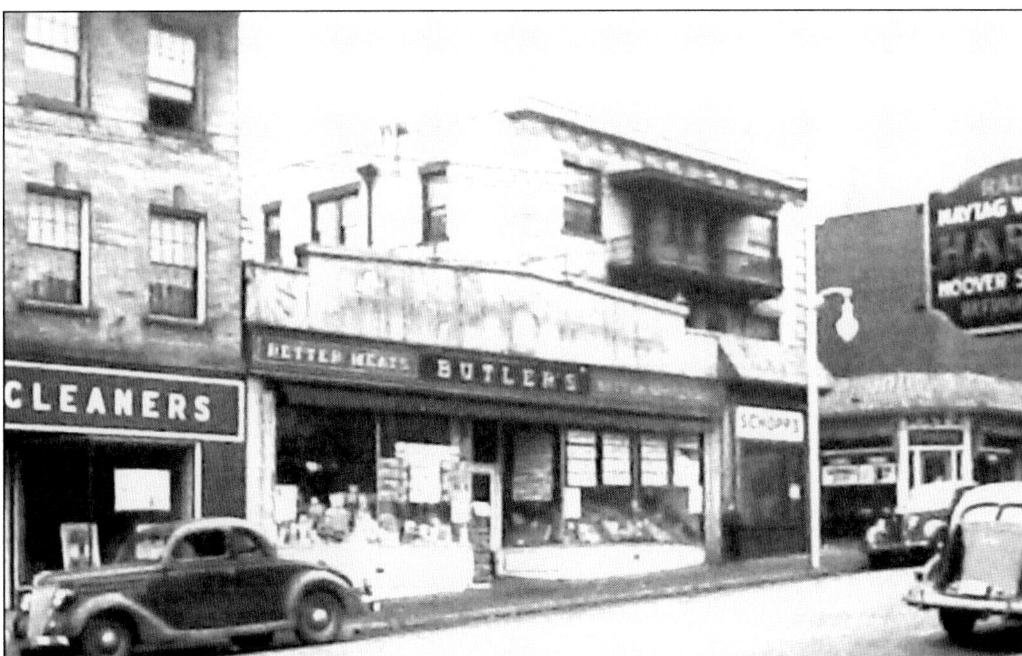

Different grocery stores, such as Giant Eagle, Krogers, and Thorofare, were located in various buildings on Potomac Avenue through the years. This Butler store was at 1435–1439 Potomac Avenue from 1934 until 1937.

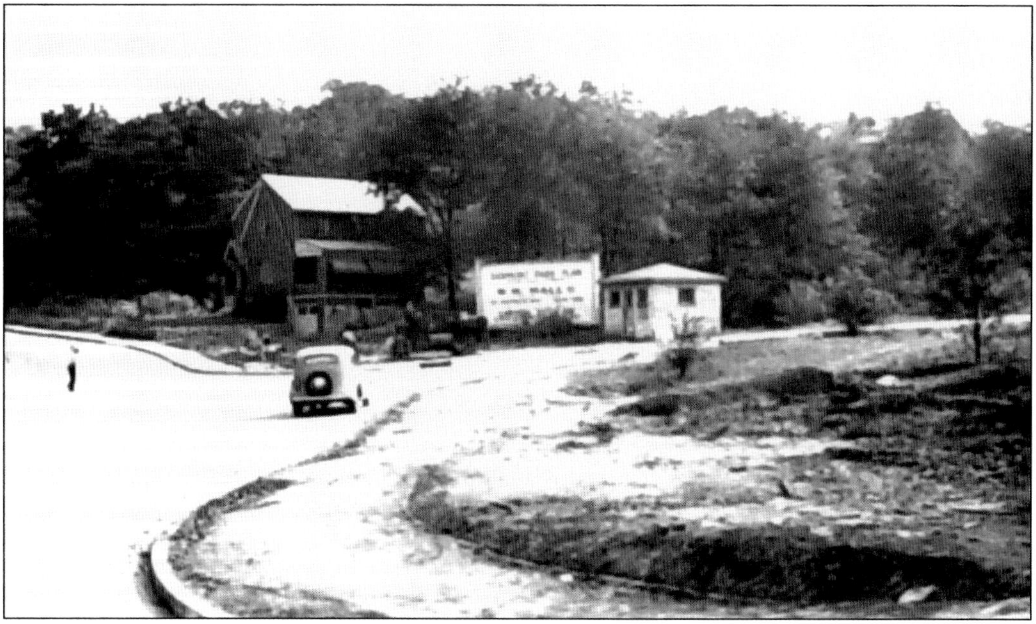

Lots in the Park Plan, the borough's final residential development, were being advertised when this picture was taken in 1938. The plan was so named as one side extends the length of Dormont Park; the other sides are bordered by Annapolis, Kelton, and Dwight Avenues. Most of the houses in the plan were built between 1927 and 1950.

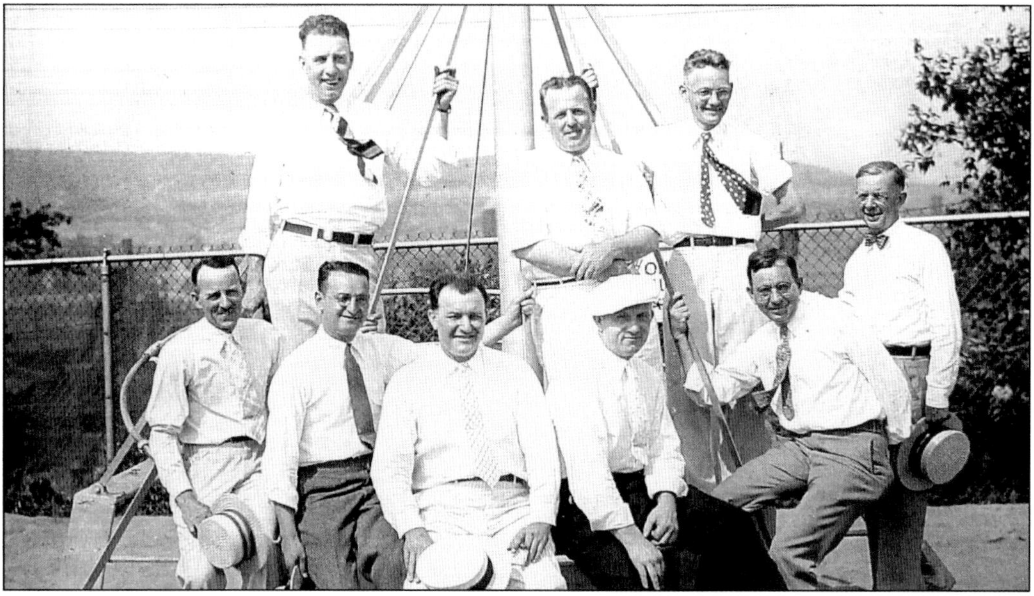

Six of the borough's prominent businessmen and two of its policemen pose for this picture in the 1930s. Seen from left to right are (first row) unidentified; Joseph Rubenstein, Dormont Variety Store; Casey Hasley, police officer; Charles Paull, *Liberty Ledger* publisher; George Hards, Hards Appliances; and L. C. "Sim" Price, Price's Men's Shop; (second row) Charles "Jake" Thomas, Thomas' Formal Wear and Flags; Ralph Miller, chief of police; and Robert Elton, Elton on Kelton, an automobile accessory and electrical repair shop.

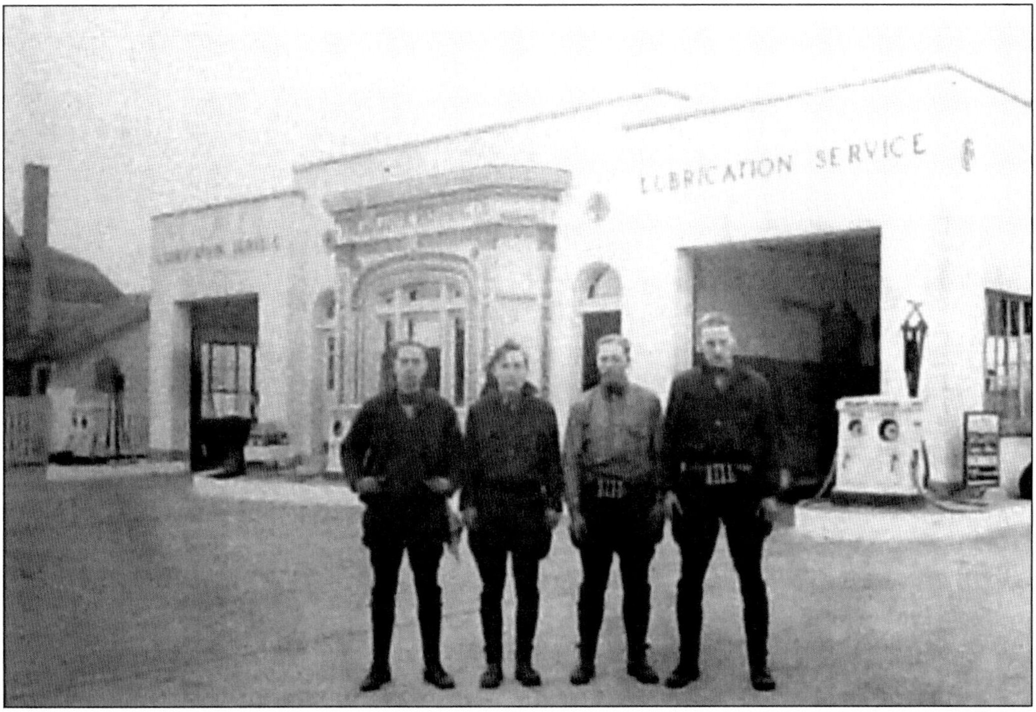

Before the mid-1940s, most gas stations were owned by their companies. Atlantic owned this one, at the corner of Dormont and West Liberty Avenues, before William Siegfried bought it.

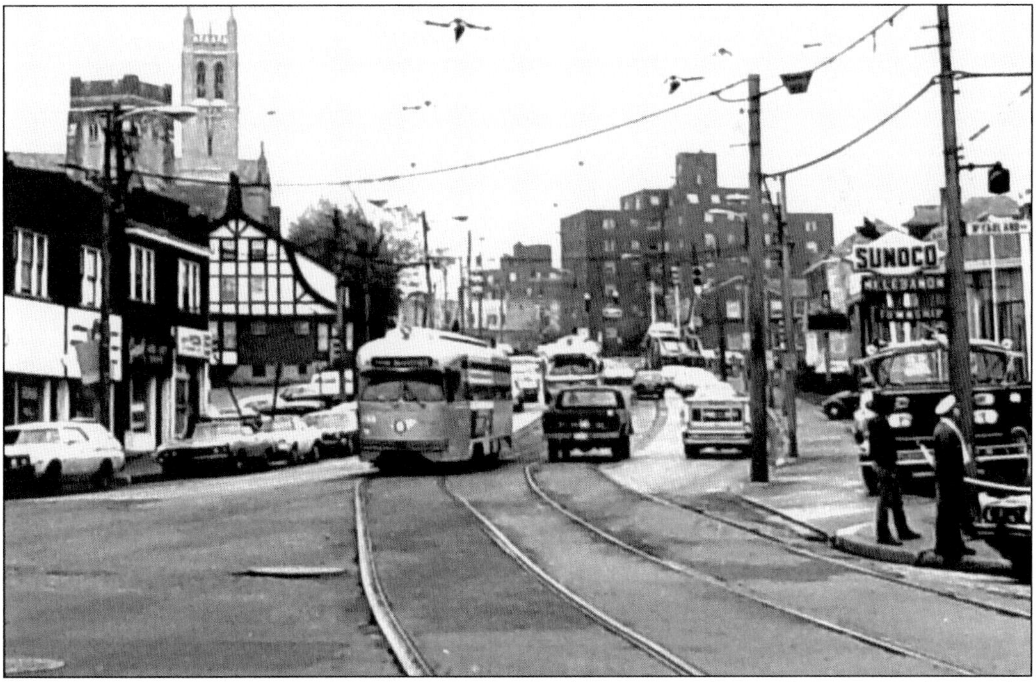

Streetcars heading toward Pittsburgh from Mount Lebanon turned onto the Dormont line at the junction near McFarland Road after Pittsburgh Railways paved over the tracks on West Liberty Avenue in the 1960s.

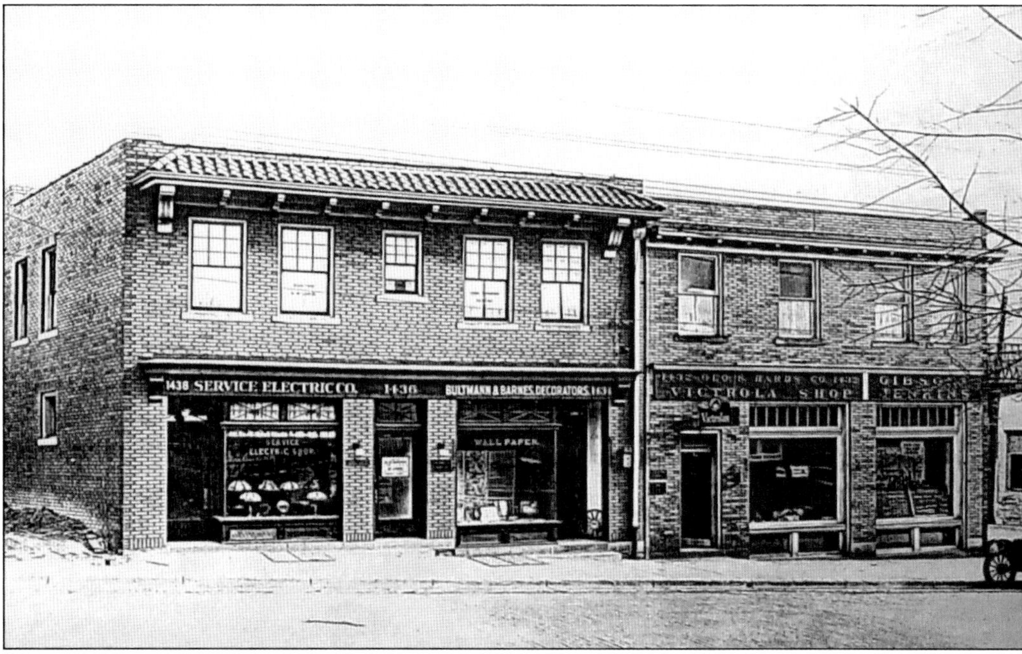

George Hards opened a store at 1441 Potomac Avenue to sell Victrolas and records in 1919. That same year, he moved his business to the building across the street at the corner of Potomac and Glenmore Avenues and added radio and electrical appliances. The store was closed when he retired in 1951.

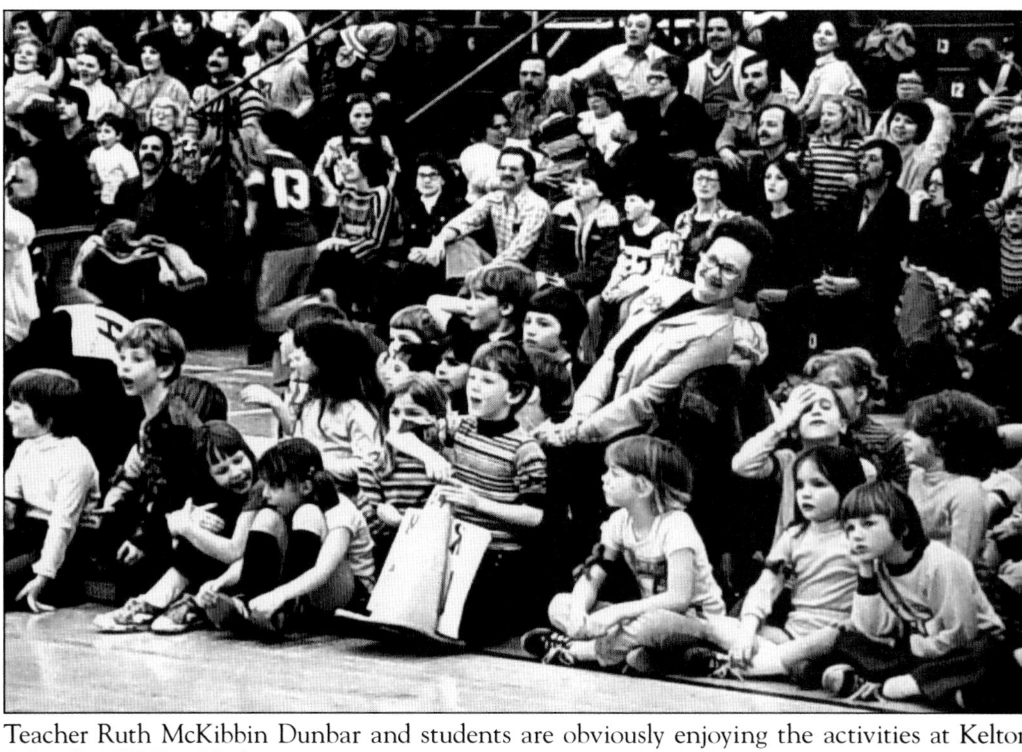

Teacher Ruth McKibbin Dunbar and students are obviously enjoying the activities at Kelton School's 1977 Fun Night.

James Wiedt displays the football and scrapbook he donated to the Dormont Historical Society. The game ball had been awarded to him after Dormont's 12-0 defeat of archrival Mount Lebanon in 1937.

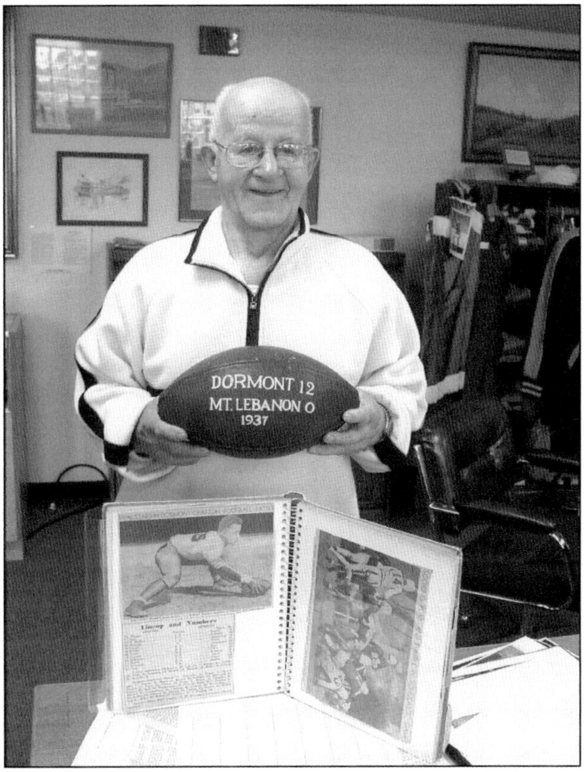

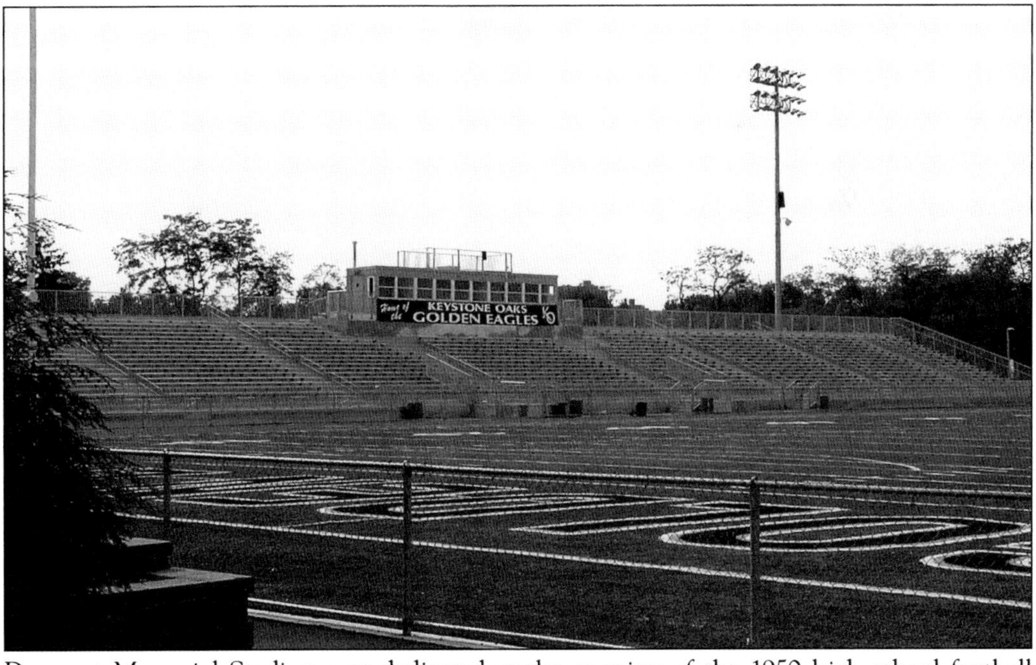

Dormont Memorial Stadium was dedicated at the opening of the 1950 high school football season. Some of the improvements made when it was renovated in 2006 included replacing the wooden bleachers with metal ones, moving and updating the concession stands, and widening the field to accommodate soccer games.

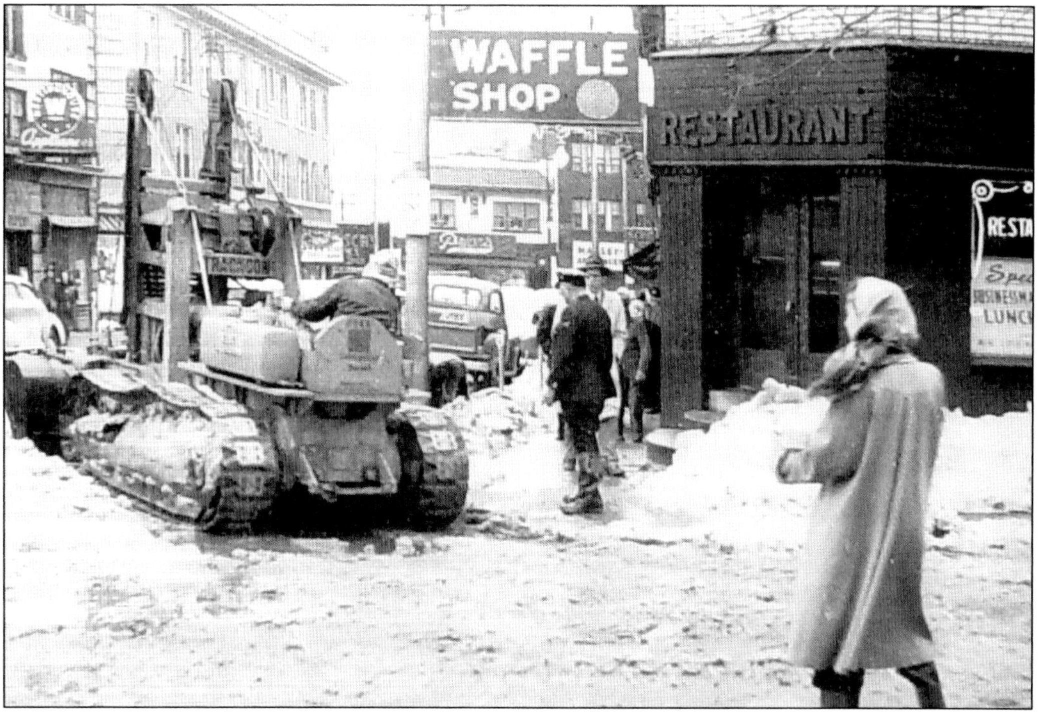

The deep snow that covered the area at Thanksgiving in 1950 created a major problem for the street crew, as seen at the corner of Potomac and Glenmore Avenues.

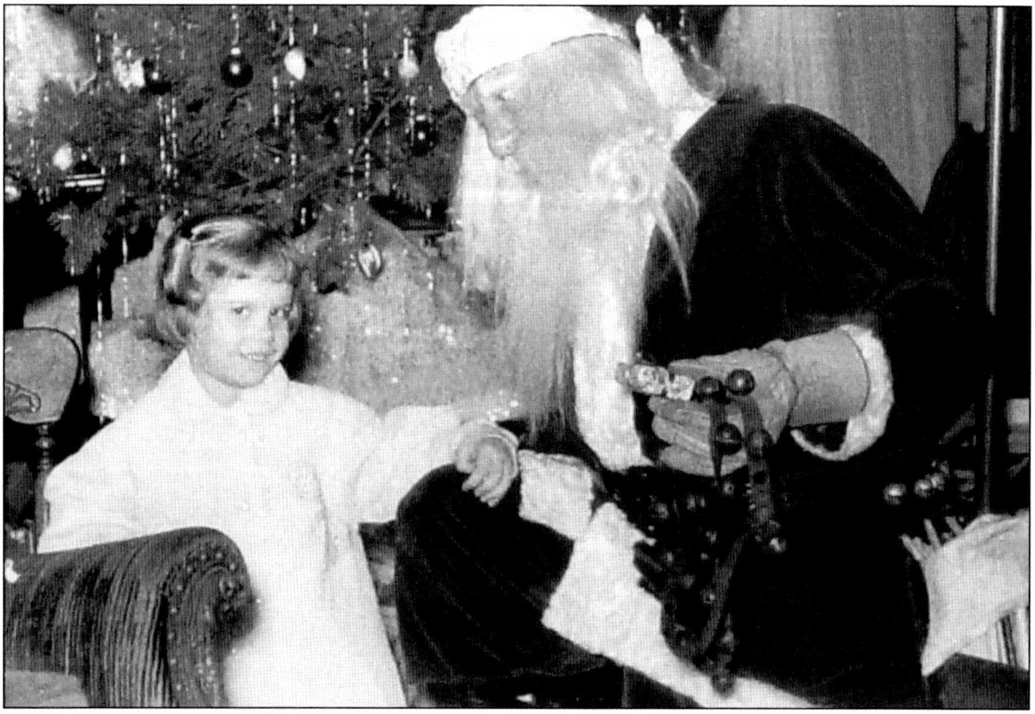

Dormont businessman Charles "Jake" Thomas devoted many hours each holiday season to being Santa for the fire department, charitable groups, and friends.

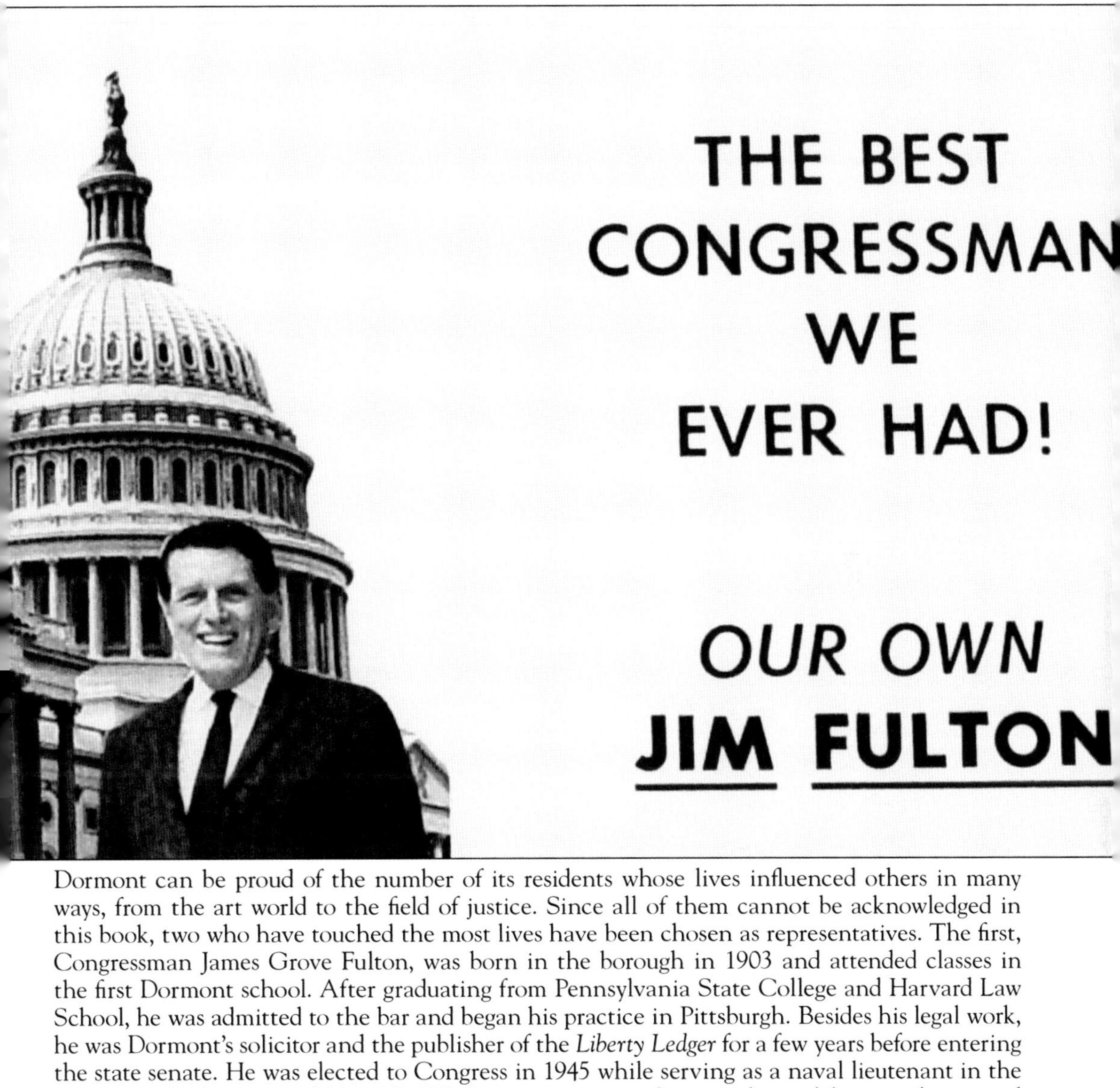

Dormont can be proud of the number of its residents whose lives influenced others in many ways, from the art world to the field of justice. Since all of them cannot be acknowledged in this book, two who have touched the most lives have been chosen as representatives. The first, Congressman James Grove Fulton, was born in the borough in 1903 and attended classes in the first Dormont school. After graduating from Pennsylvania State College and Harvard Law School, he was admitted to the bar and began his practice in Pittsburgh. Besides his legal work, he was Dormont's solicitor and the publisher of the *Liberty Ledger* for a few years before entering the state senate. He was elected to Congress in 1945 while serving as a naval lieutenant in the South Pacific during World War II. While a congressman, he served as a delegate, adviser, and chairman of many conferences and commissions until his death in 1971.

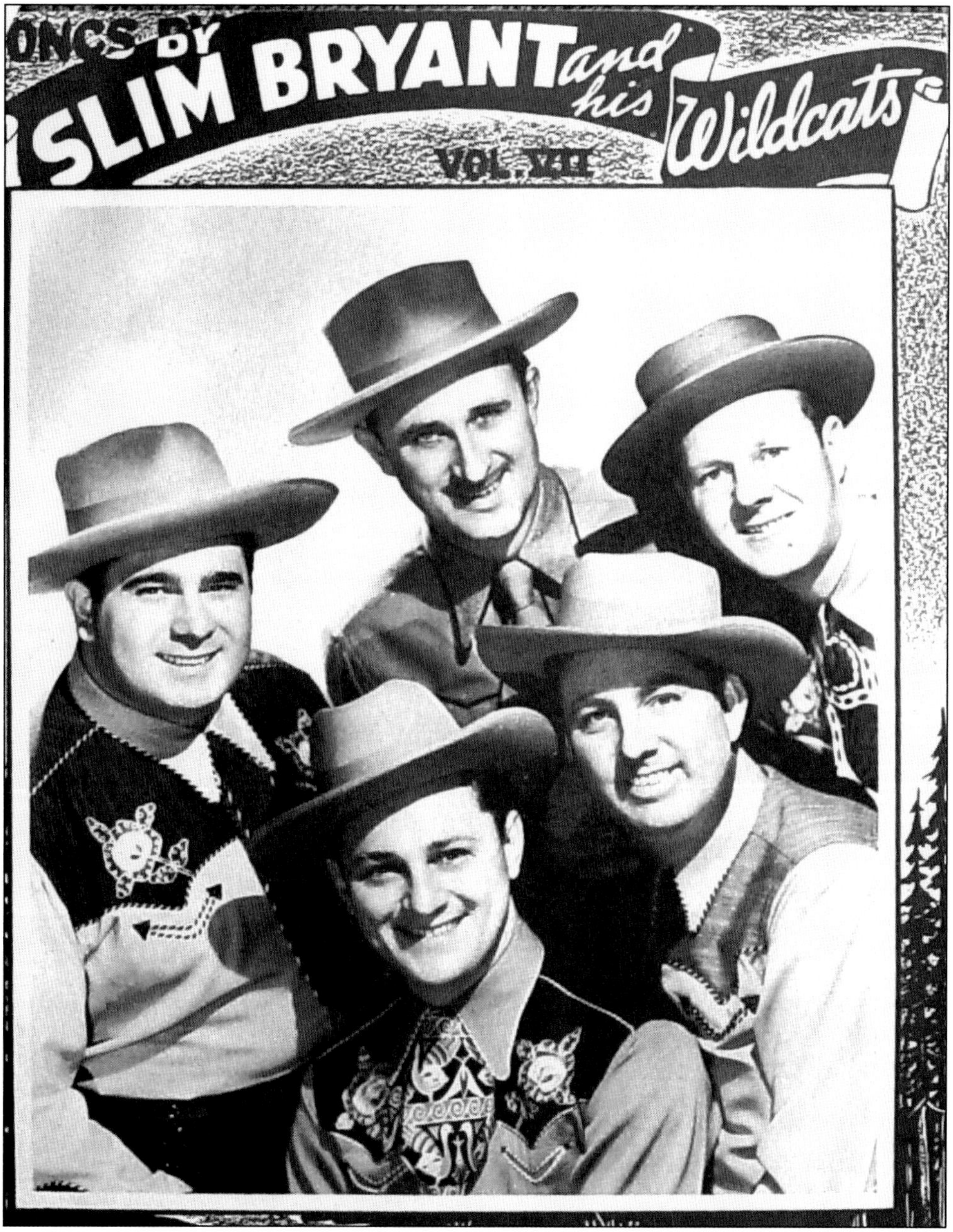

When Thomas H. "Slim" Bryant graduated from a Georgia high school, he had no idea that he would become an internationally known country musician. Recognized as one of the most progressive guitarists in country music, he has written more than 200 songs, one for his longtime friend Gene Autry and another for his friend Jimmie Rodgers. At one time, over 500 radio stations around the world played recordings by Slim and his Wildcats. Some still do. In 1940, Slim moved to Dormont when he joined the staff of KDKA radio. He and the Wildcats played on KDKA for 19 years and on television for 10 years, besides traveling to make personal appearances. For 30 years they recorded for Decca, Columbia, and MGM and made 289 Thesaurus Transcriptions. In 1999, Slim was inducted into the Country Music Hall of Fame. He is standing center back on the cover of this songbook.

Two

SCHOOLS

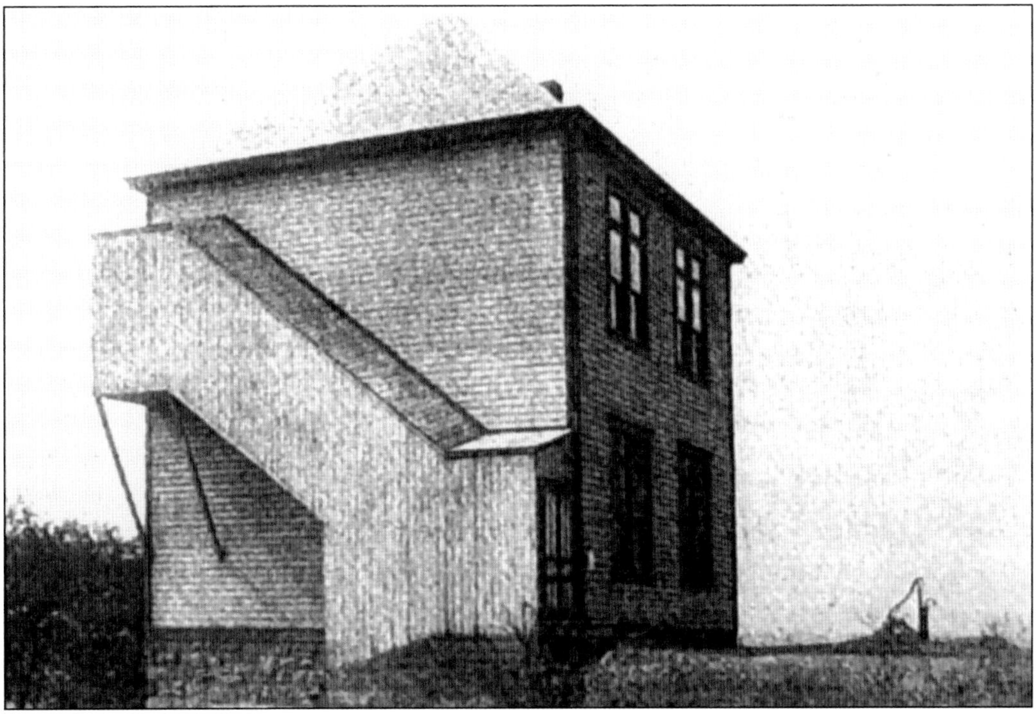

The first school for Dormont children was the wooden one built on Snyder Avenue (later renamed Hillsdale Avenue) in 1905 at a cost of $3,000. Although it was named Snyder School, some references call it the Espy School because it was in the Espy Plan of lots that had been laid out in the borough. Besides servicing 22 pupils, the building was used for council meetings, to house the fire department's equipment, and for Sunday school classes of the Presbyterian Church. It was demolished after Dormont Public School was built.

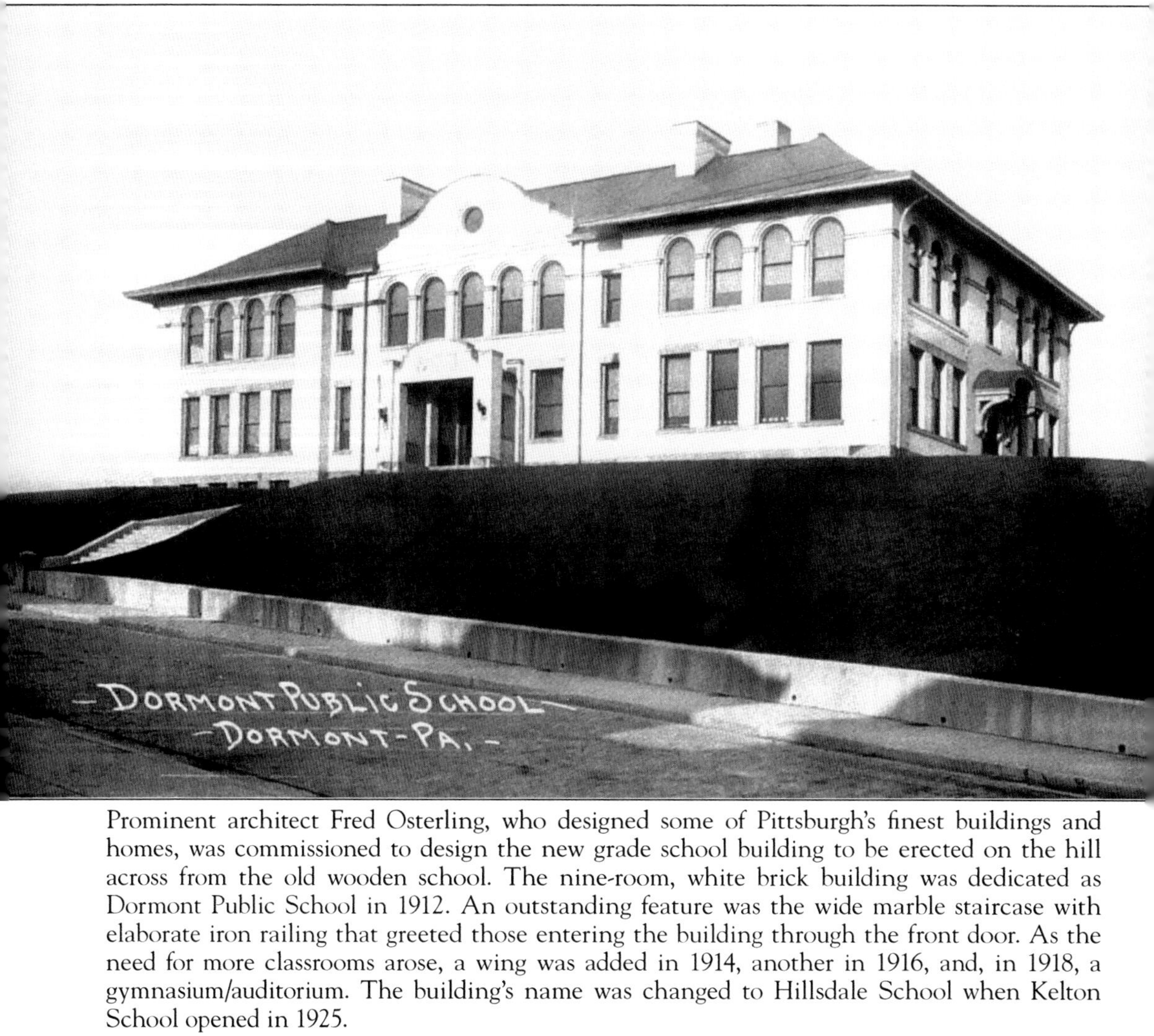

Prominent architect Fred Osterling, who designed some of Pittsburgh's finest buildings and homes, was commissioned to design the new grade school building to be erected on the hill across from the old wooden school. The nine-room, white brick building was dedicated as Dormont Public School in 1912. An outstanding feature was the wide marble staircase with elaborate iron railing that greeted those entering the building through the front door. As the need for more classrooms arose, a wing was added in 1914, another in 1916, and, in 1918, a gymnasium/auditorium. The building's name was changed to Hillsdale School when Kelton School opened in 1925.

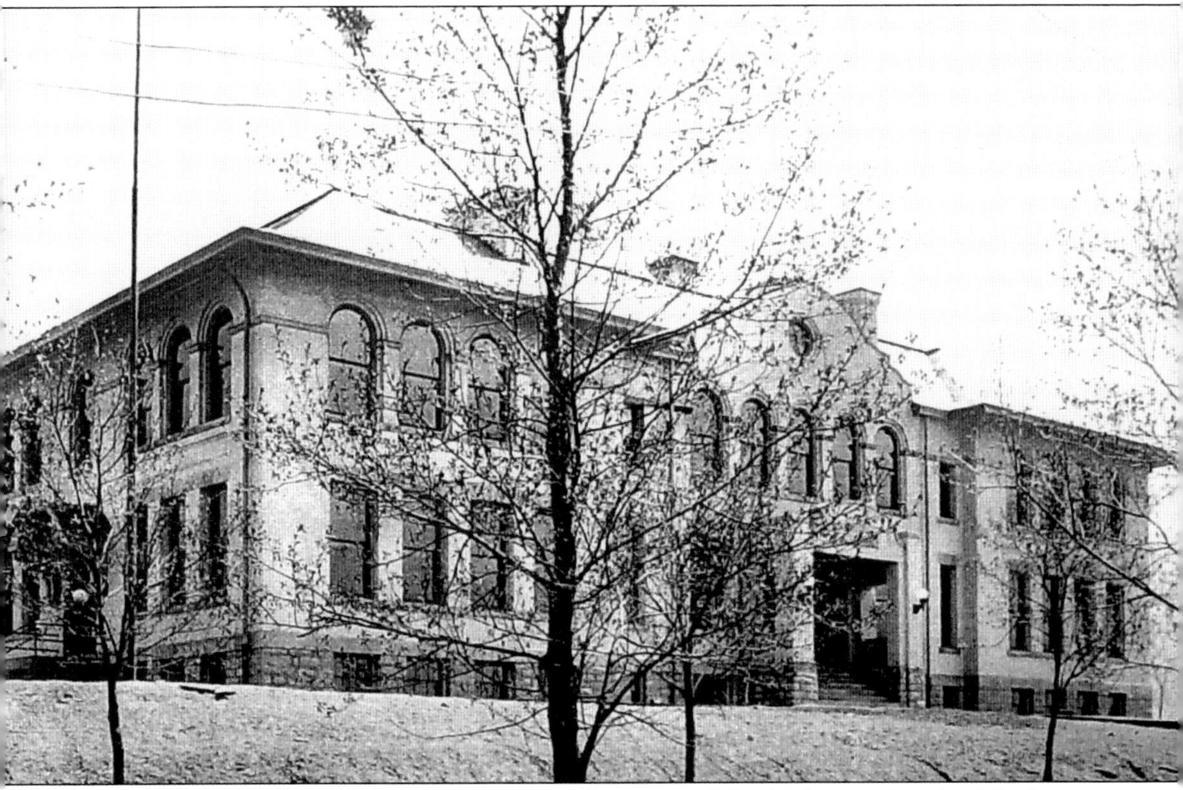

The Hillsdale School building, which is situated on one of the highest points in Allegheny County, is shown here in the 1950s before a microburst damaged its roof severely. While the roof was being replaced with a flat one, the entrance to the building was remodeled. Besides being used for gym classes and school programs, its large gymnasium/auditorium was frequently used for public events. The school was closed in 1996 after Dormont Elementary School was built. It sat empty until being completely renovated and reopened as Dormont's municipal center in 1999.

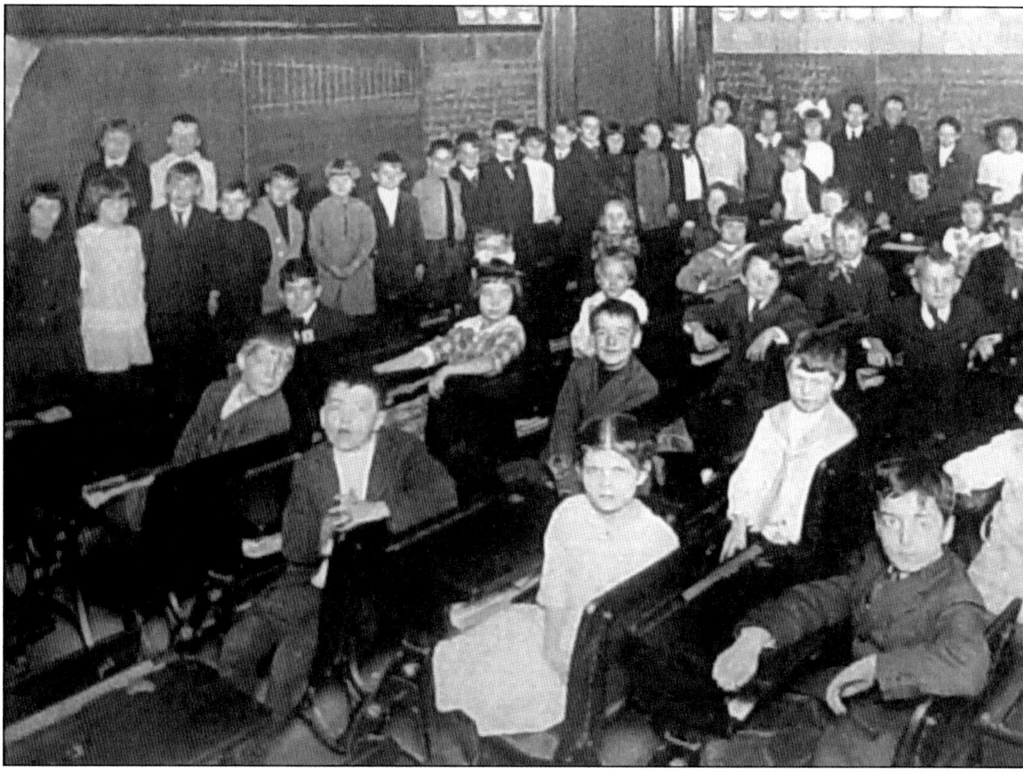
Boys and girls are seen in their Hillsdale classroom in 1920.

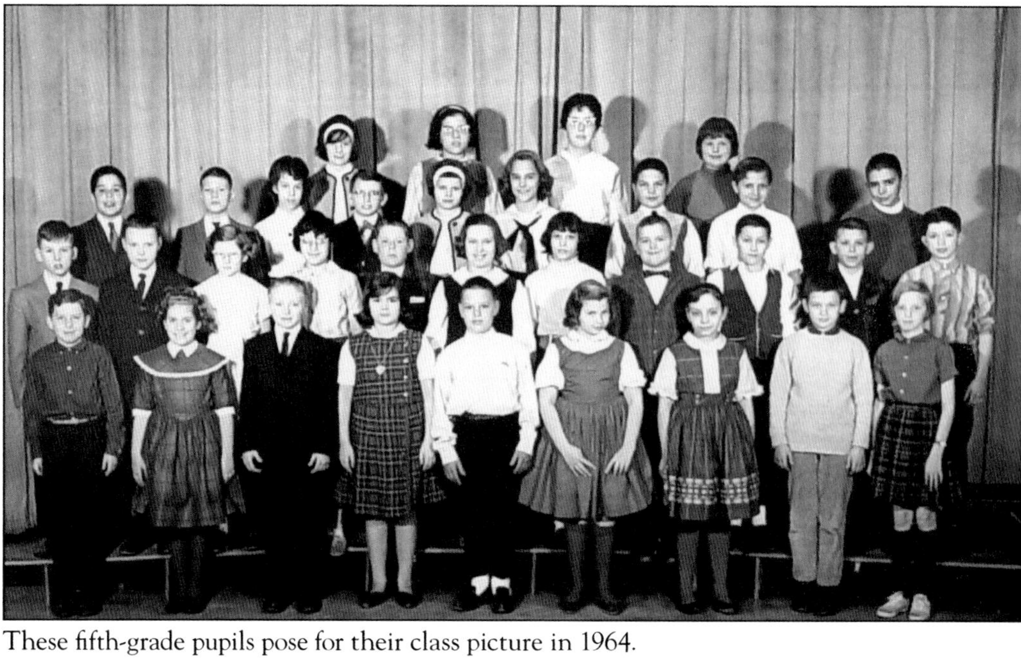
These fifth-grade pupils pose for their class picture in 1964.

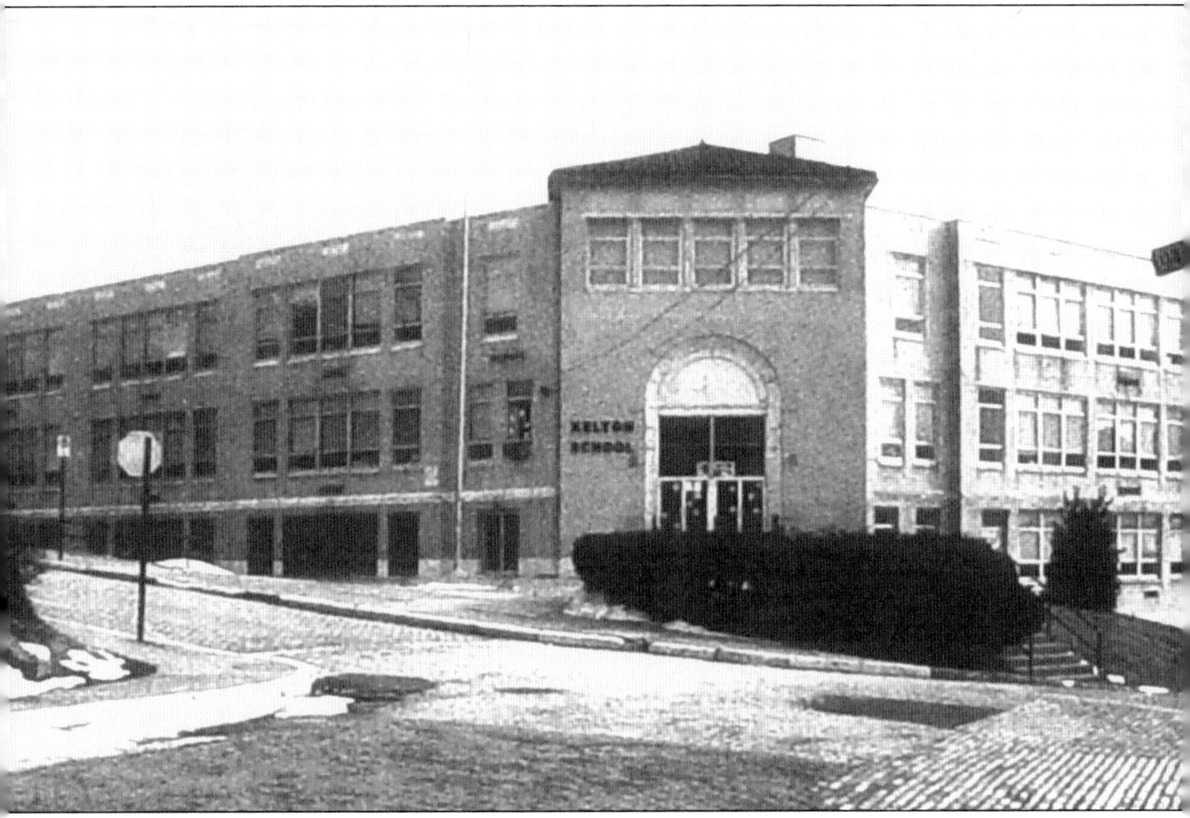

Kelton Grade School, at the corner of Kelton and Delwood Avenues, serviced the children on the east side of the borough so they would not have to cross busy West Liberty Avenue on their way to school. Dedicated in 1925, its second story was added in 1931. The building had facilities for shop, cooking, and sewing classes that were used by both Hillsdale and Kelton seventh and eighth graders. It was closed and razed in 1996 when Dormont Elementary School opened.

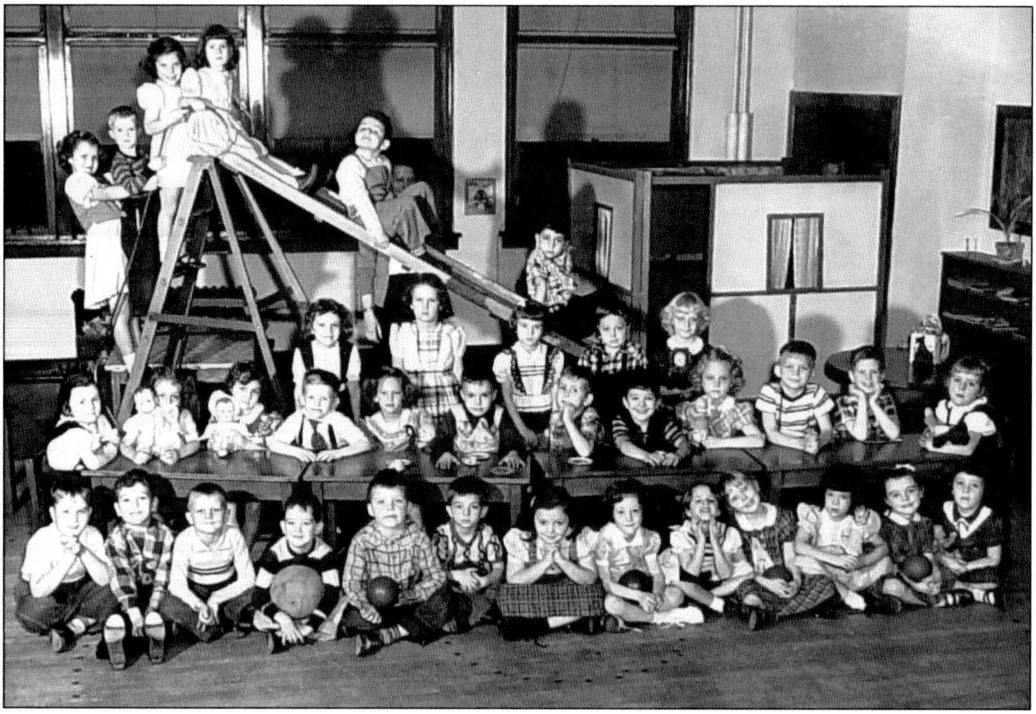

The 1950–1951 kindergarten class is shown with some of the things that made school days fun.

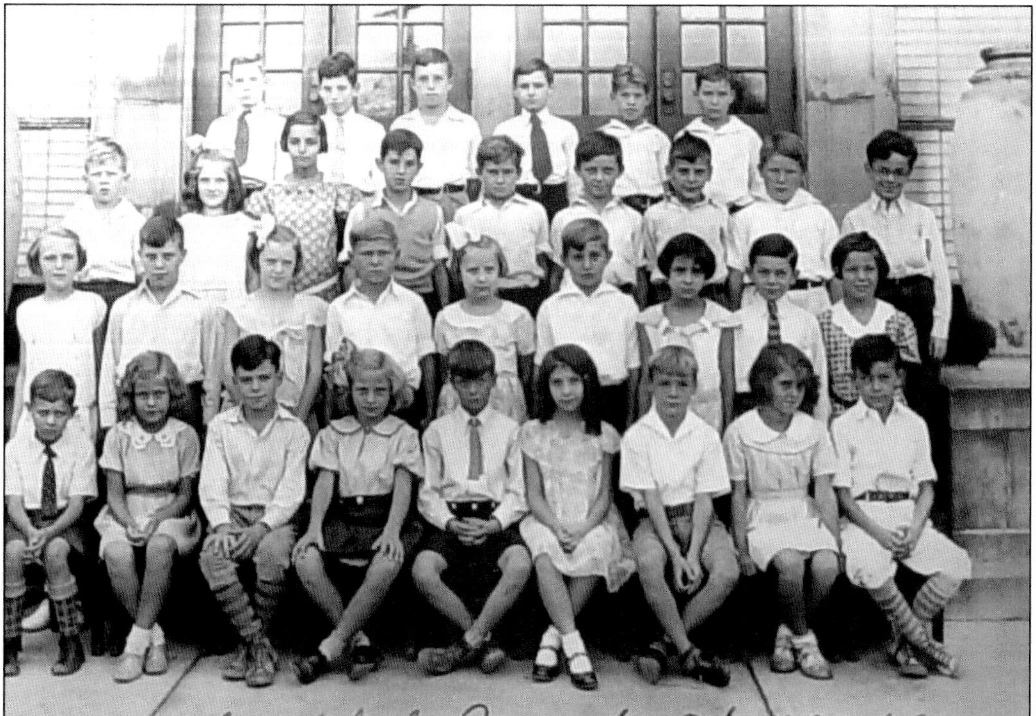

These boys and girls were fifth graders in 1934.

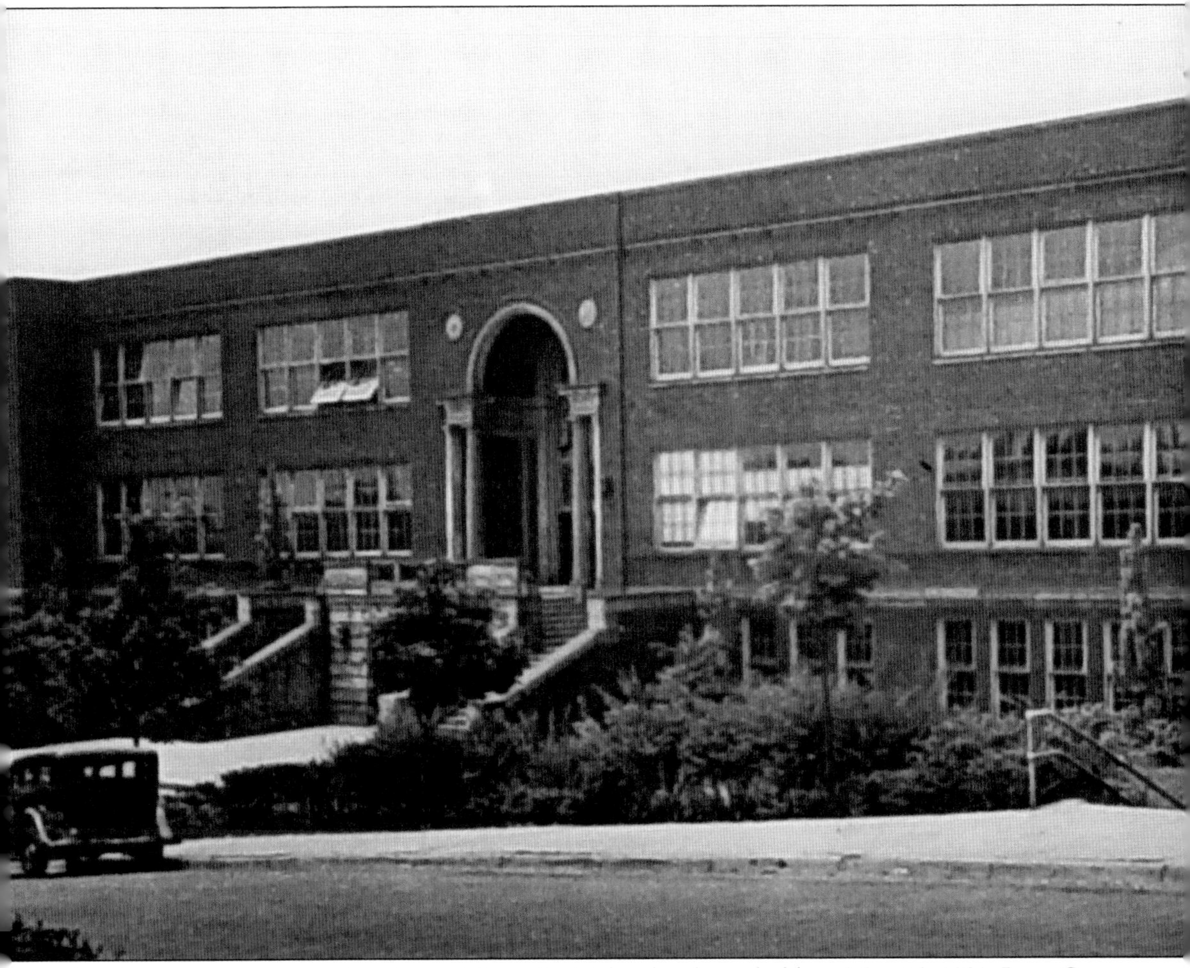

The first meeting concerning the building of a high school was held on May 16, 1921. Press C. Dowler was chosen to be the architect. When the redbrick Dormont High School, at the intersection of Grandin and Annapolis Avenues, opened for classes on September 5, 1922, it accommodated 26 faculty members and 521 students. Some of those students were from Mount Lebanon, as they had no high school of their own at that time. A state-of-the-art building, the school offered a wide variety of classes, including one in millinery. Among its features were a model dining room, sewing department suite, and drafting room. In 1926, the three and one-half acres next to the school were developed into an athletic field for sports events. A new gymnasium, shop, and cafeteria section were added in the early 1940s. Dormont's schools became part of the Keystone Oaks School District in 1964. When a new high school was dedicated in 1969, this building was used as Jay Neff Middle School until it was closed and razed in 1996.

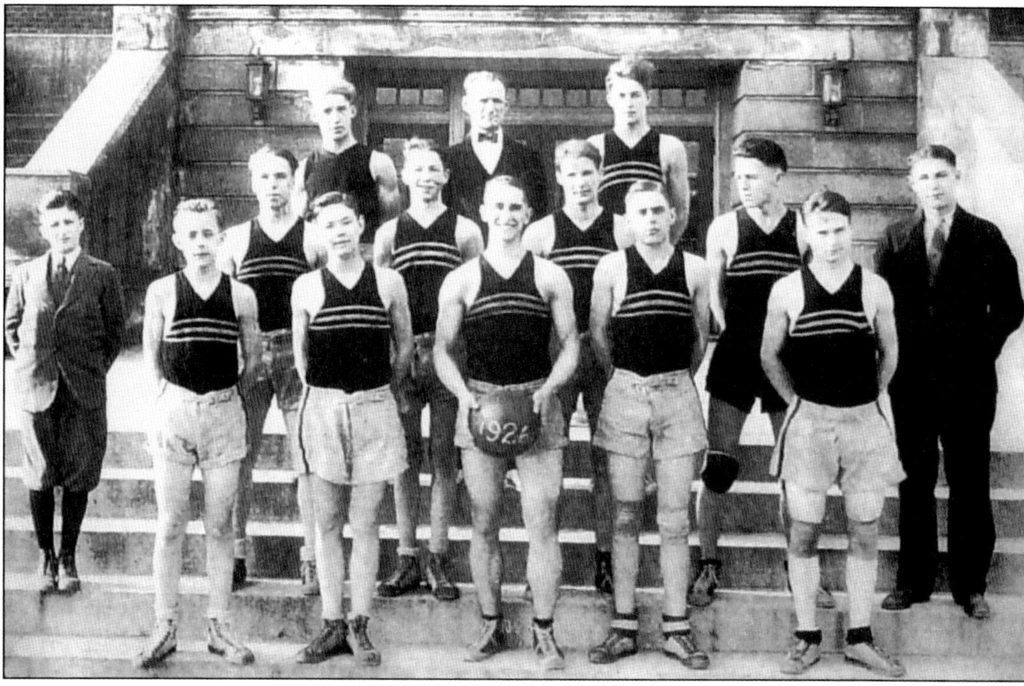

Teacher Clarence E. Glass coached this 1926 high school basketball team. In 1927, he became the high school's principal, a position he held until his retirement in 1955.

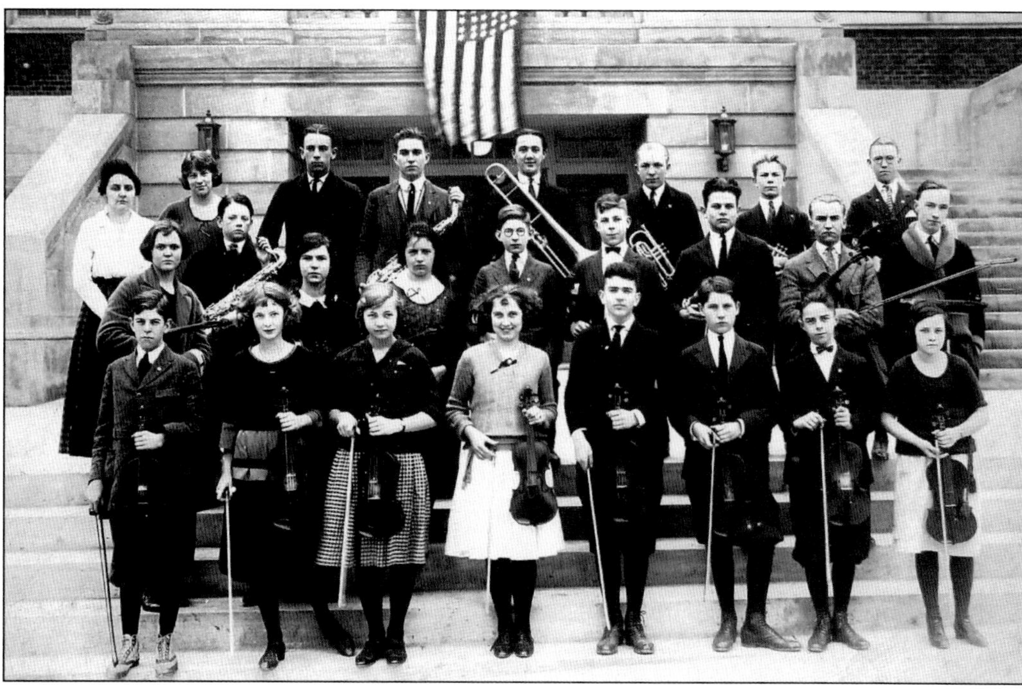

Dormont High School's first orchestra and band were organized in 1932 by a Mr. Thalheimer, the music director. When the band made its first major public performance, only 35 members could participate for lack of enough uniforms.

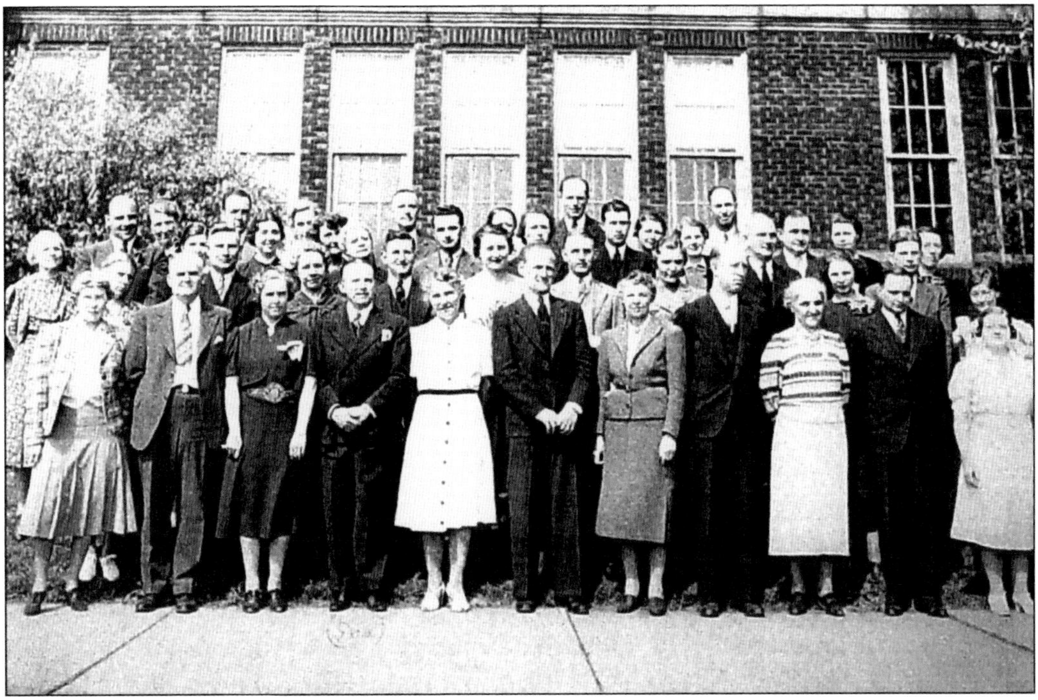

The faculty assembled for this picture in 1939. Many of these teachers were part of the original faculty and taught at the high school until they retired.

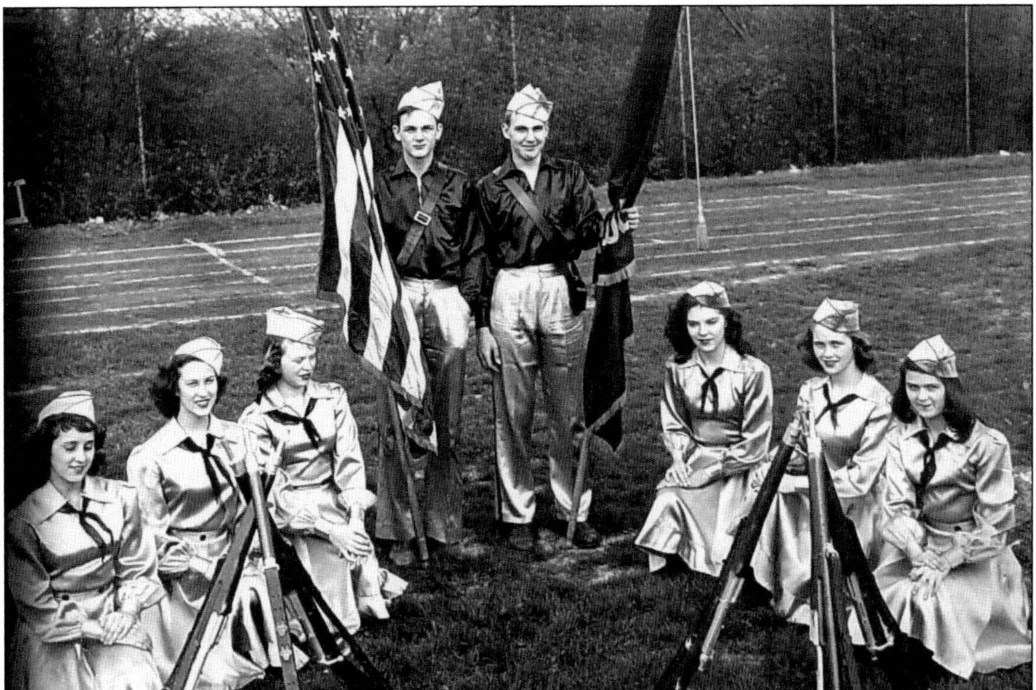

In 1949, the color guard and flag bearers are, from left to right, Mary Lou Mendel, Betty Paxton, Joan Logie, Charles Krauss, Donald Keller, Muriel Shreve, Nancy Stafford, and Faye Greiner.

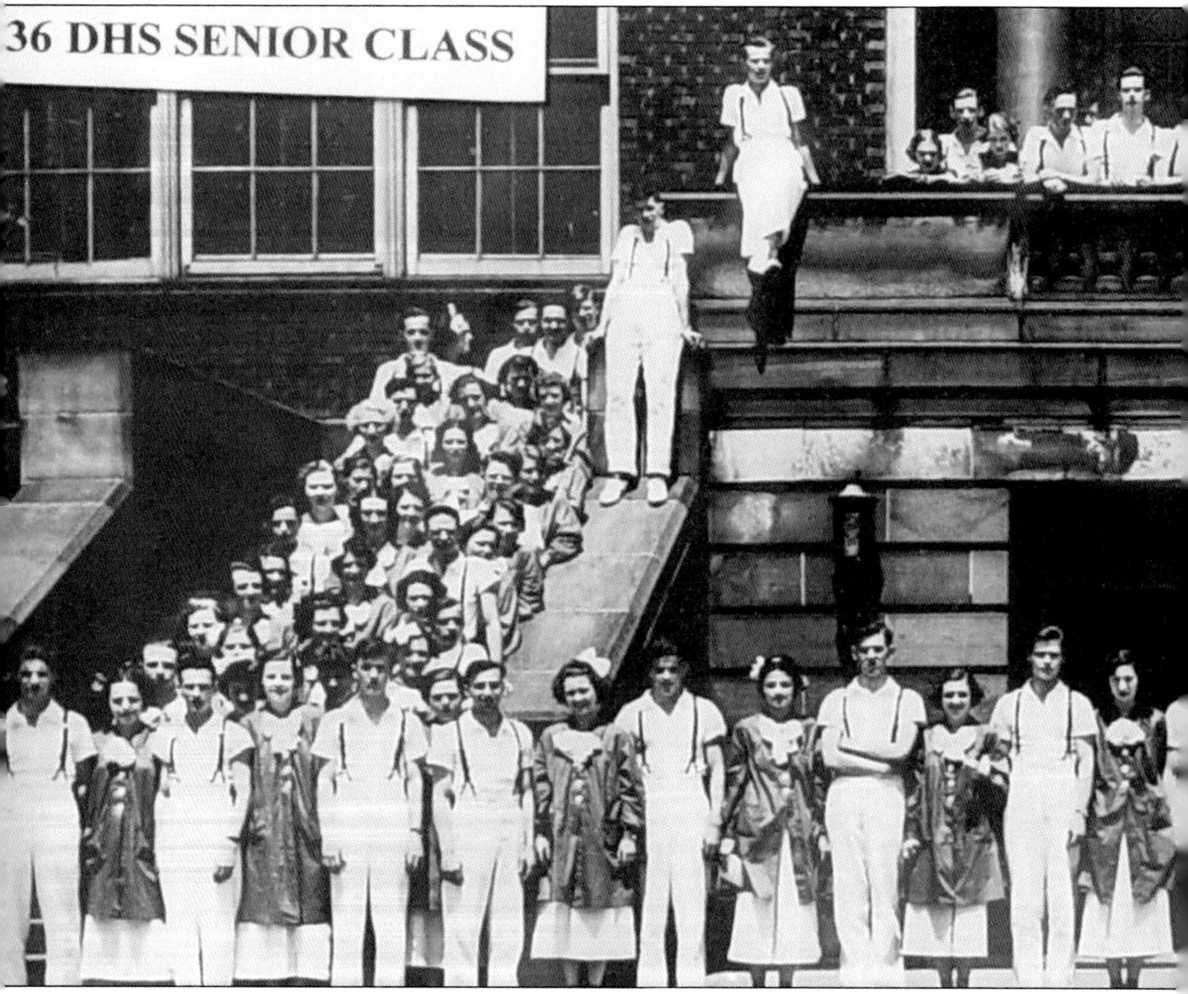

Class Day was a special time for the members of each senior class from the early years of Dormont High School until the late 1940s. Committees spent weeks planning the celebration to be held on their last day at the high school. They chose colors to represent their class and agreed on outfits that class members would wear. An original class song was composed or words were adapted to a favorite song of that time. An auditorium program was written to be presented

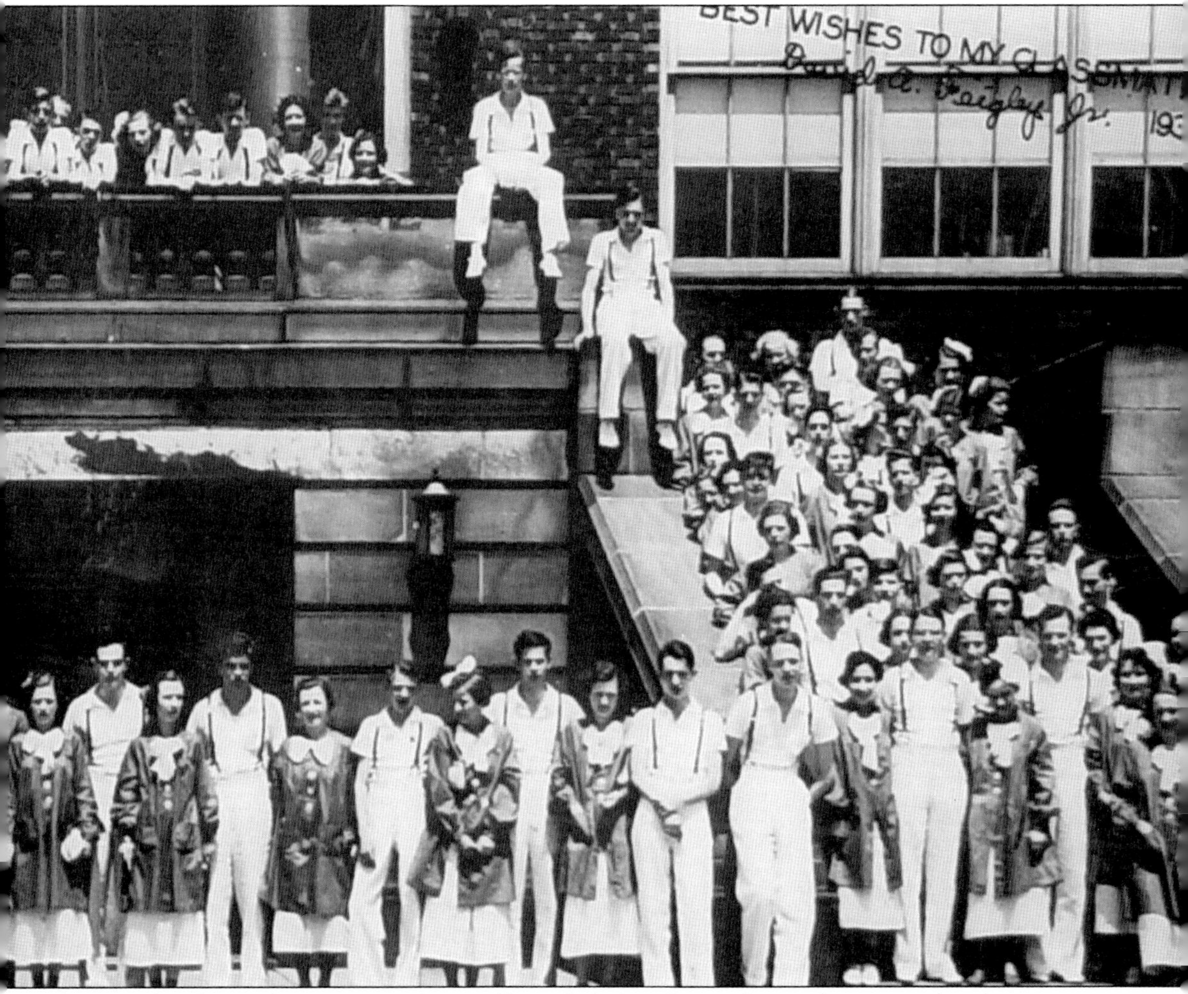

during schooltime that morning. It usually included a play or skits, talent acts, the class song, and lots of humor. Members of the class of 1936, dressed in their blue and gray Class Day outfits, took time from their festivities to gather outside the main entrance to the school for this picture to be taken.

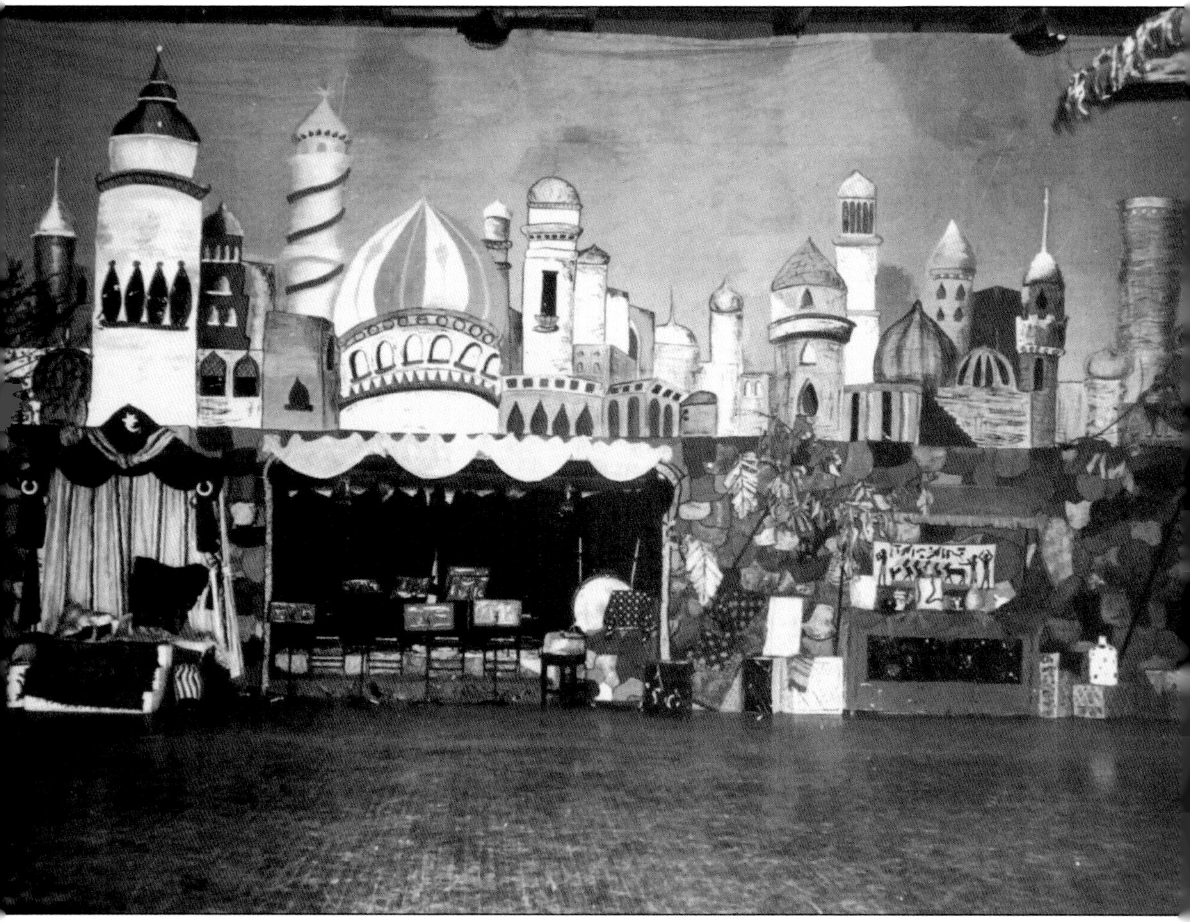

Scenery always played a major part in the success of Dormont High's annual "Varieties" productions, which were held in the gymnasium. After the choosing of a theme, the art students, under the direction of their teacher William Reed, spent many hours planning and painting the backdrop, which would completely conceal the end of the gymnasium where the members of the acts waited until it was their turn to perform. This scenery for the 1946 "Arabian Nights" shows the amount of time and talent that had been devoted to it.

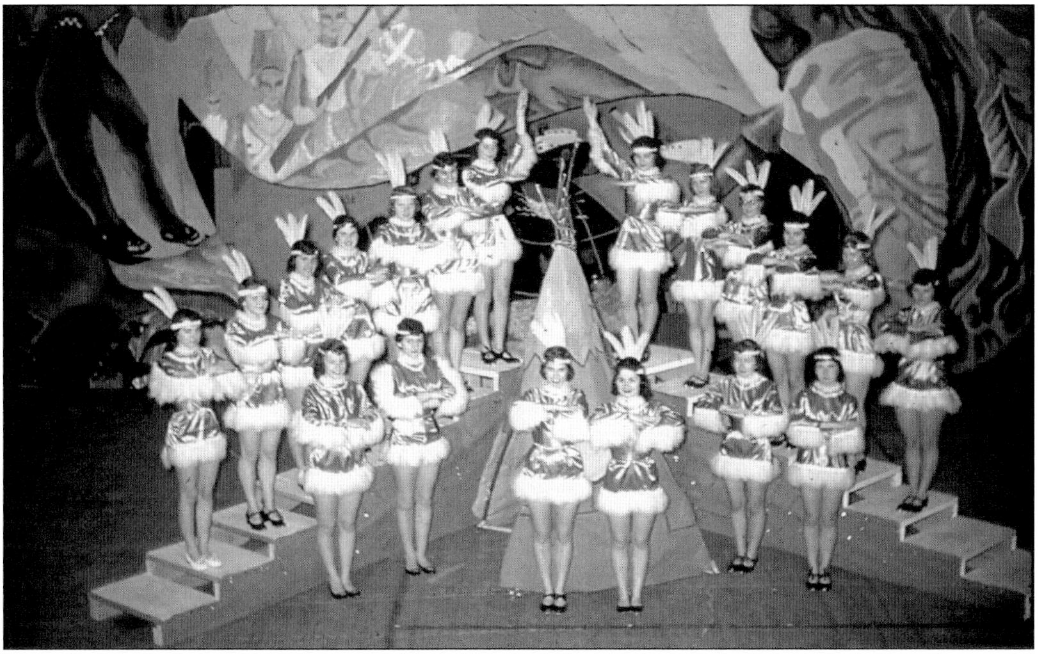

Performing in "Varieties" was a thrill. Those whose acts were chosen spent hours planning their costumes and practicing their routines. Each year the programs were varied, but they always included numbers by a tap chorus like the 1958 one shown here.

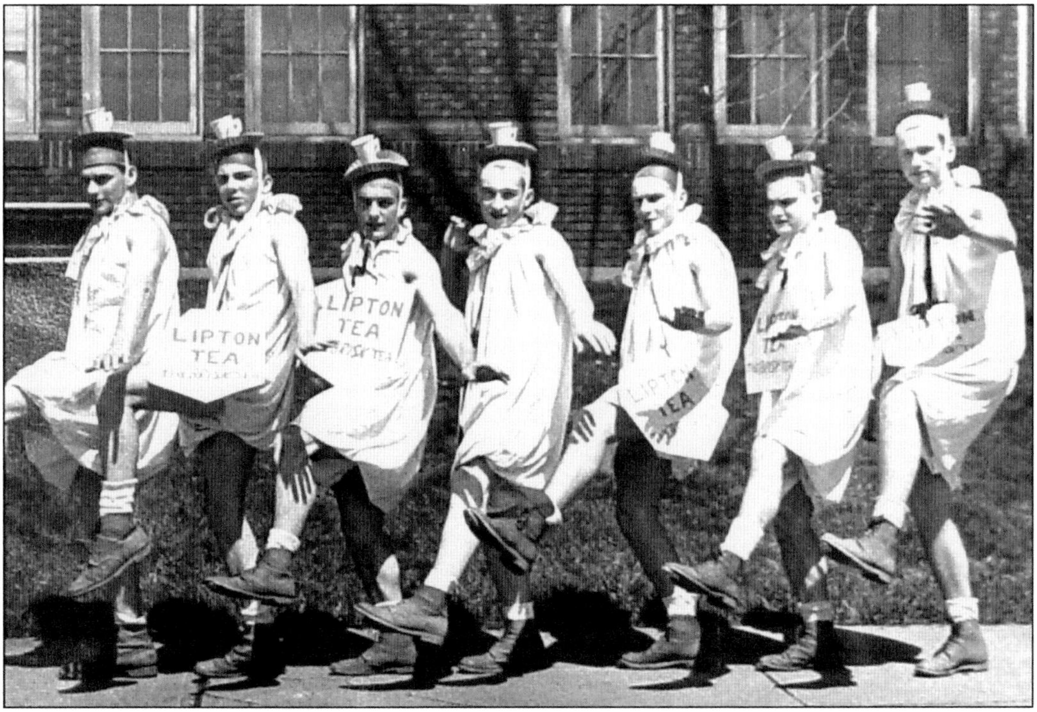

The football teams added humor to the productions. "Tea for Two" was the 1949 team's act. Some of its performers are shown here: from left to right, Thomas Wyke, William Strazza, Richard Pardini, Russell Eastwood, Fred Loeffler, William Green, and James McAnulty.

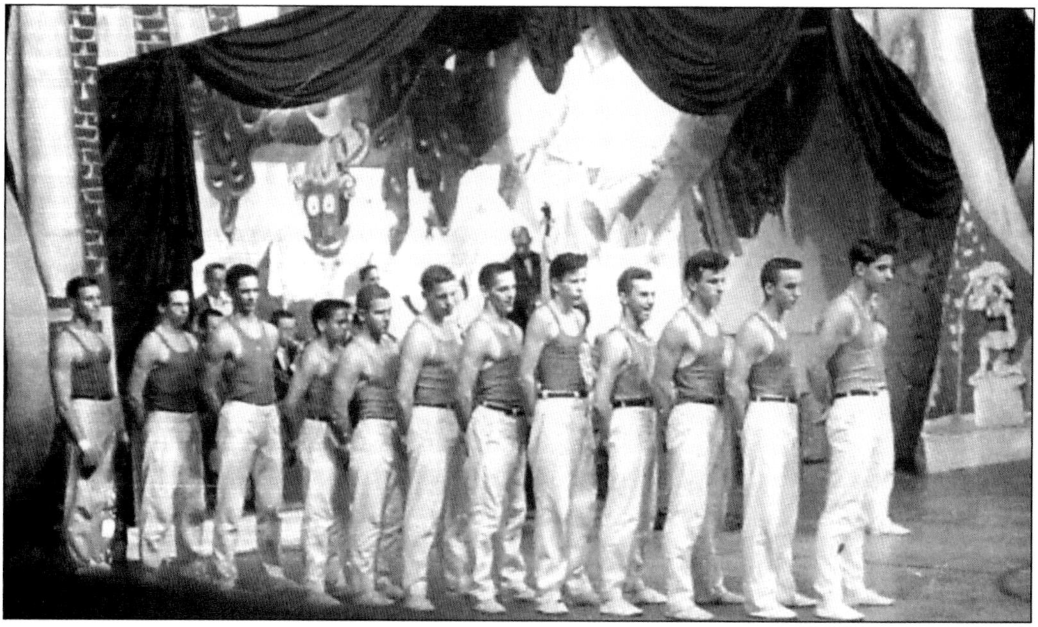

Exciting demonstrations of gymnastics by the tumbling teams, under the direction of coach Lynn Kling, provided the grand finales.

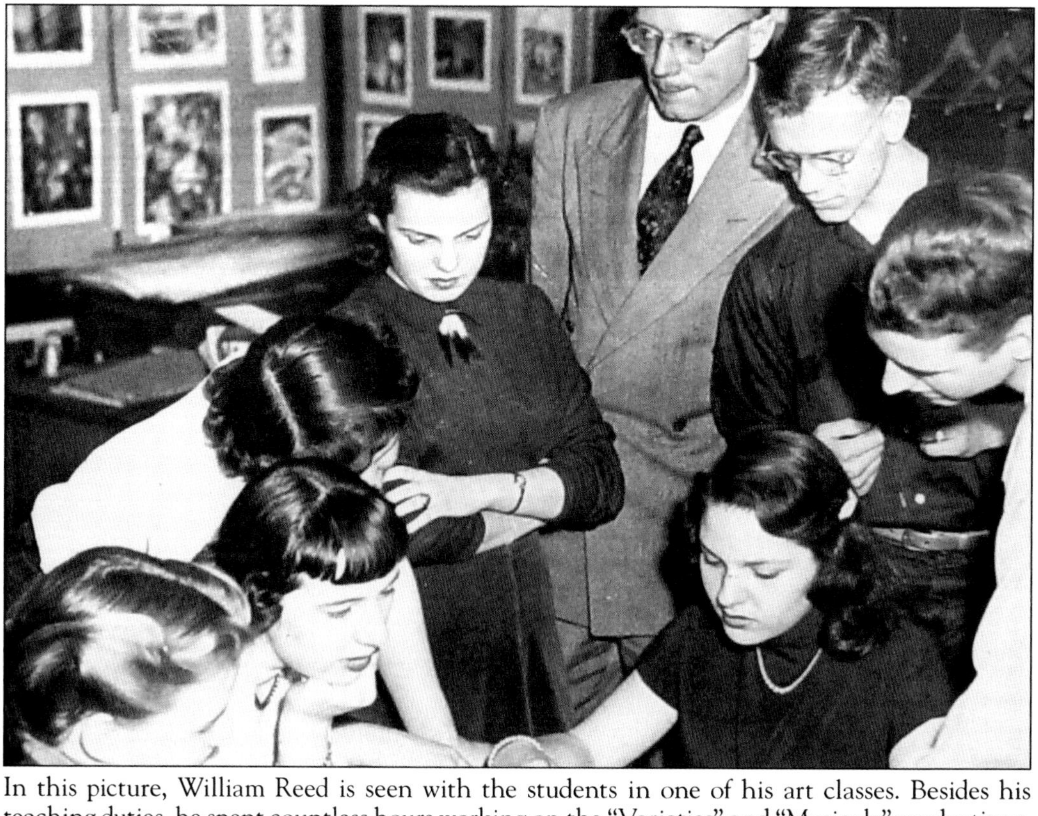

In this picture, William Reed is seen with the students in one of his art classes. Besides his teaching duties, he spent countless hours working on the "Varieties" and "Musicale" productions, directing the cheerleaders, and helping with many other school activities.

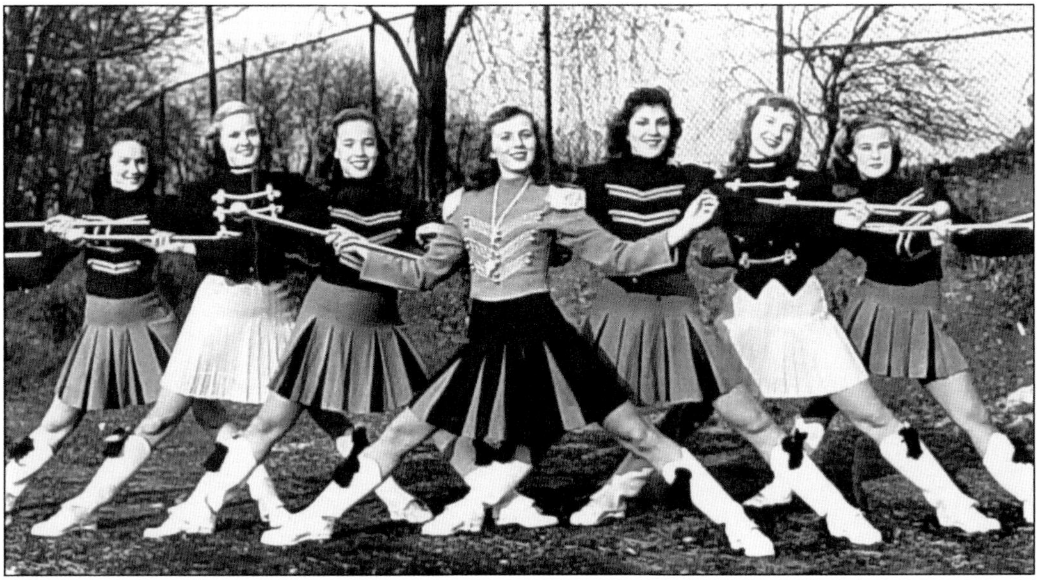

The majorettes for 1948–1949 are, from left to right, Shirley Hunter, Sarah Huddleson, Joanne McGall, Henrietta Bowden, Marie Pelino, Ann Bowden, and Janet Vaughn.

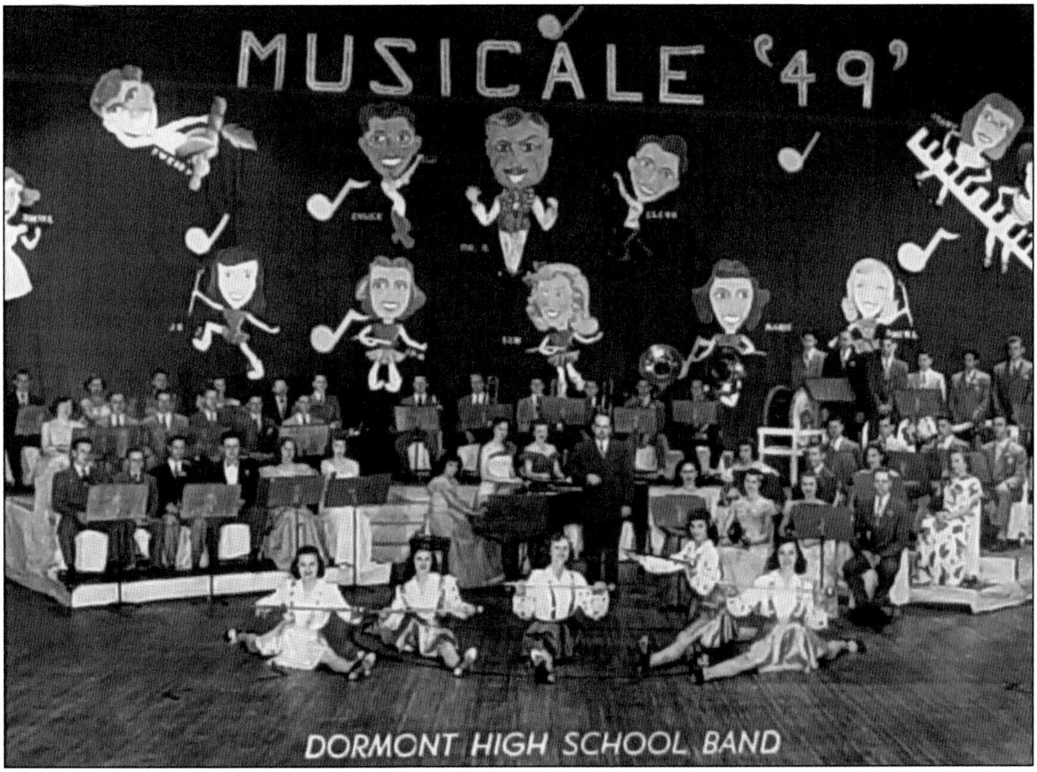

Each year, band members and majorettes joined in presenting the "Musicale" in the high school gymnasium. John Rumbarger, director and Dormont High alumnus, stands center front.

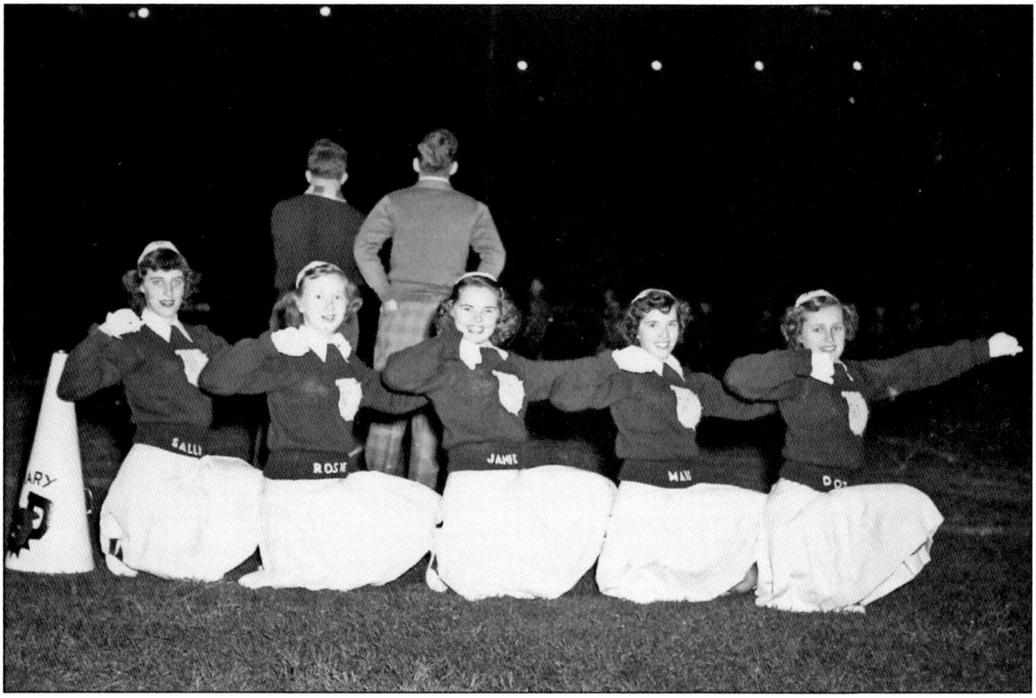

From left to right, Sally Patton, Rosemary Nalitz, Janie Laurin, Mary Prezioso, and Dorothy Minnich are cheering for Dormont's football team to beat Crafton on September 30, 1949.

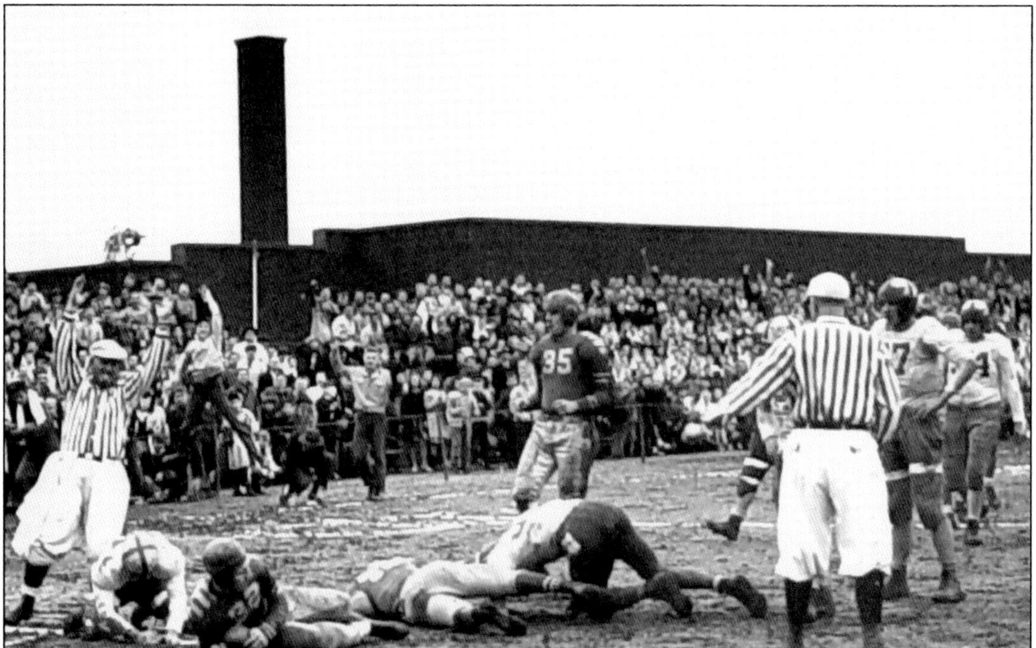

Home football games were played on the field adjoining the high school Friday afternoons at 3:00. Lucky students were driven to the away games; others went by streetcar or bus. This picture shows Don Ivol scoring a touchdown for Dormont in a 1946 home game.

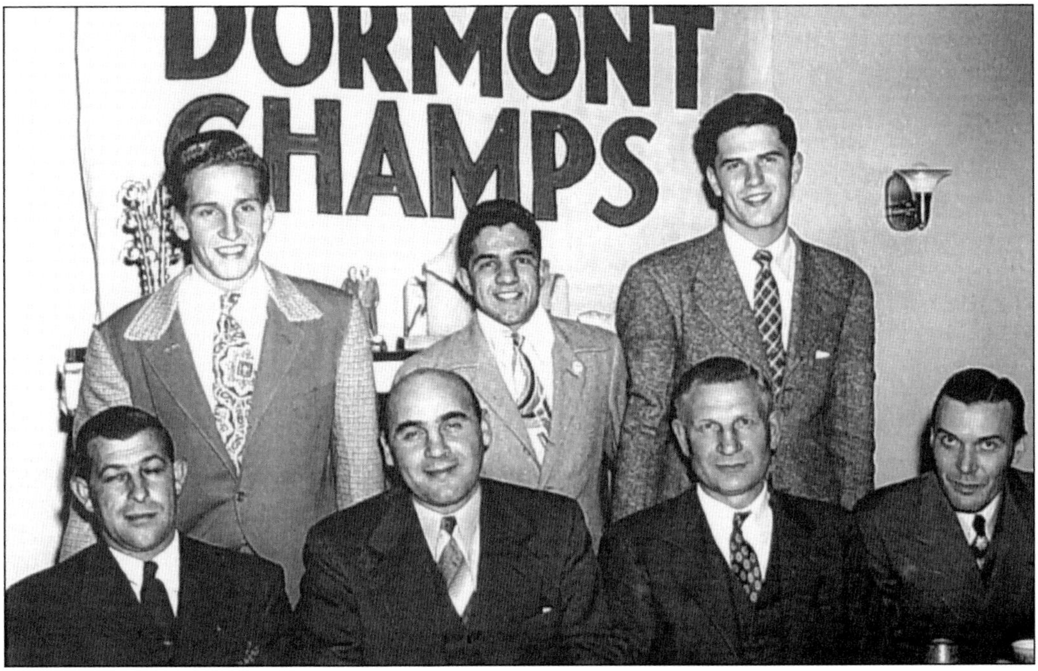

Dormont's football teams were championship contenders during the 1940s. Part of the 1947–1948 team is pictured at that year's championship banquet. Seated at the table are, from left to right, coaches Lynn Kling, Samuel Smith, and Fred Loeffler, and team physician Dr. Frank Robeson. Standing from left to right are team members Robert Boucher, John Prezioso, and Donald Smith.

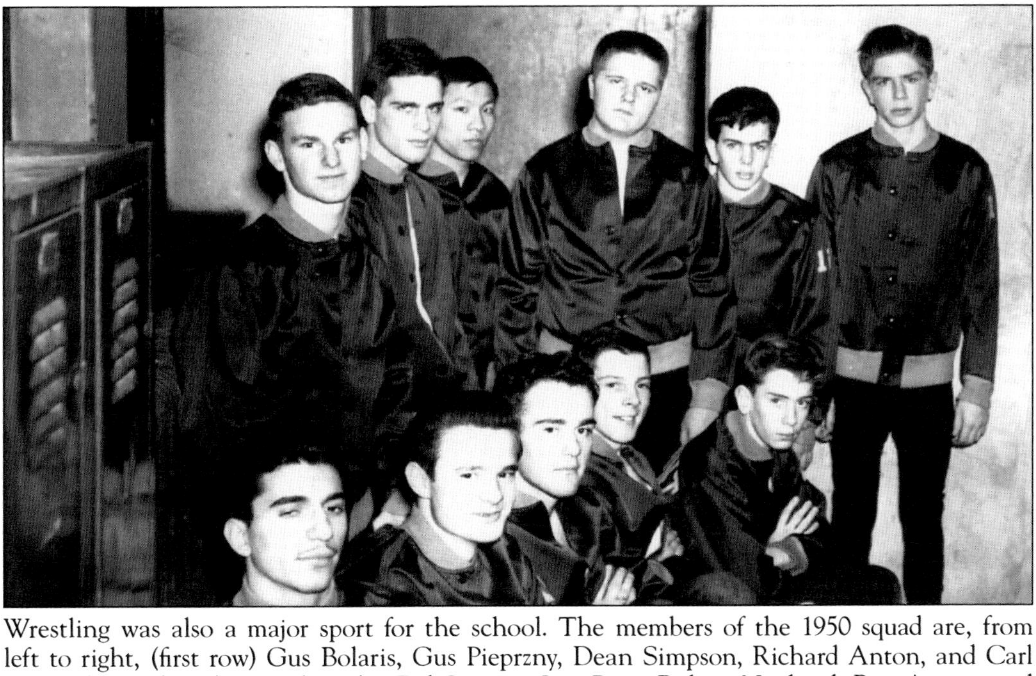

Wrestling was also a major sport for the school. The members of the 1950 squad are, from left to right, (first row) Gus Bolaris, Gus Pieprzny, Dean Simpson, Richard Anton, and Carl Muck; (second row) Daniel Little, Ted Stinner, Lee Ping, Robert Neuhard, Ray Anton, and Donald Kelso.

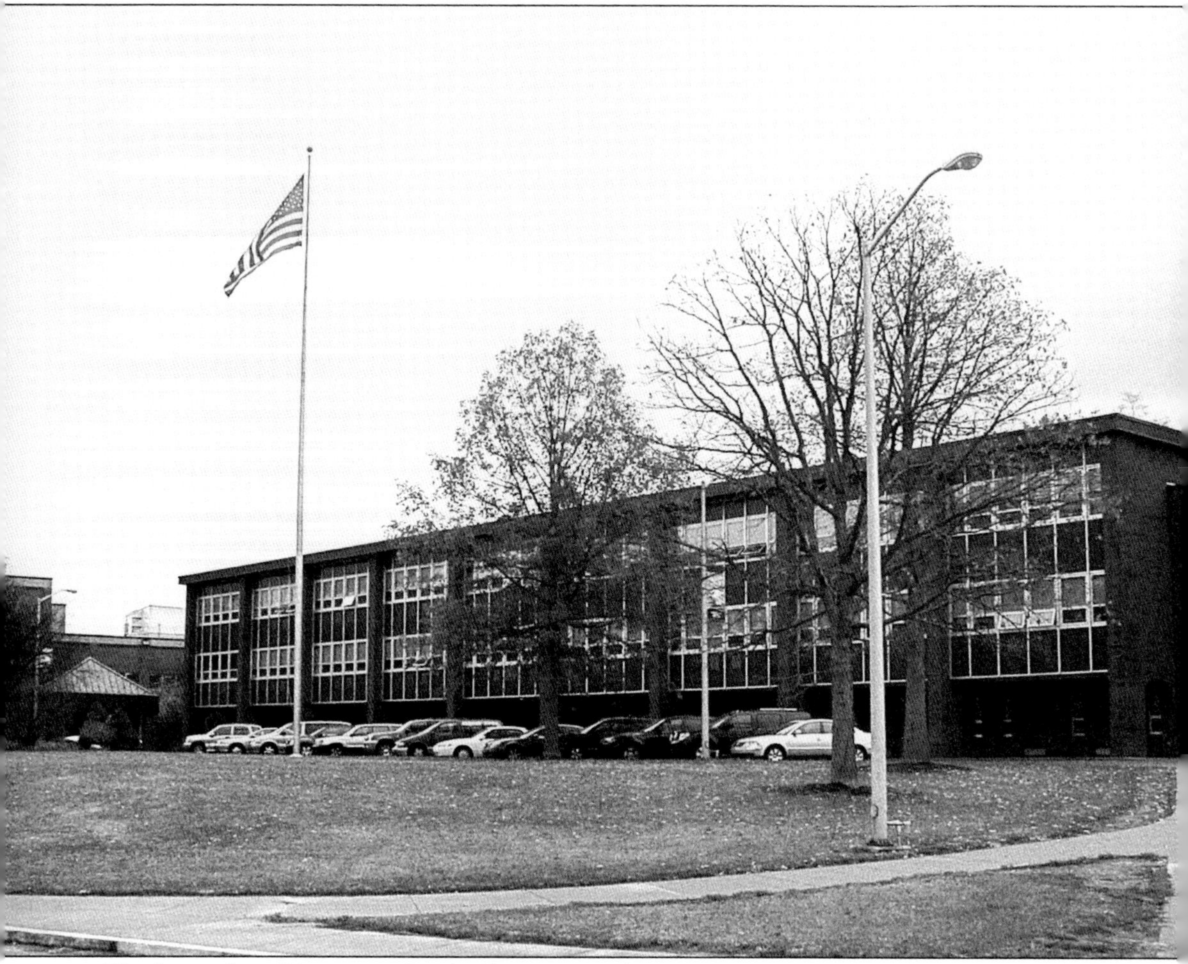

The boroughs of Dormont, Castle Shannon, and Green Tree incorporated their school systems into the Keystone Oaks School District in 1964. The new district's name combines the idea of a key to the door in Dormont, a stone from the castle in Castle Shannon, and an oak tree in Green Tree. A high school was built in 1969 at the end of Kelton Avenue on what had been a section of Morton's farm. When it opened, the old high school was used as Jay Neff Middle School until it was razed in 1996. The Keystone Oaks Middle School section was added to the building in that same year.

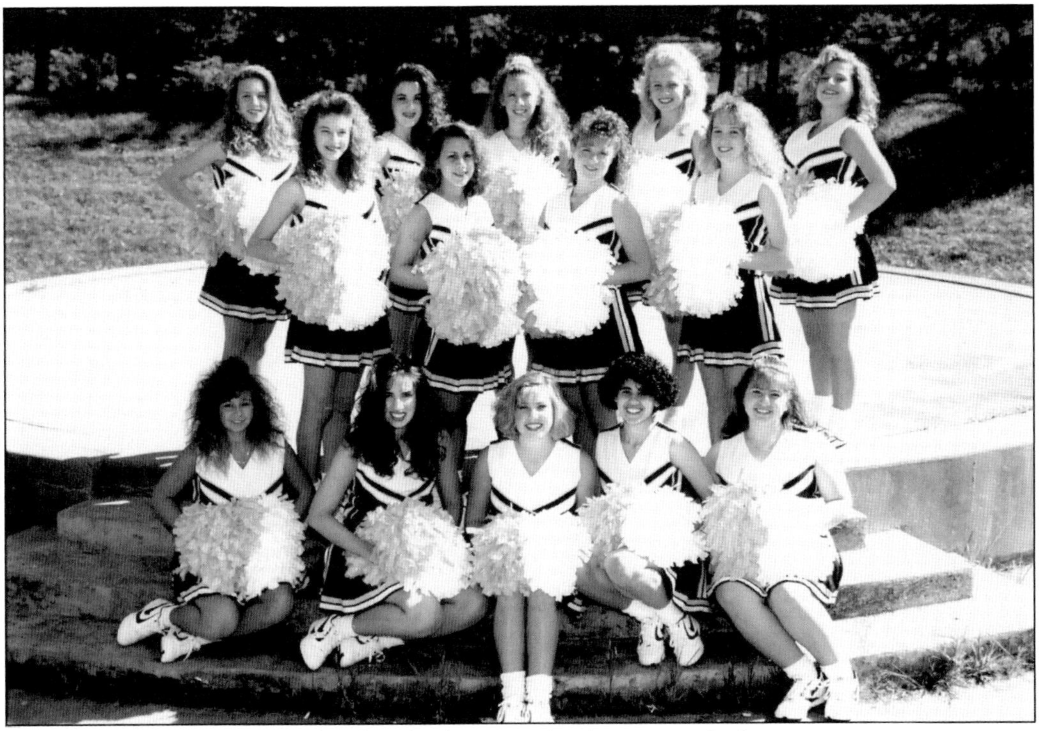

The 1992–1993 Keystone Oaks cheerleaders pose for this picture before a game.

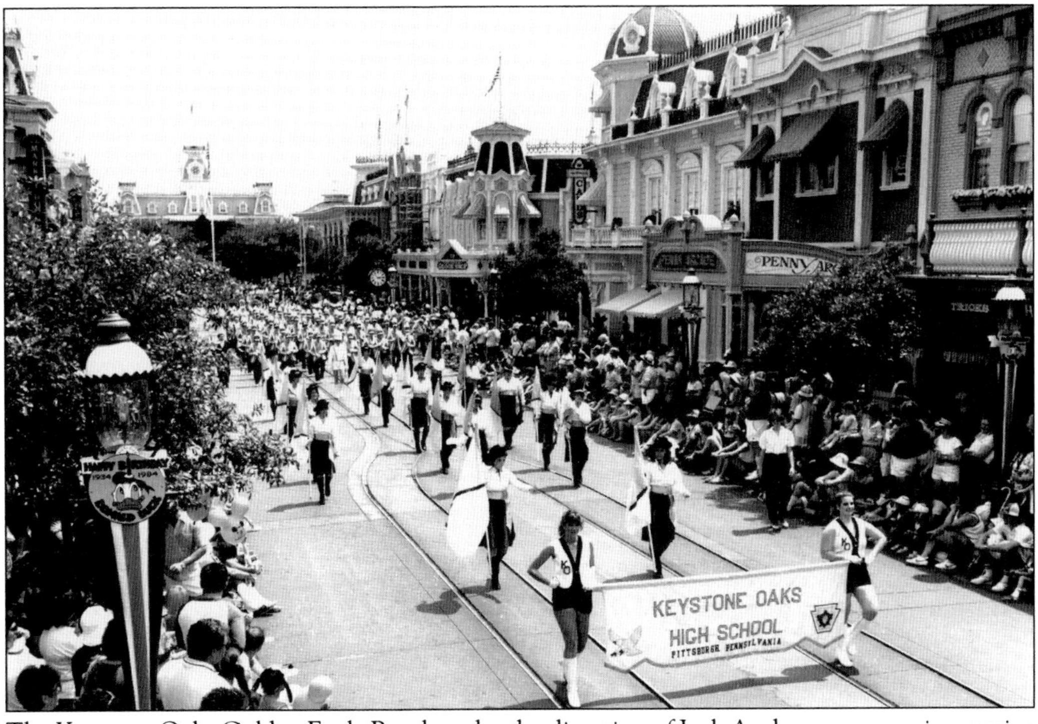

The Keystone Oaks Golden Eagle Band, under the direction of Jack Anderson, was an impressive sight as it marched through the streets of Disney World in 1984.

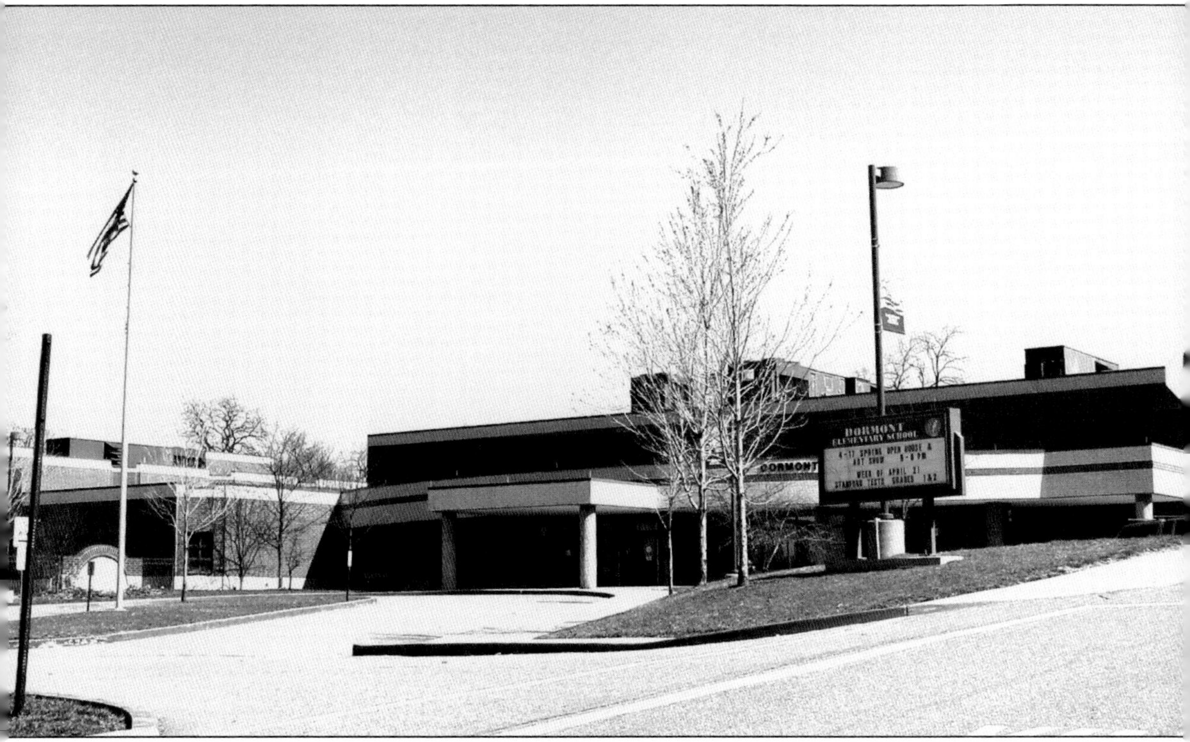

The 5.7-acre site of Dormont High School and its athletic field became the location of Dormont Elementary School, which opened in 1996. Its classrooms for kindergarten through fifth grade are arranged by pods. The stage in the large combination gymnasium/cafeteria is used for school productions and special programs. A playground, butterfly garden, sports field, and large parking area flank the building.

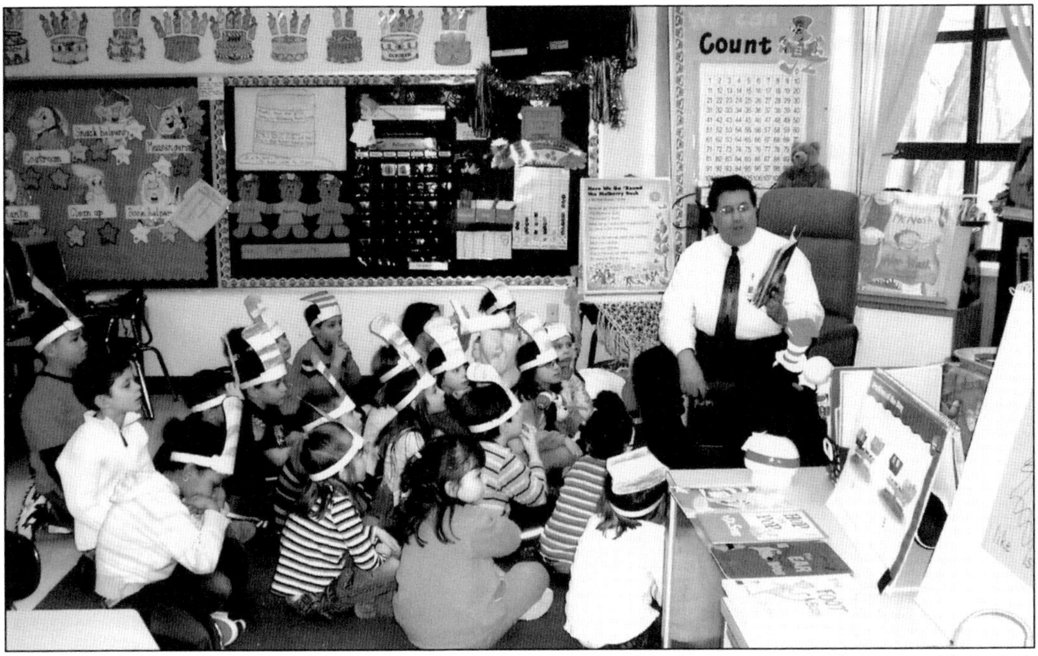

Guest readers are invited into the classrooms during the school year. Principal George Shevchik reads to these children in 2005.

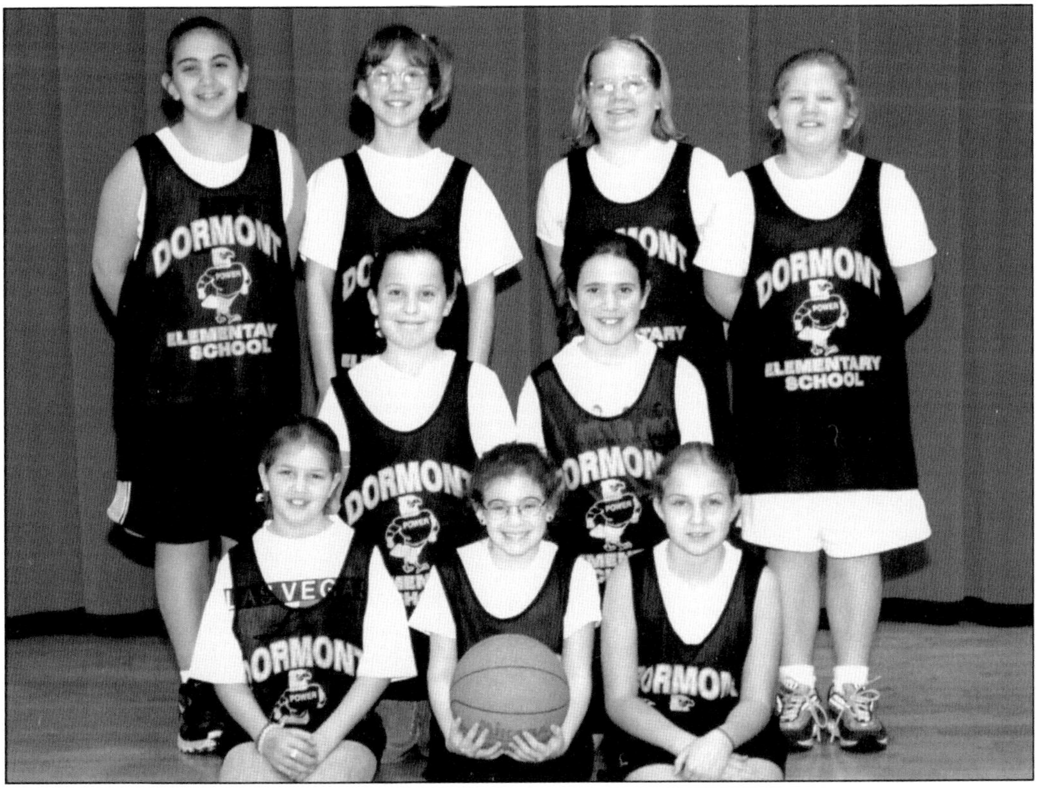

These players represent the 2000 basketball team.

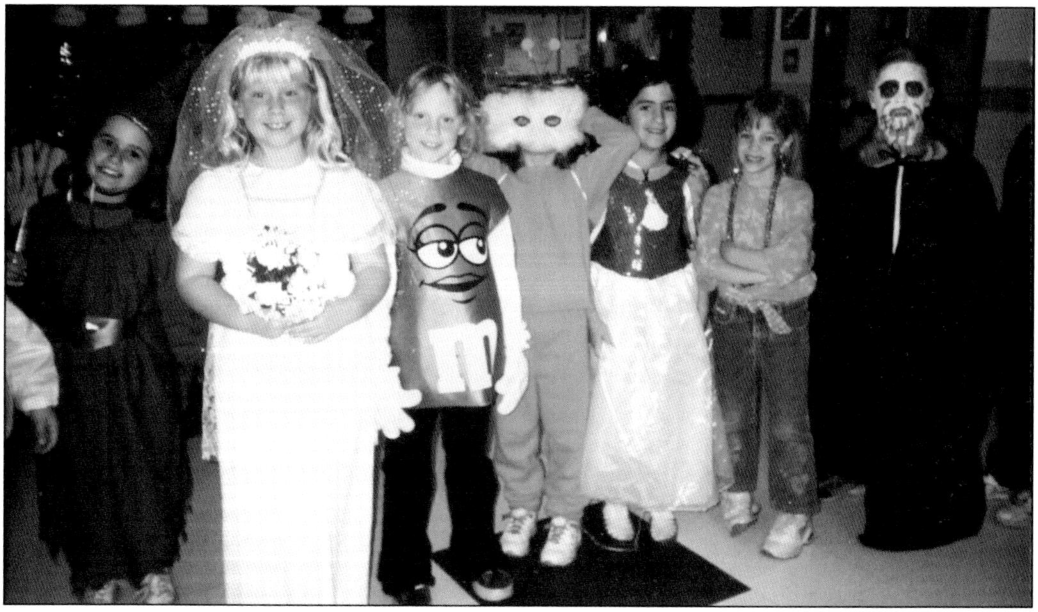

Elementary children wear their Halloween costumes for the schooltime parades that have been a Dormont tradition for many years. In 2000, these second graders, from left to right, Brittany Natto, Rachael Vietmeir, Kayla Huetter, Britteny Palashoff, Georgia Yamalis, Kara Kreeply, and Zack Acopora, waited while their teacher, Donna Killmer, took this picture before they joined the parade.

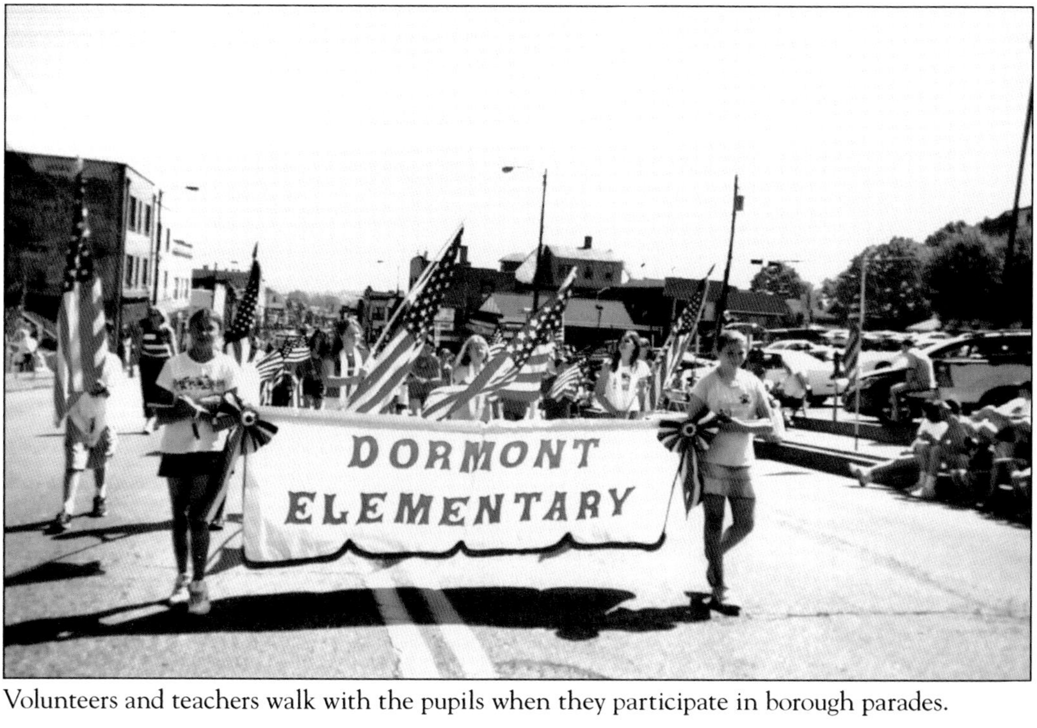

Volunteers and teachers walk with the pupils when they participate in borough parades.

Three

BUSINESSES

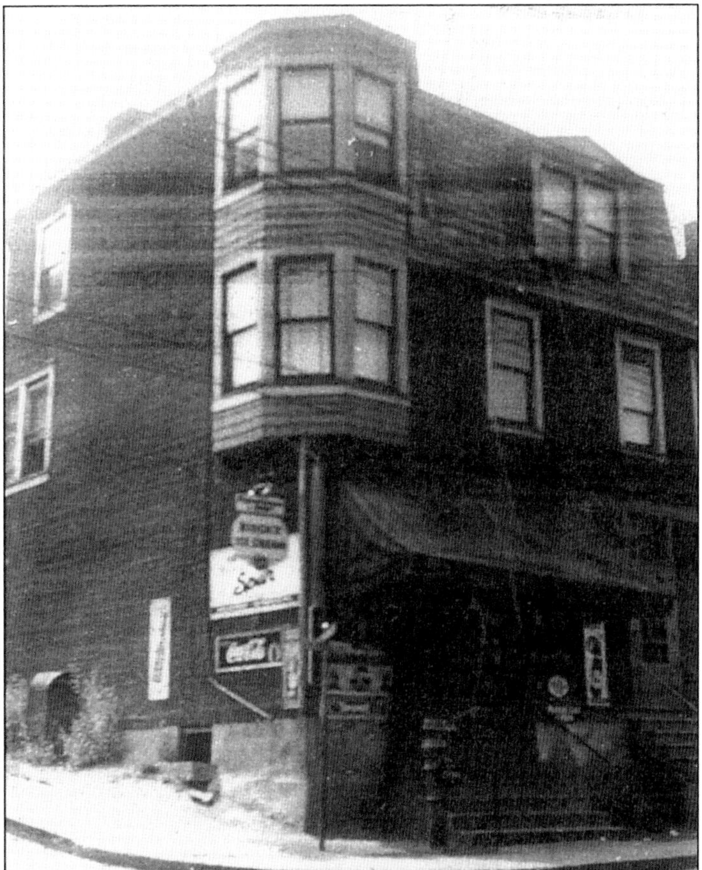

Independent mom-and-pop stores, like Sobotsis' at the corner of Illinois and Annex Avenues, were located within walking distance for borough residents from the earliest years until the 1970s. Some had cases filled with penny candy that made them favorite places for children to stop as they walked home from school. When ownership of automobiles became common after World War II and South Hills Village was built, neighborhood stores such as these began to disappear.

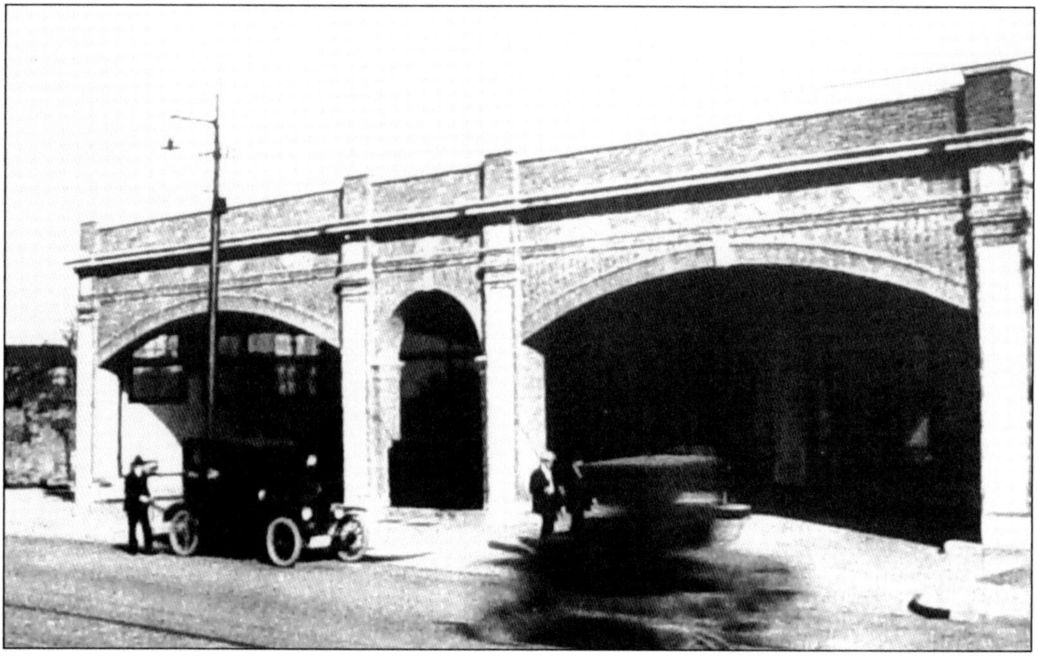

Montgomery-Rohrich Packard occupied this building at the corner of West Liberty and Dormont Avenues in the 1920s. Other car agencies were located there before the building was remodeled for other uses.

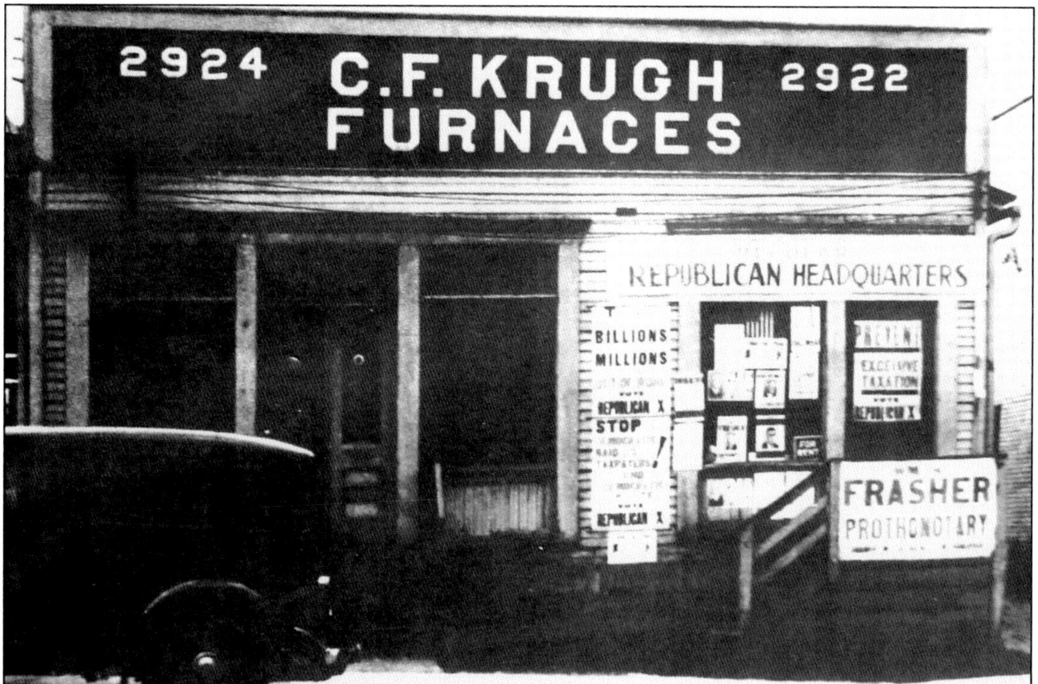

A Mr. Krugh was a tinsmith making ducts and flues for furnaces when he opened his business at 2924 West Liberty Avenue in 1910. After the business closed in 1959, the borough bought the property for a public parking lot. This picture was taken in 1935.

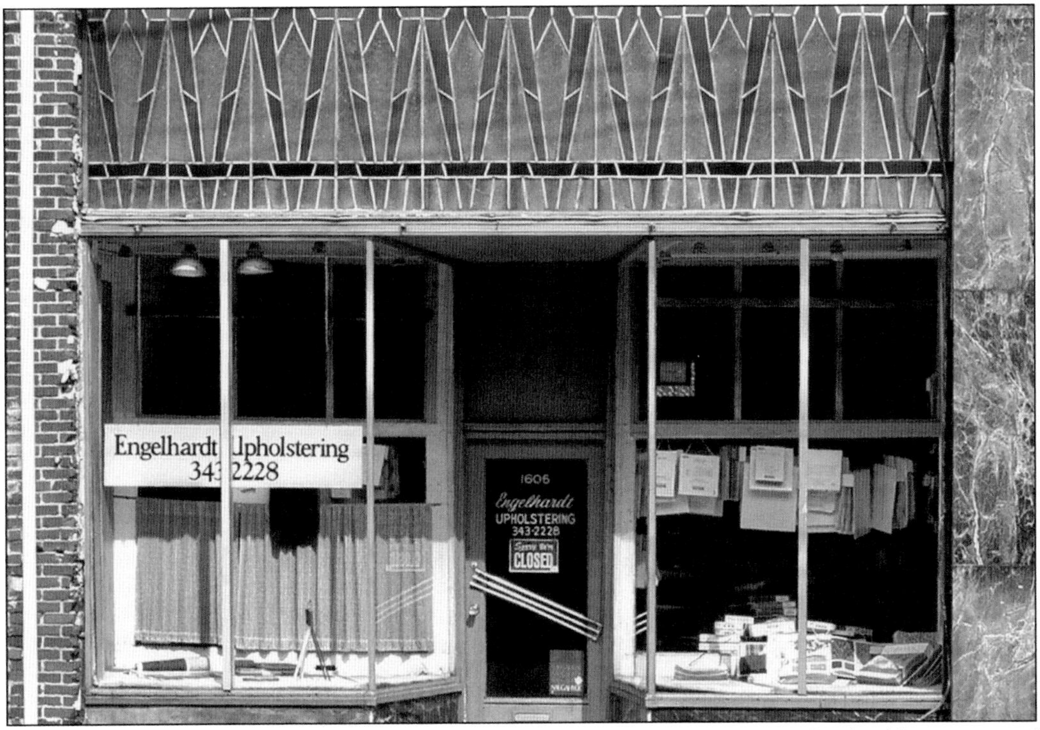

Engelhardt Upholstering has been at 1606 Potomac Avenue since 1971. This building is one of two in the borough that still have their interesting art deco glass designs across the front.

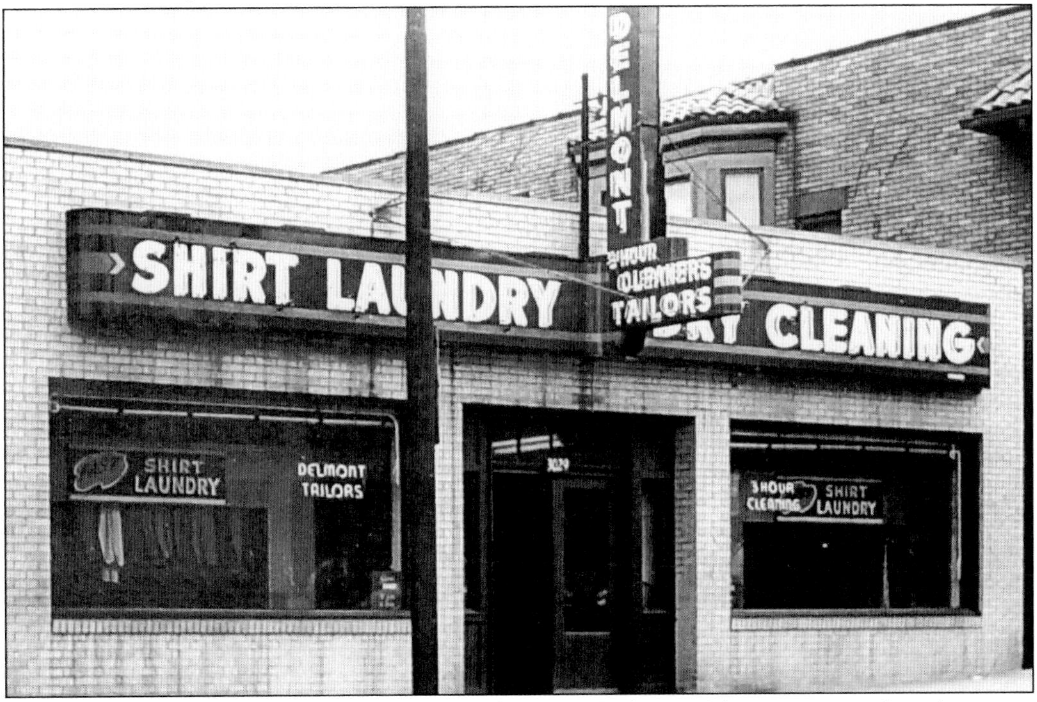

From the time it opened in 1929 until it closed in 1965, Delmont Cleaners was in three locations on West Liberty Avenue: 3235, then 3211, and finally 3029.

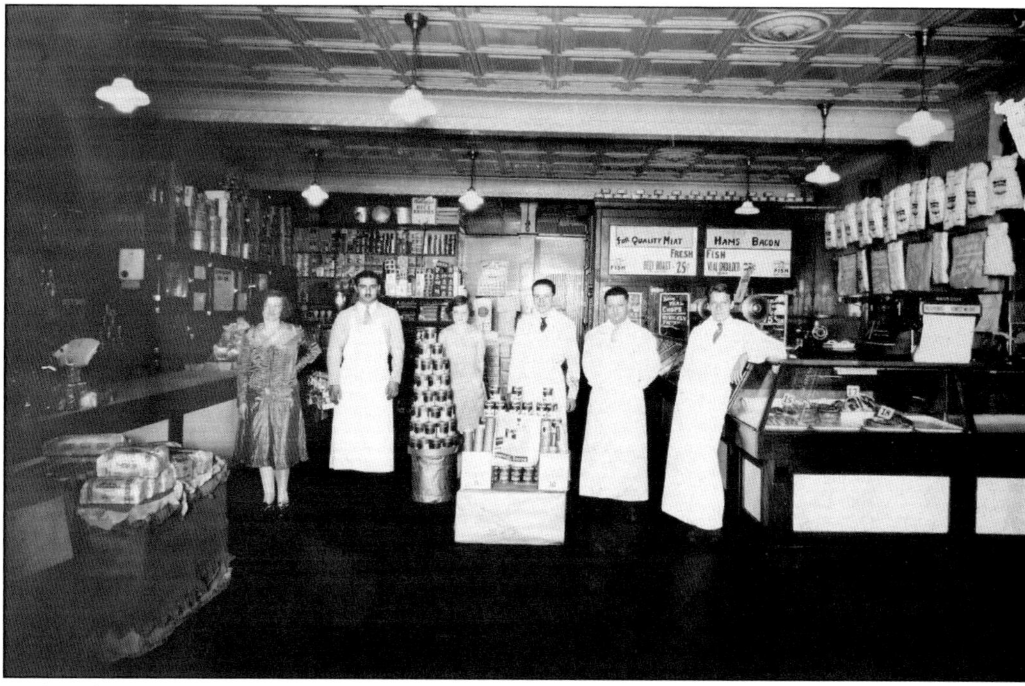

Beck's Clover Farm Market was one of the earliest businesses in Dormont when it opened at 2997 West Liberty Avenue around 1907. Here are (from left to right) Verne Bellingham Beck, Walter Beck, Dorothy Beck Connell, Carl Beck, and two employees inside the store on May 8, 1930.

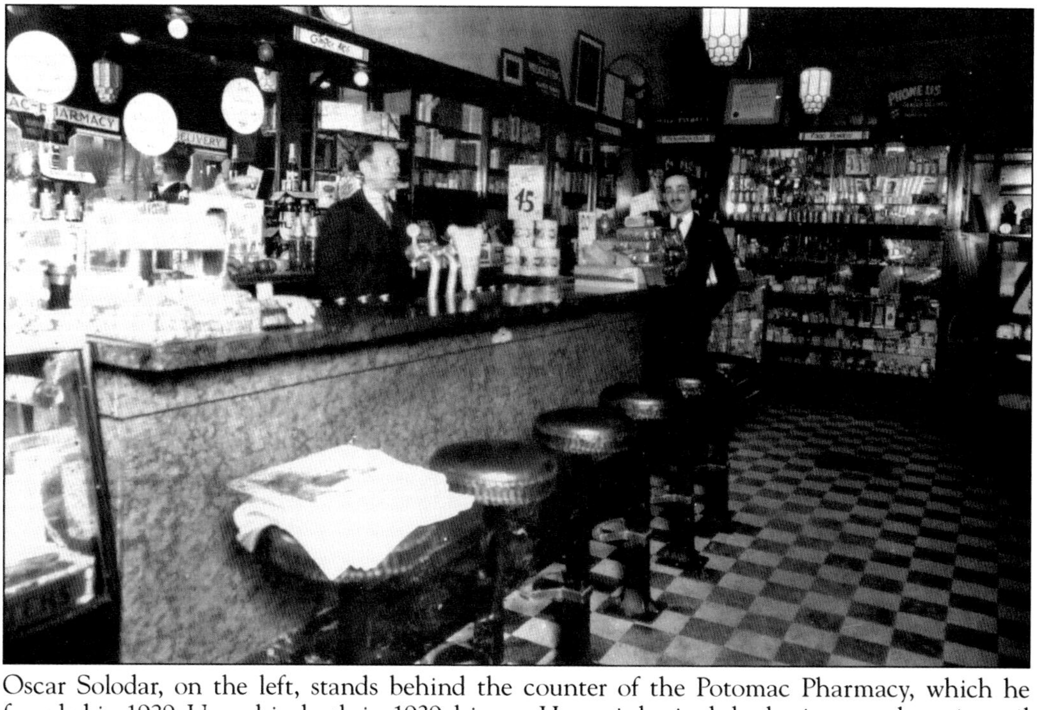

Oscar Solodar, on the left, stands behind the counter of the Potomac Pharmacy, which he founded in 1929. Upon his death in 1939, his son Henry inherited the business and ran it until 1991. The pharmacy is still there under new ownership, although its soda fountain is gone.

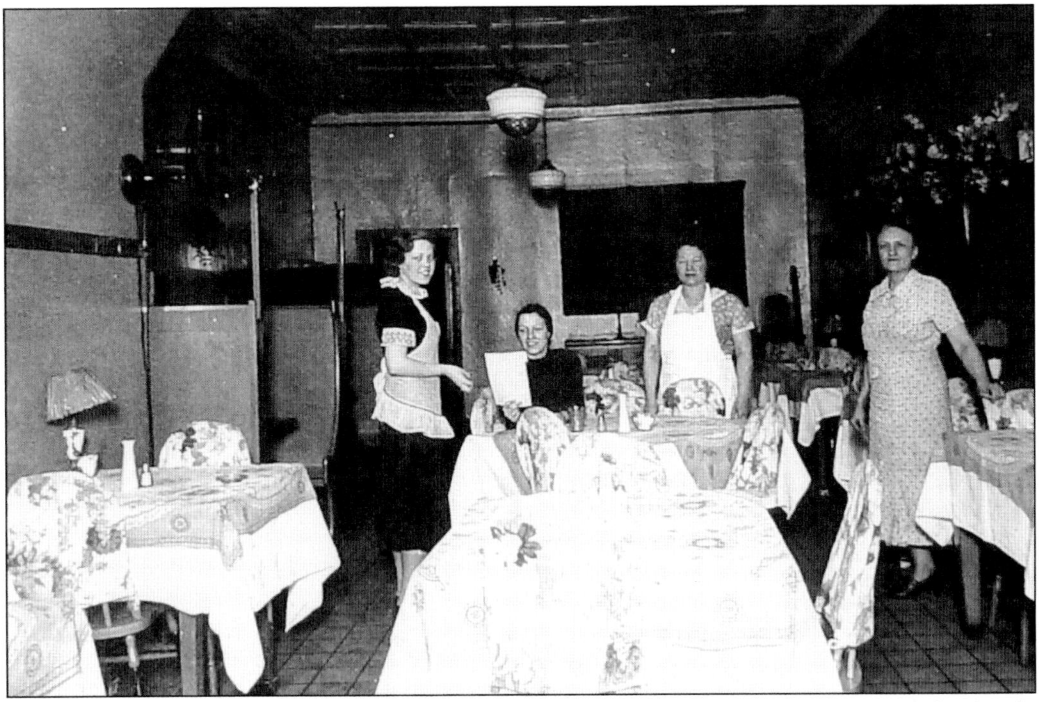

Wayside Inn, located at 3267 West Liberty Avenue in the early 1930s, was one of the family restaurants that used to be in the borough. In this picture, Donna Lohen, the owner's wife, is standing on the right.

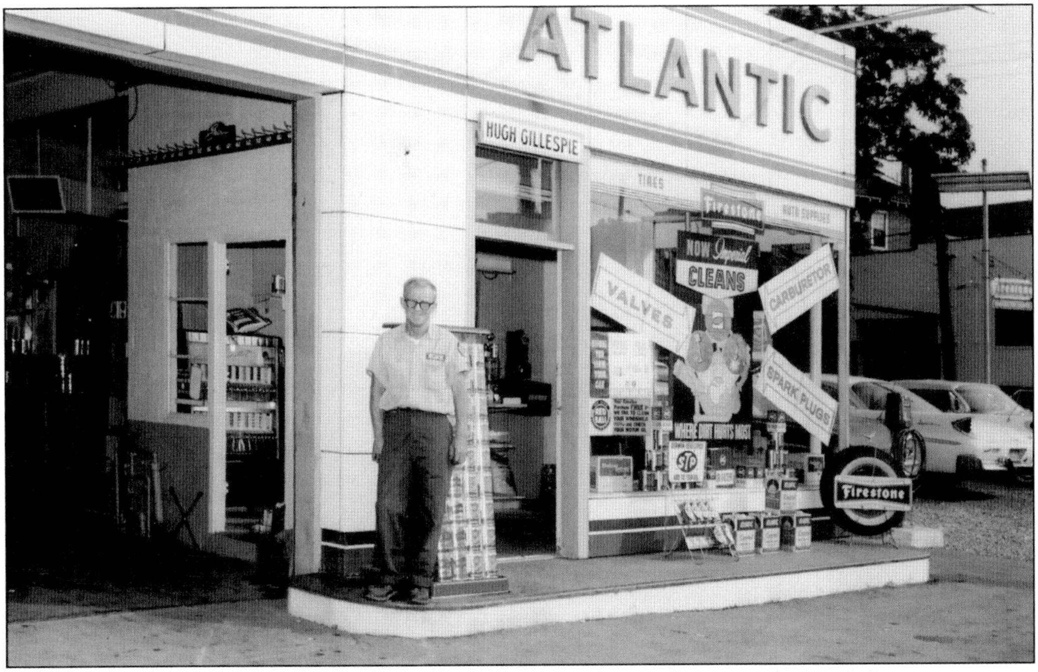

In 1965, Hugo "Red" Gillespie waited while this picture was taken outside his Atlantic station at the corner of West Liberty and Dormont Avenues. After opening the business in 1958, he was there for more than 20 years.

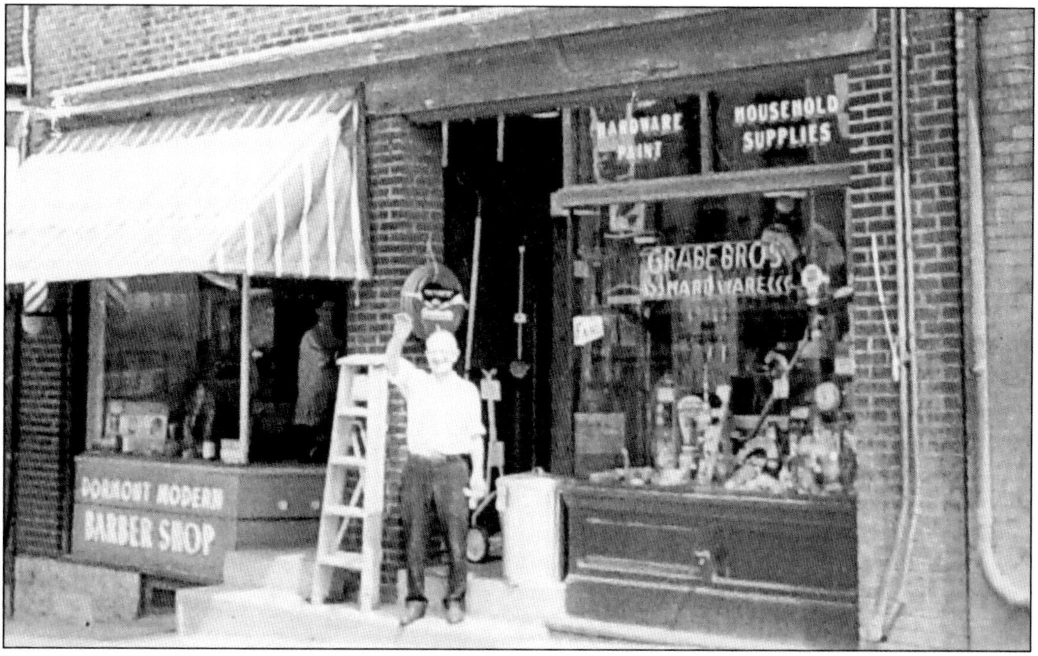

Lou Grabe stands in front of Grabe Brothers Hardware, 2927 West Liberty Avenue. Shortly after it opened, the store's complete stock and friendly service made it a favorite shopping place of South Hills residents. When customers wanted something not in one of the many drawers or on the shelves, one of the Grabes would open the trapdoor and go into the basement to get it. The store closed in 1978.

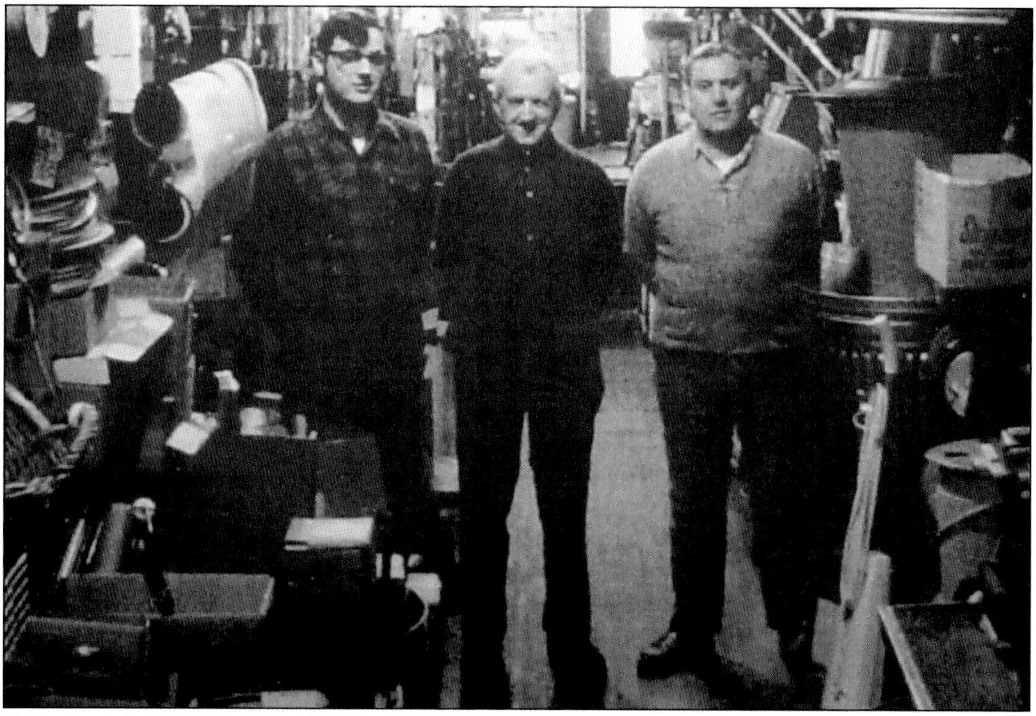

George Grabe, center, poses for this picture inside the store with two friends.

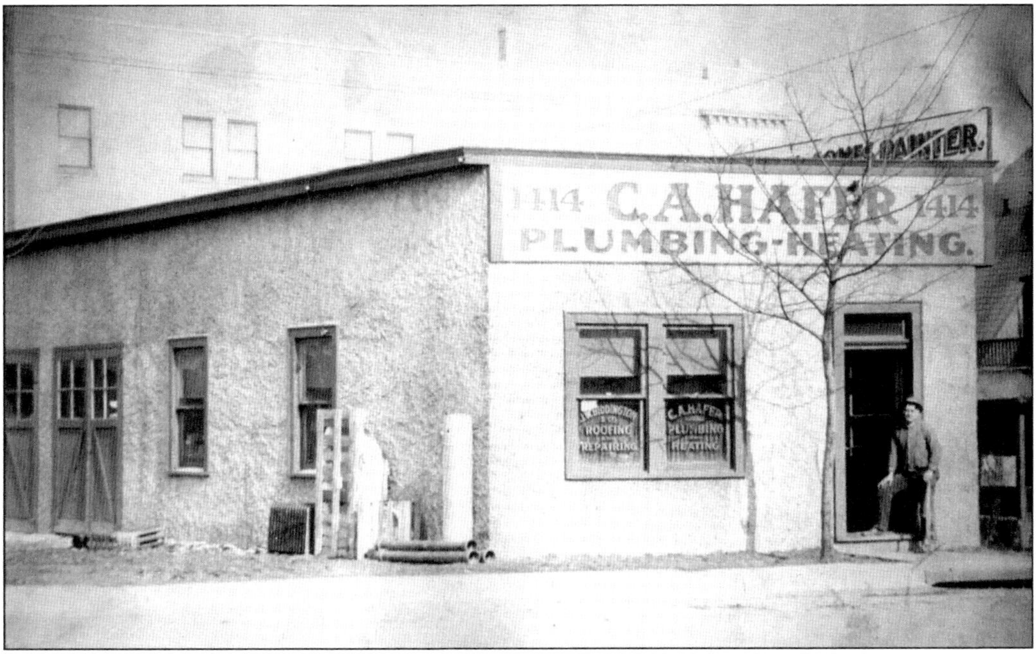

This is the building in which Charles Hafer opened his plumbing and heating business in 1908. The business stayed in the family for generations. Charles Hafer Jr. (with briefcase) and his siblings are seen here in front of the store with their employees.

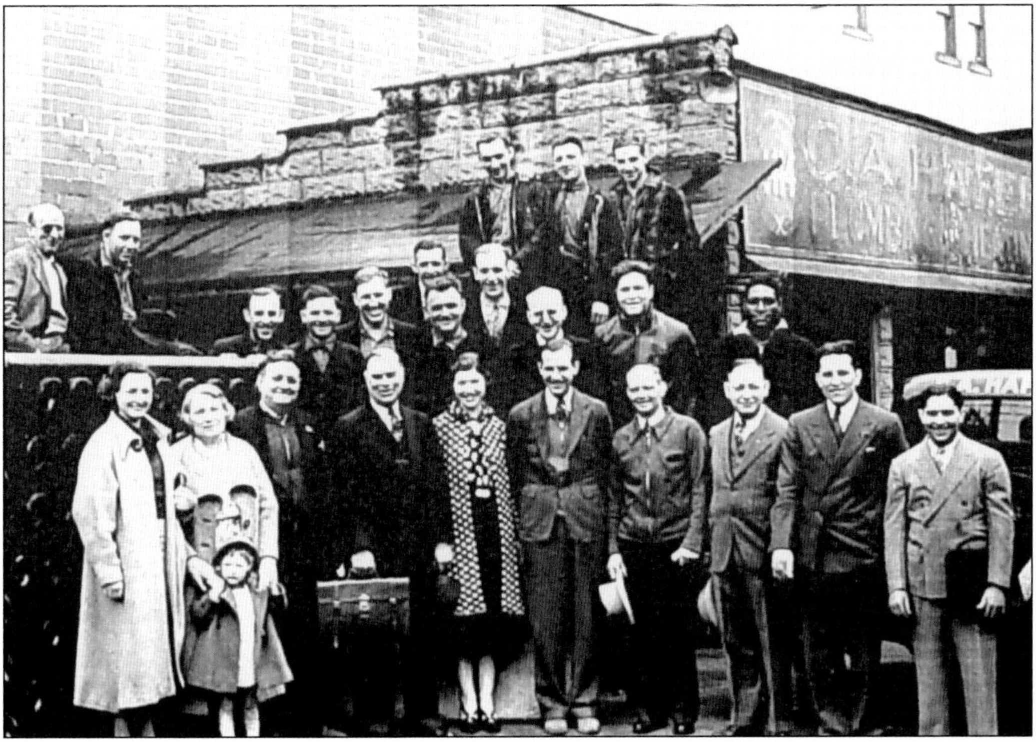

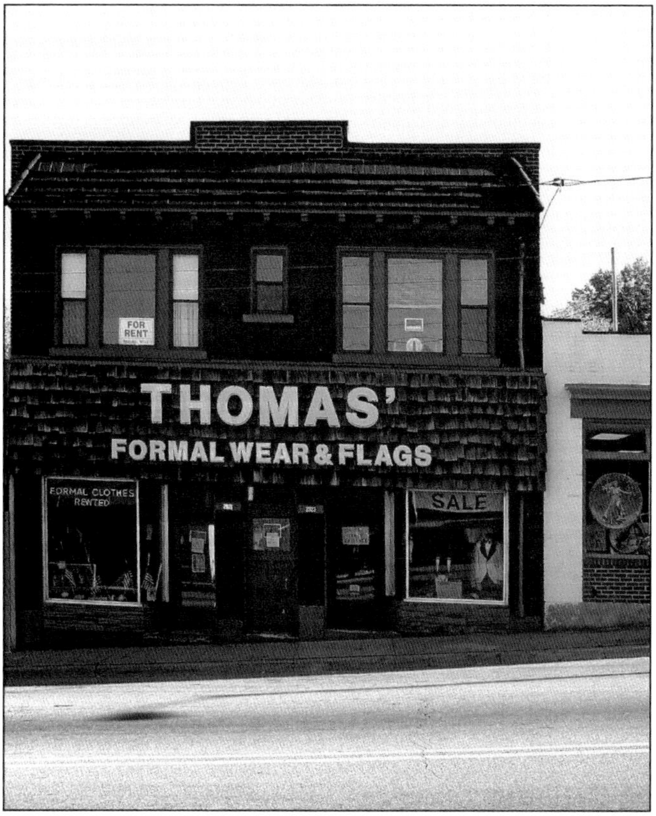

Charles "Jake" Thomas opened his first cleaning and tailoring shop in 1906. He changed its location three times before moving it into this building at 2921 West Liberty Avenue. Through the years, Jake became better known for tuxedo rentals and the sale of flags. When he died in 1968, his son Charles Jr. ran the business until 2007.

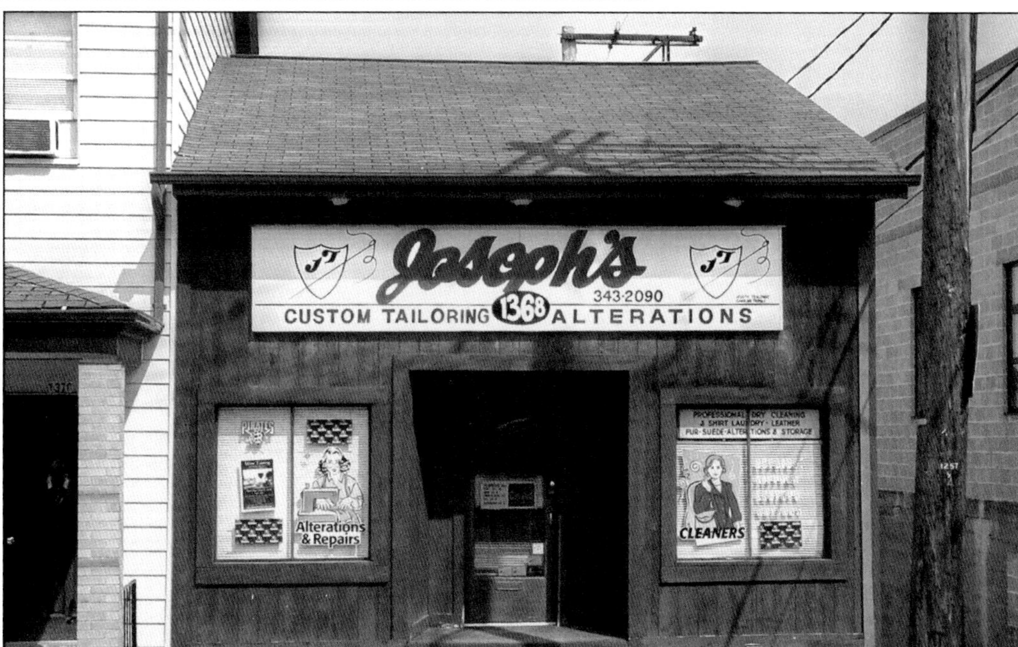

Various businesses were located at 1368 Tennessee Avenue before Joseph's Custom Tailoring and Alterations moved there around 1980.

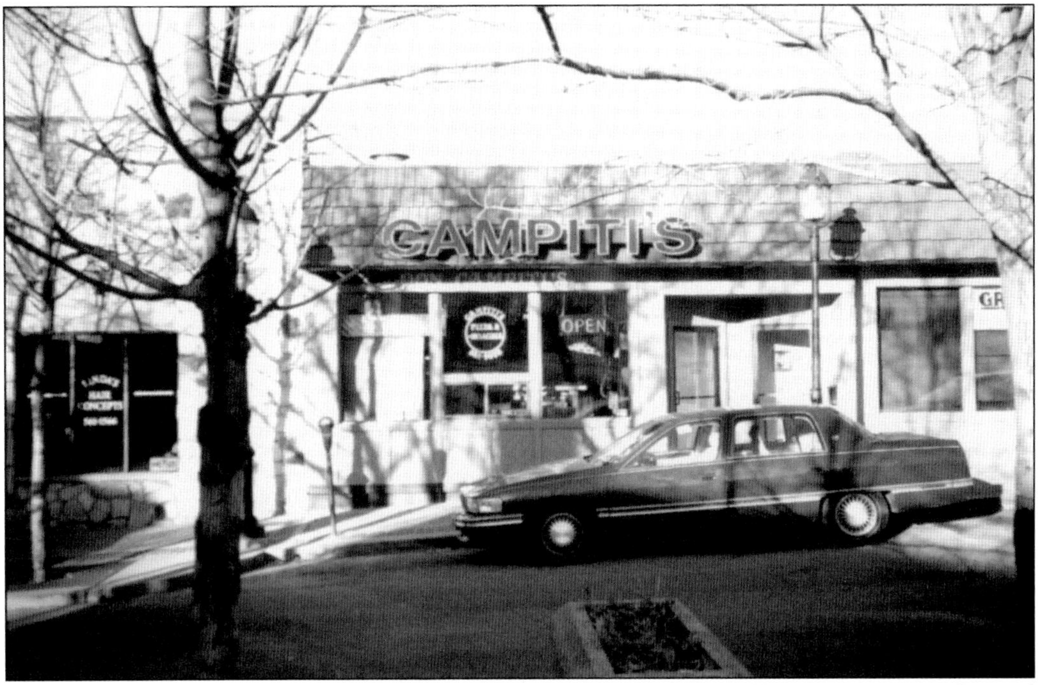

No. 1509 Potomac Avenue has been a favorite place of pizza-loving folks since Campiti's located its business there in 1962. Former residents still go there for pizza or hoagies when they are in this area.

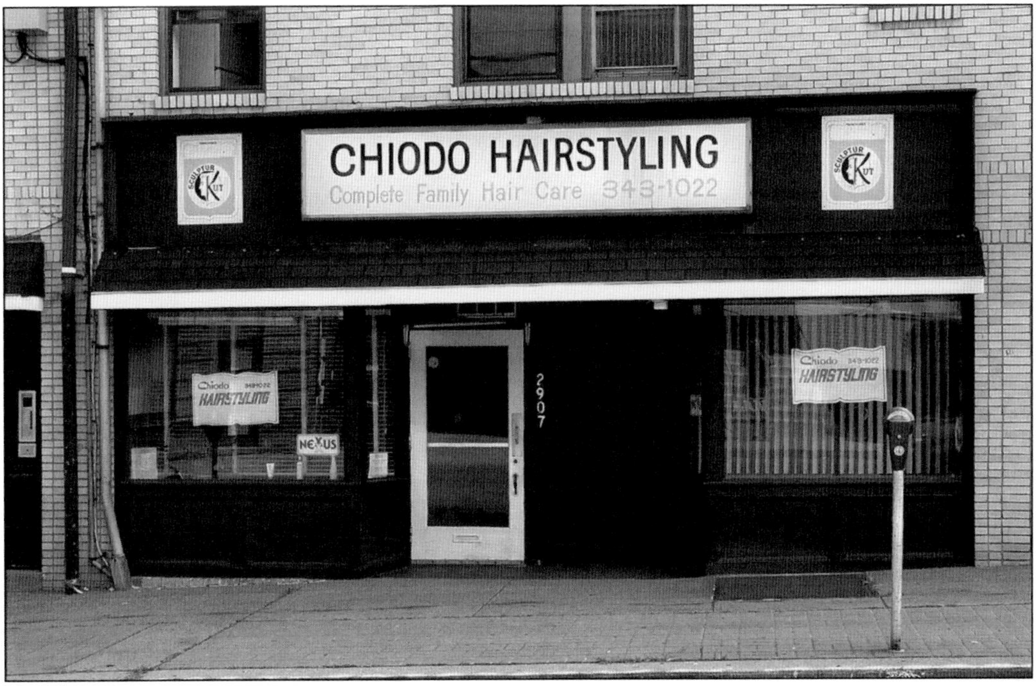

When Peter (Pete) Chiodo opened his barbershop at 2907 Glenmore Avenue in 1950, it had but one chair and men's haircuts cost 50¢. Regular customers are still keeping Pete busy.

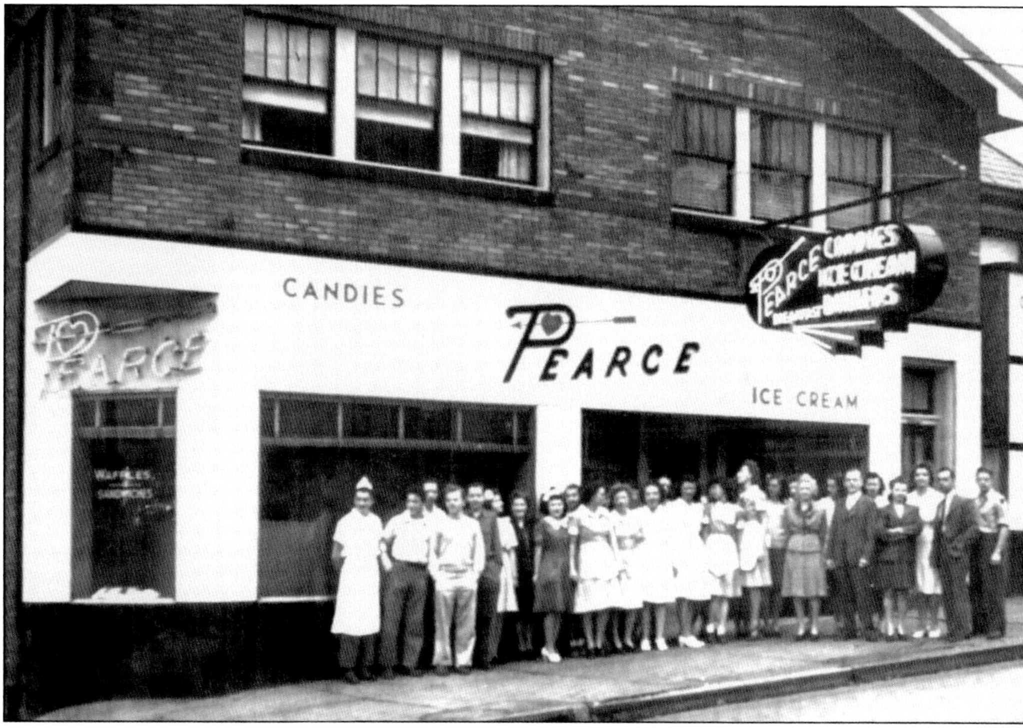

Pearce's, at 3039 West Liberty Avenue, was known for its sandwiches, ice-cream treats, and especially its homemade candy. Those who were hungry enough to eat a very large banana split would be awarded a pin proclaiming, "I was a pig at Pearce's." High school students worked there during the 1940s and 1950s.

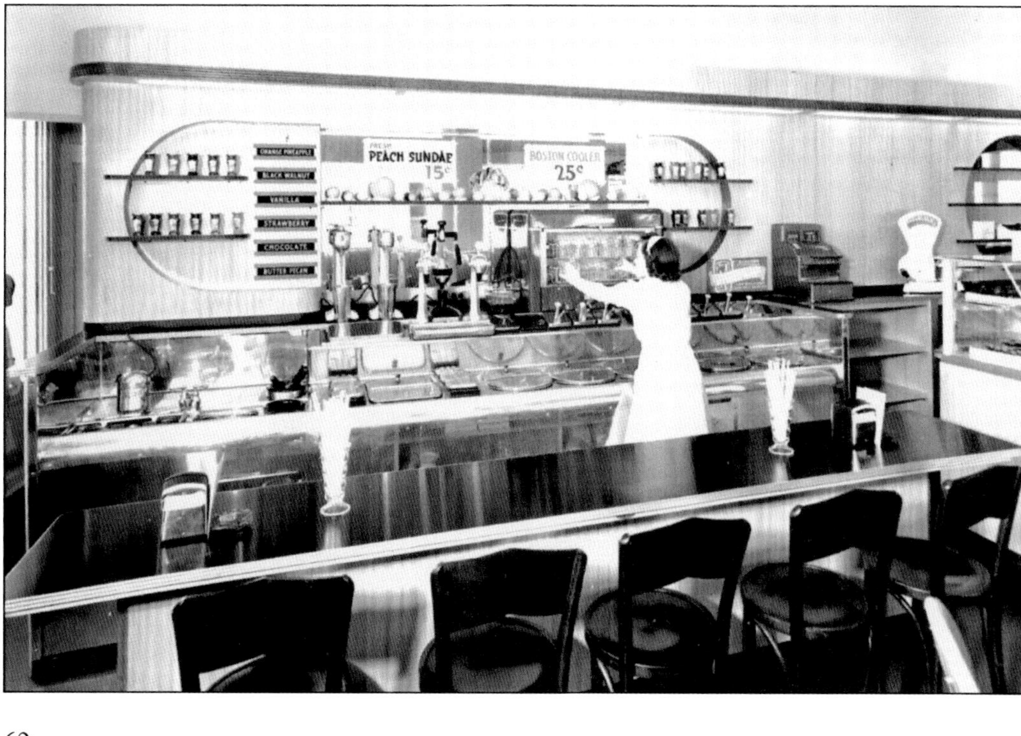

Members of Dormont's Brownlee family had their real estate and law offices at 3117 West Liberty Avenue for many years.

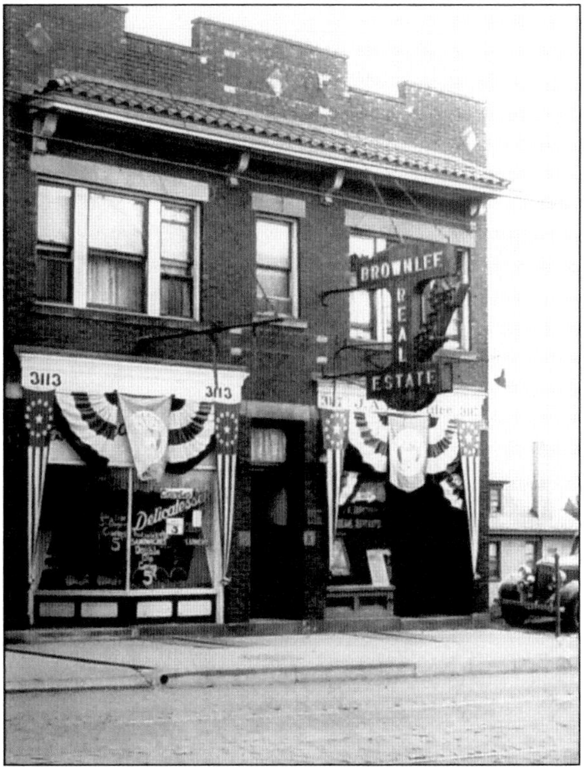

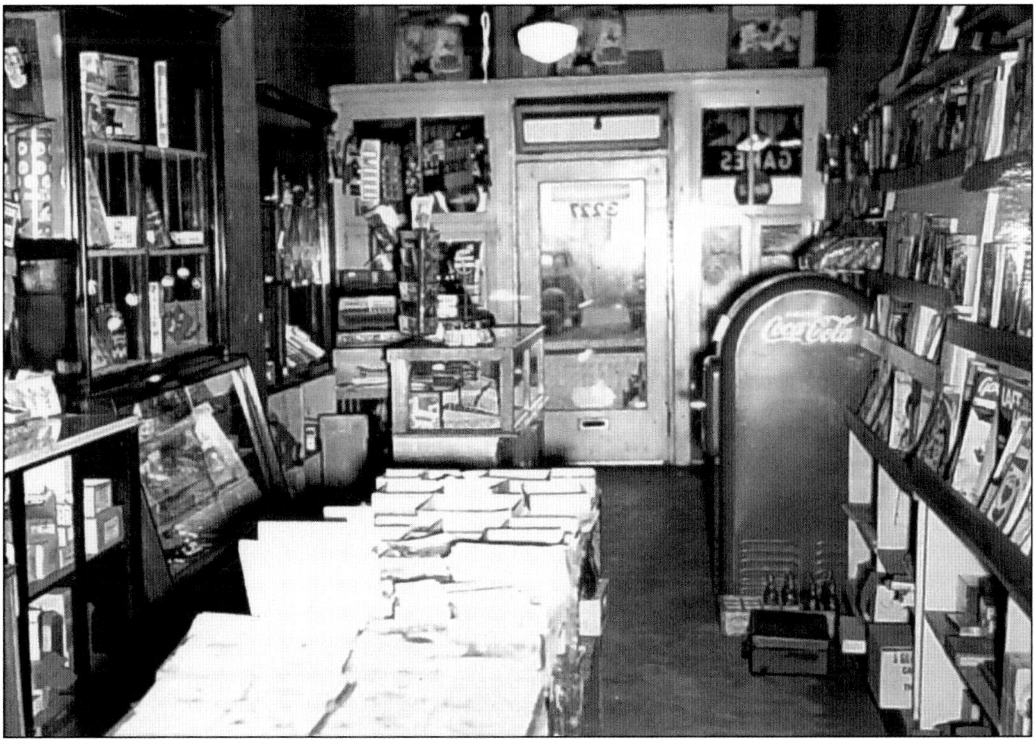

West Liberty News was located at 3227 West Liberty Avenue during the 1940s and 1950s.

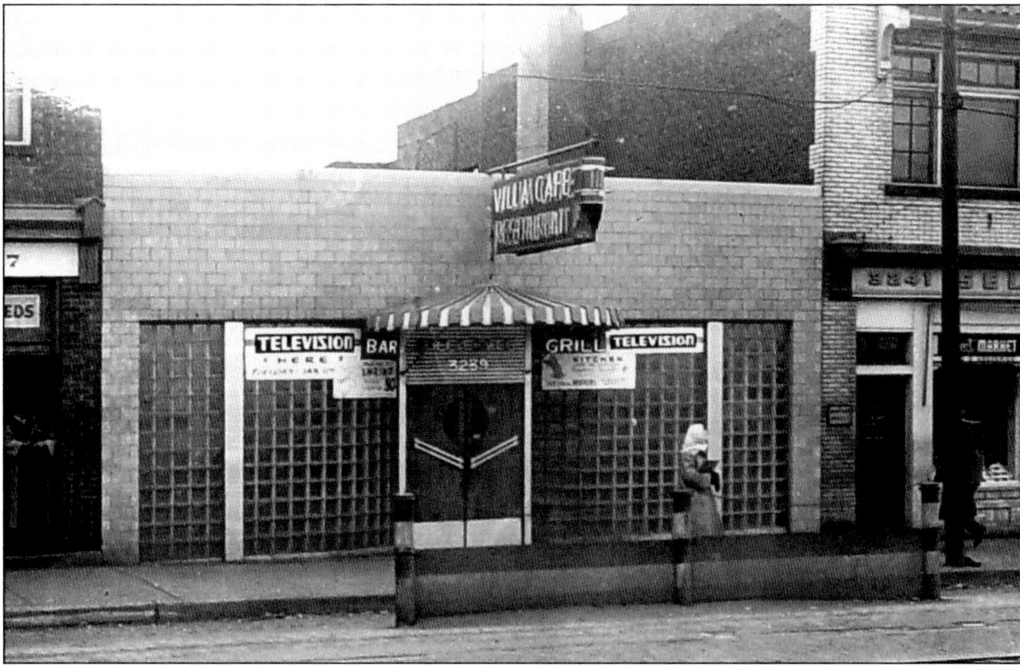

From 1961 until the early 1970s, Villa Café was located at 3239 West Liberty Avenue. Cain's-A-Saloon is located there now.

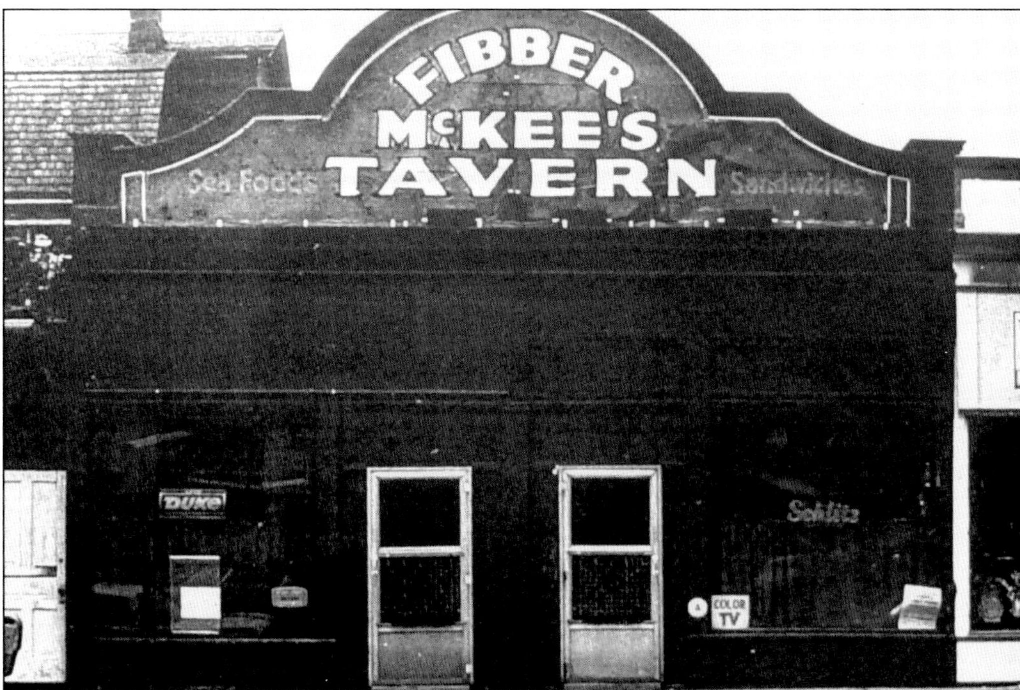

"The best shrimp and fish sandwiches in town" was one of Fibber McKee's claims to fame for the restaurant/bar he opened in 1937. The building at 1533 Potomac Avenue was one of those razed for the light-rail transit station.

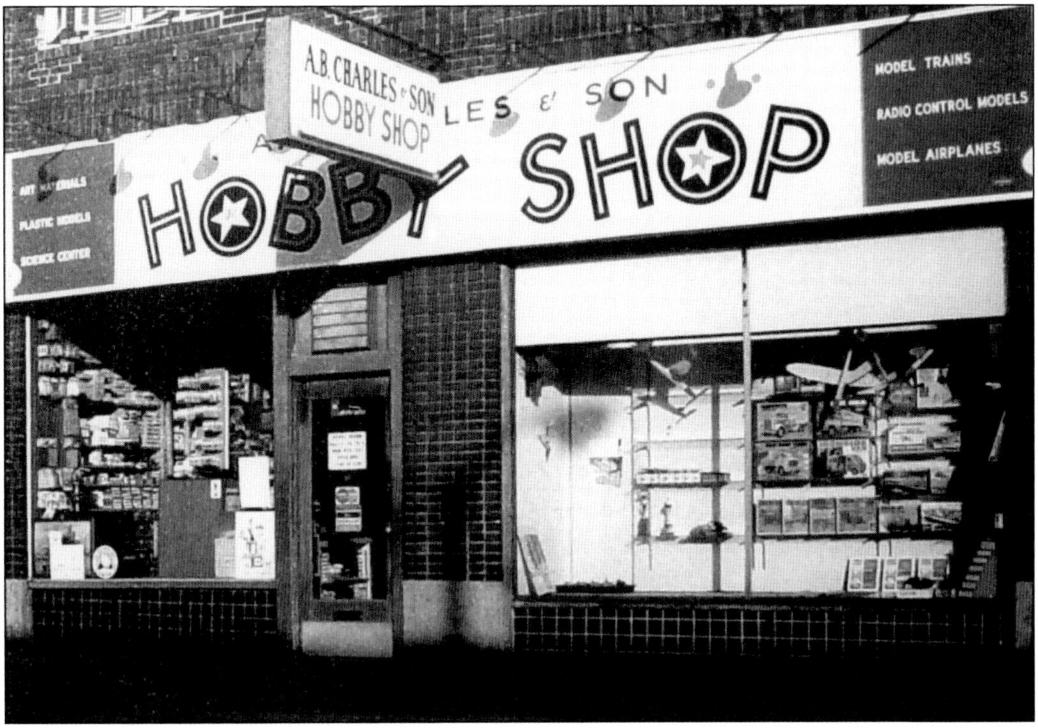

A. B. Charles Hobby Shop, which opened in 1945, soon outgrew its original location and moved to 3213 West Liberty Avenue. Although it was best known for its model railroad supplies, all kinds of items were available for both model builders and buyers. Local shoppers, and those from a distance, were keenly disappointed when the shop moved out of the borough in 2006 because the building had been sold.

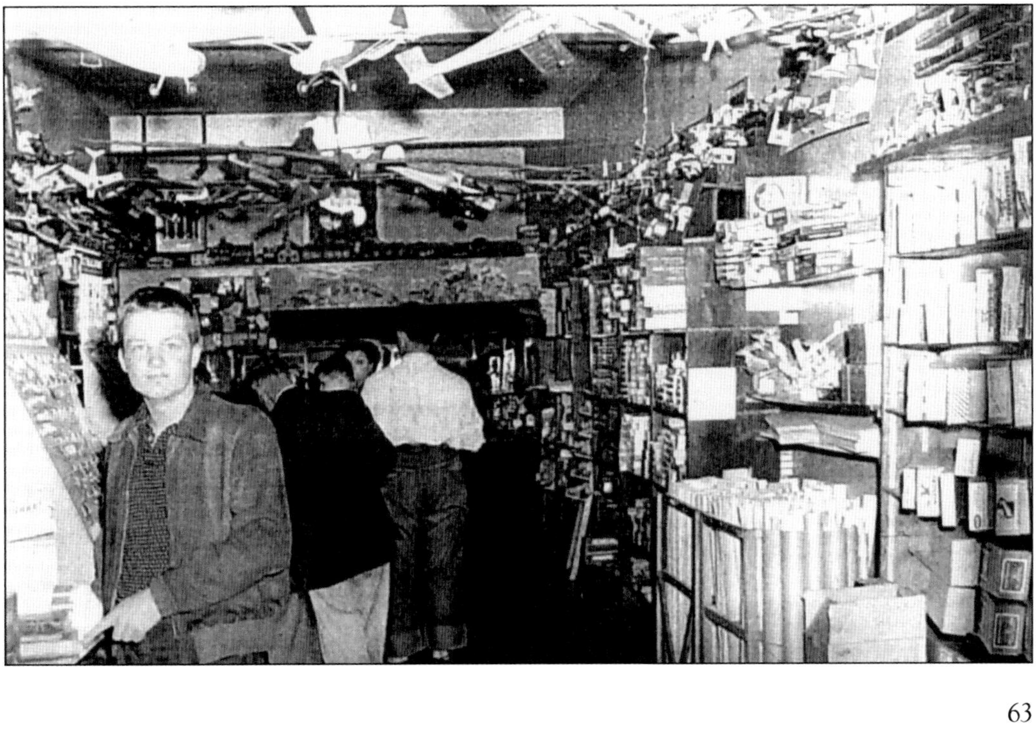

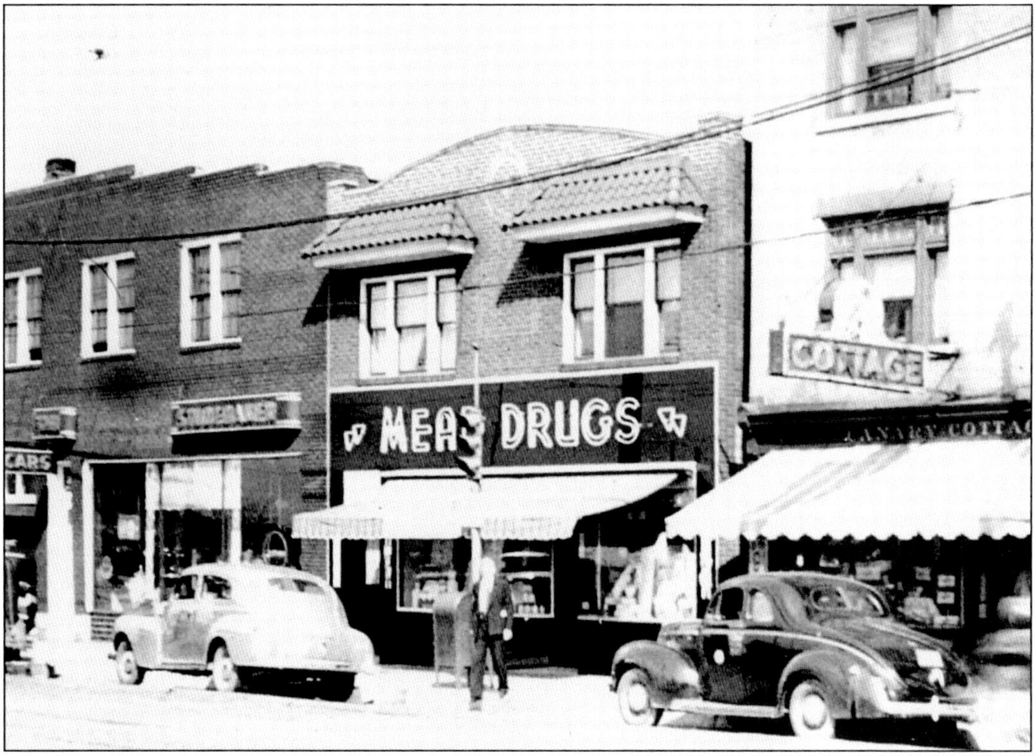

Mead Drugs opened at 3071 West Liberty Avenue in 1923. It later moved to 3263, where it was until it closed in 1982. Evelyn McCoff worked there while in high school and for many more years.

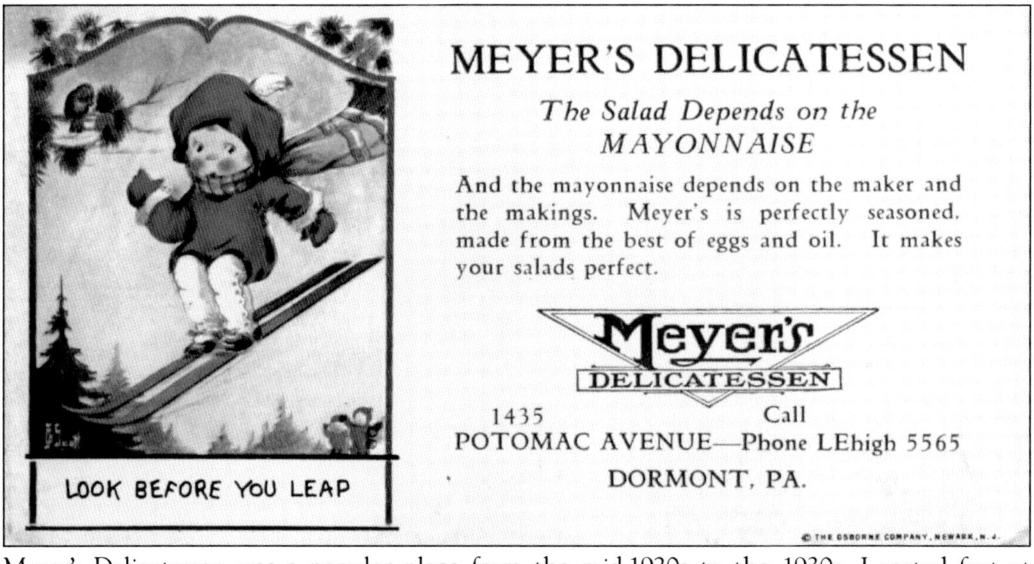

Meyer's Delicatessen was a popular place from the mid-1920s to the 1930s. Located first at 1420 Potomac Avenue, it later moved to 1435 Potomac. Its advertisements were frequently printed on blotters such as this one. Blotters, something that younger folks probably are not familiar with, were needed to blot the excess ink when writing with ink pens before ballpoint pens came into use.

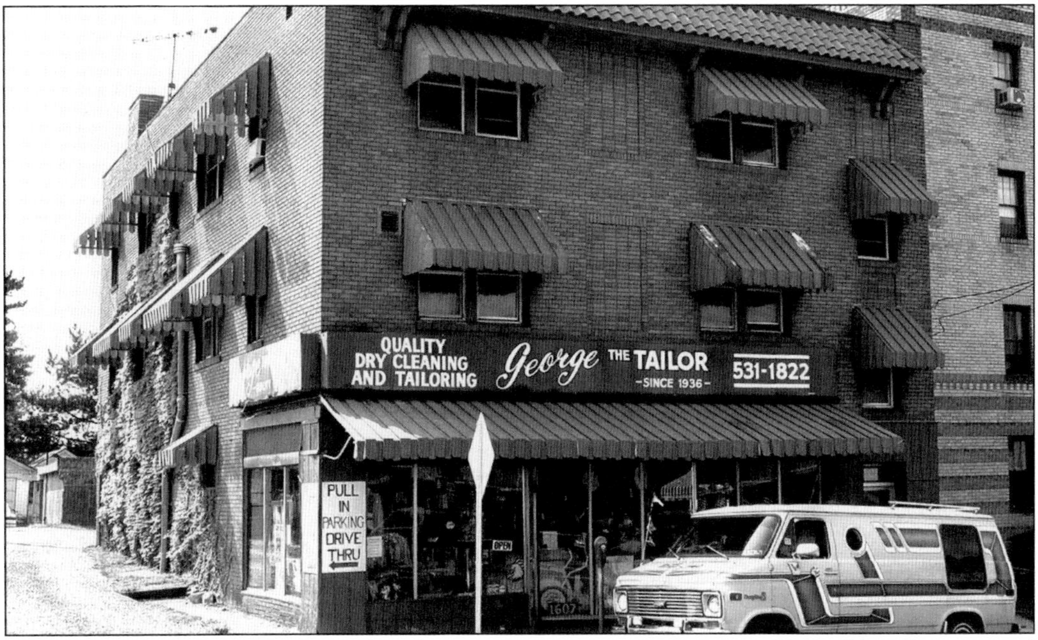

George the Tailor has been a landmark ever since George Messina established his cleaning and tailoring business at 1607 Potomac Avenue in the early 1930s. George Jr. has run the business since his father's death.

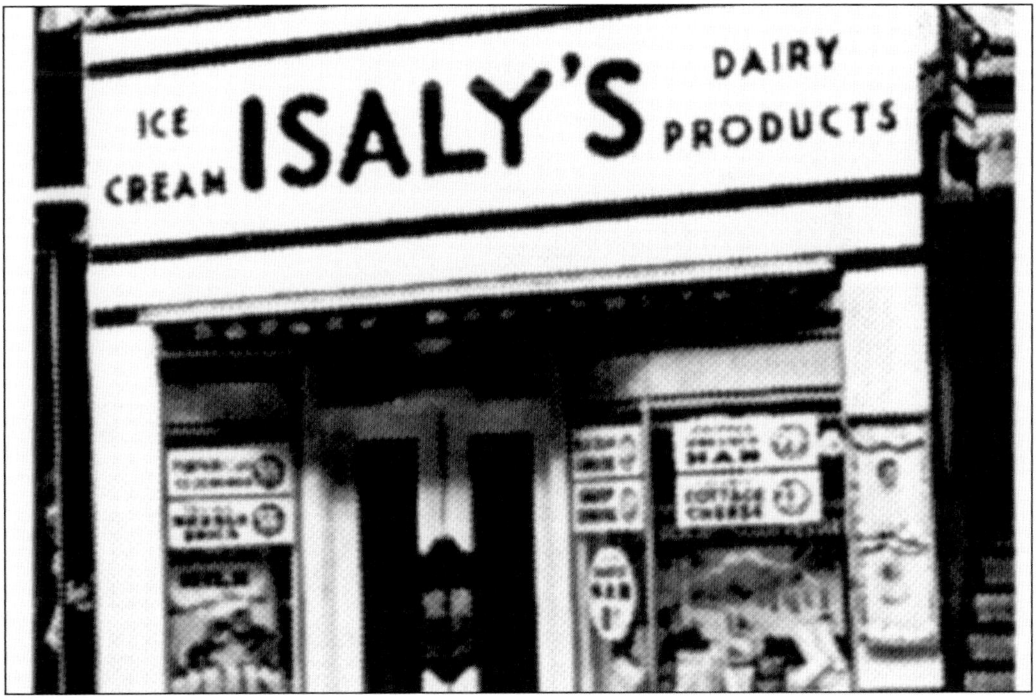

Isaly Dairy Company had two stores on West Liberty Avenue from the 1930s until the 1990s. One was at 2904, the other at 3261. Besides being known for their lunchrooms, they were popular for their skyscraper ice-cream cones, chipped ham, and the Klondikes that sometimes would have coupons or pink centers entitling the lucky buyers to another Klondike free.

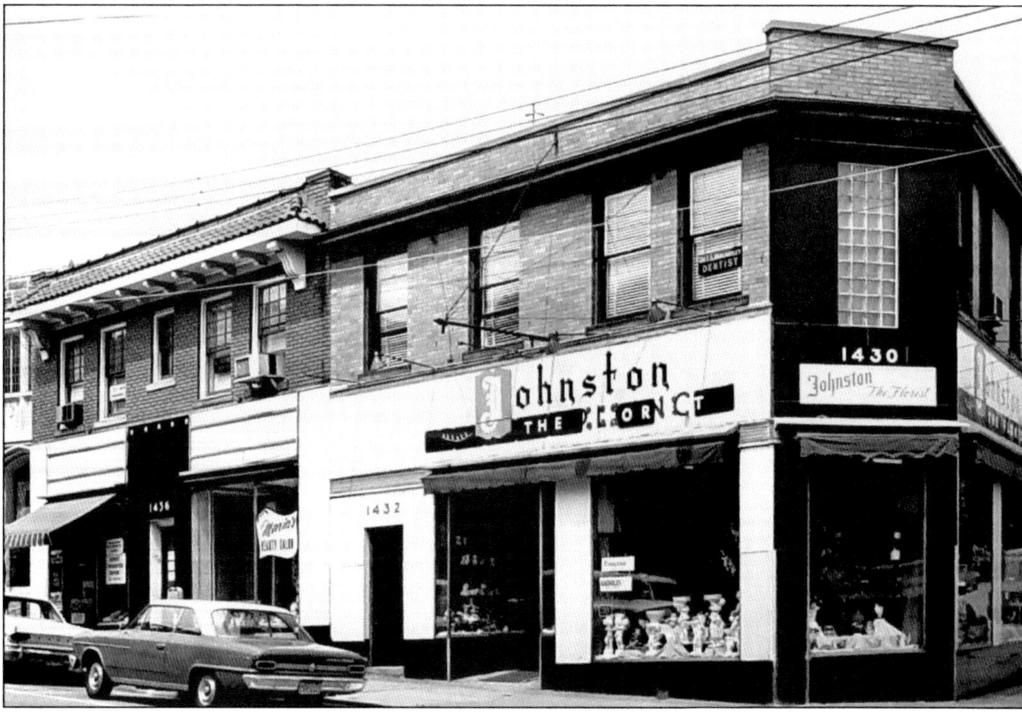

Harman Appliances opened in this building at the corner of Potomac and Glenmore Avenues after George Hards retired in 1951. Johnston the Florist moved there in 1954.

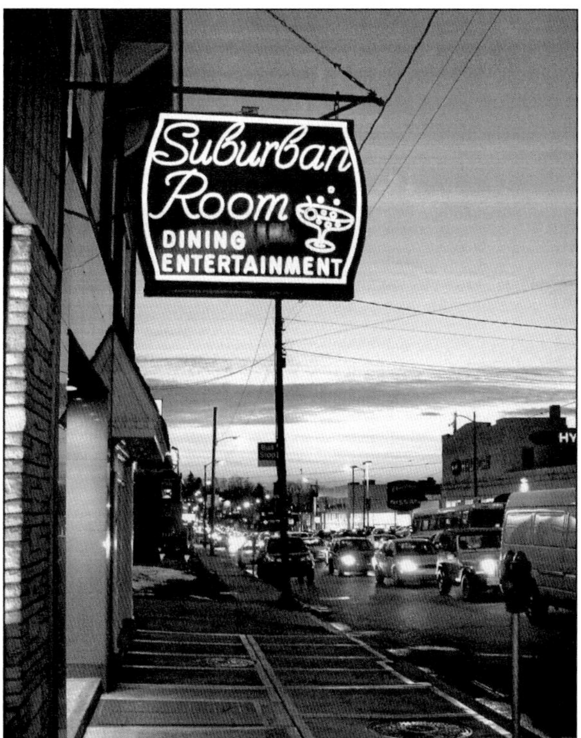

When Al Cerminara bought Berunda's Café, 3271 West Liberty Avenue, in 1954, he changed its name to Suburban Room. It is said to have been the first cocktail lounge in the South Hills.

Four

ORGANIZATIONS AND CHURCHES

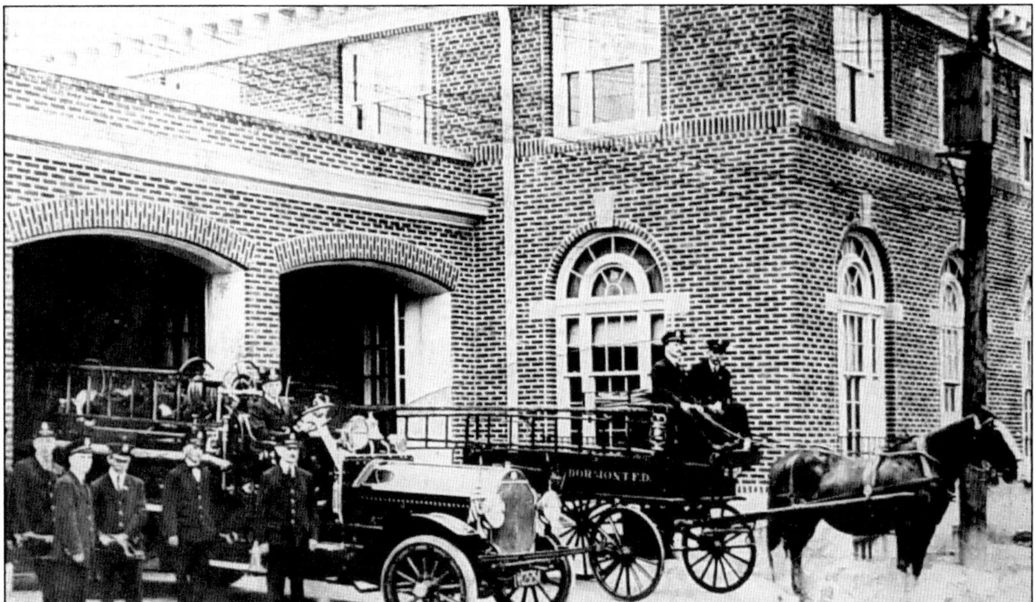

The Dormont Volunteer Fire Department was organized in 1910. Its first piece of firefighting equipment, a 45-gallon hand-drawn chemical hose wagon, was purchased by the borough in 1911. In 1913, a Gamewill air horn alerting system was placed in Barker's store at the corner of Potomac and West Liberty Avenues. When the borough building was erected in 1918, the department was housed there, and the air horn was moved to its roof. The horn blew numbers coded for different sections of the borough to alert the volunteers. This noisy system was replaced in 1963 by a group-alerting direct telephone override system installed in the volunteers' homes. A page system is used now.

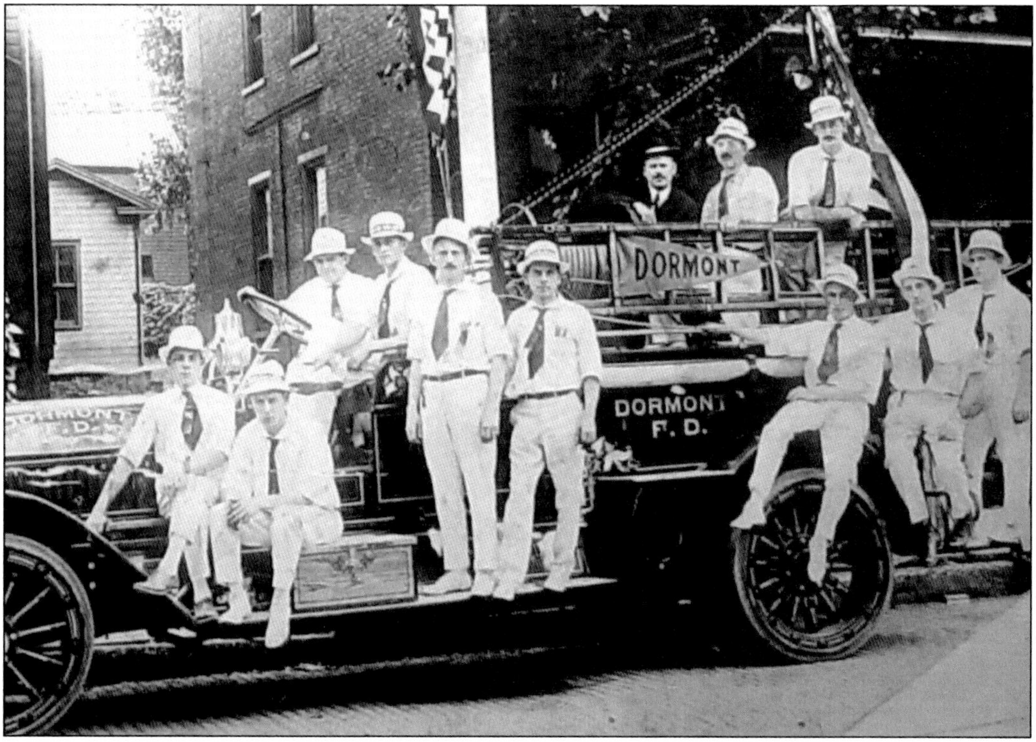

Dormont's volunteer firemen organize and participate in various parades every year. These men have returned from a parade in 1917.

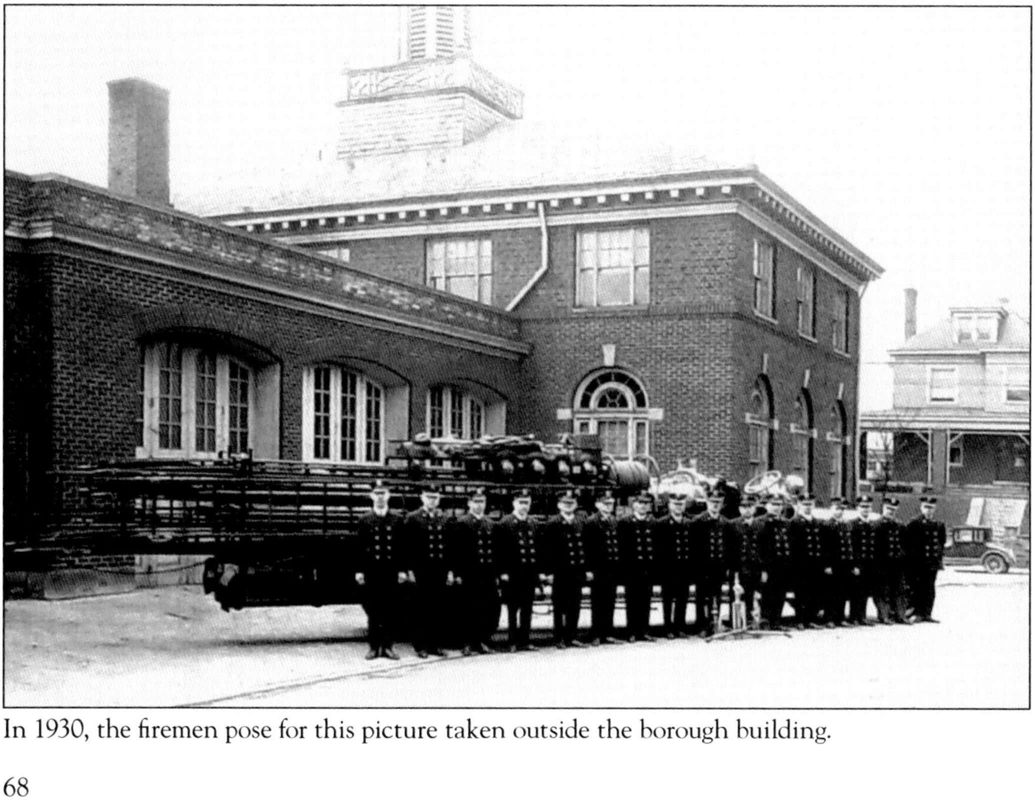

In 1930, the firemen pose for this picture taken outside the borough building.

In 1976, Charles Wilson sits at the top of the ladder while the new aerial truck is being demonstrated at Dormont Village.

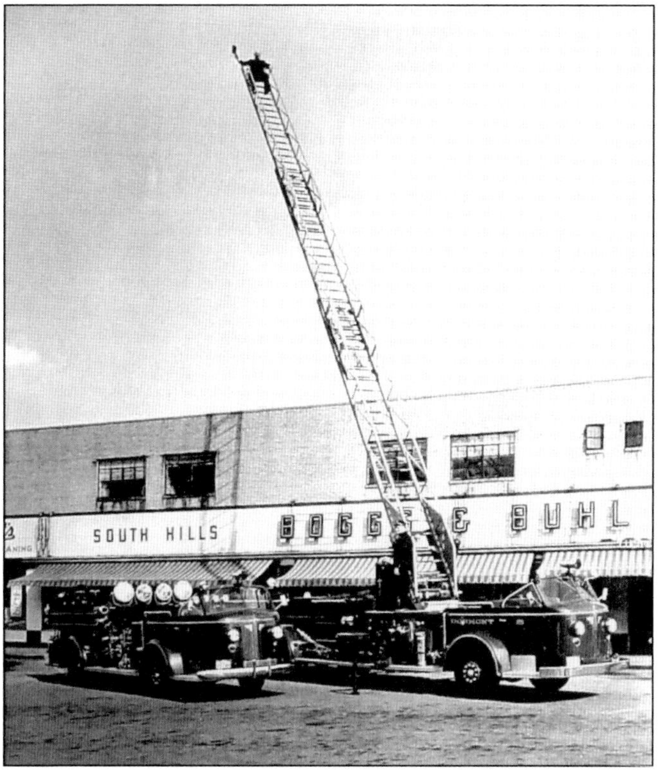

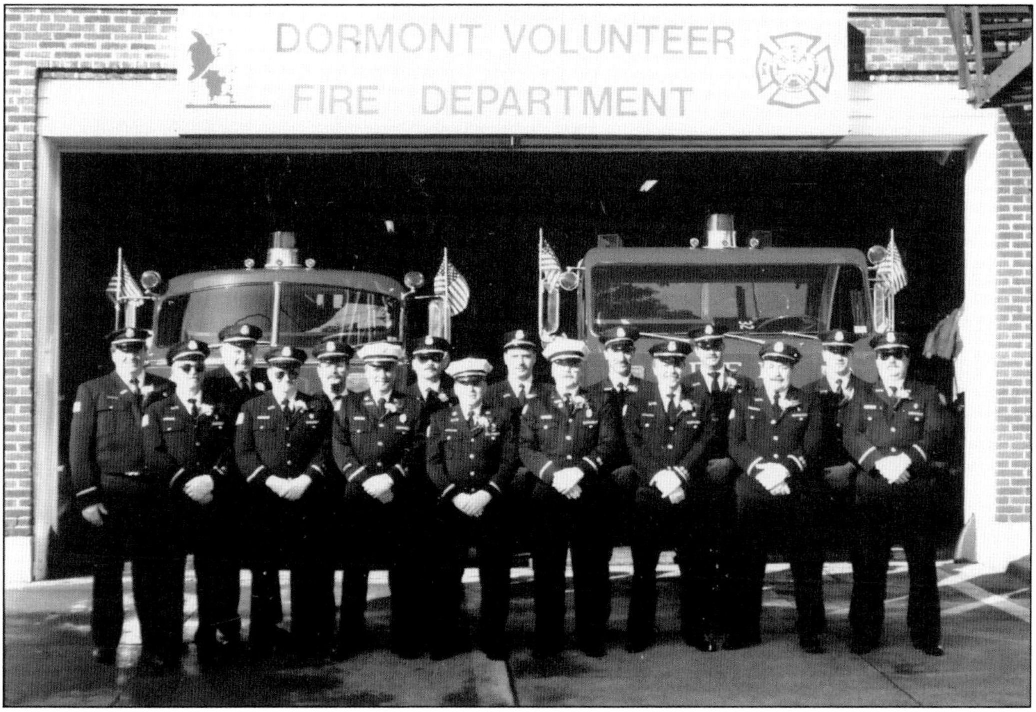

Most of the volunteers who served on the force in 1980 are pictured here. Besides their firefighting duties, the firemen have always participated in borough events.

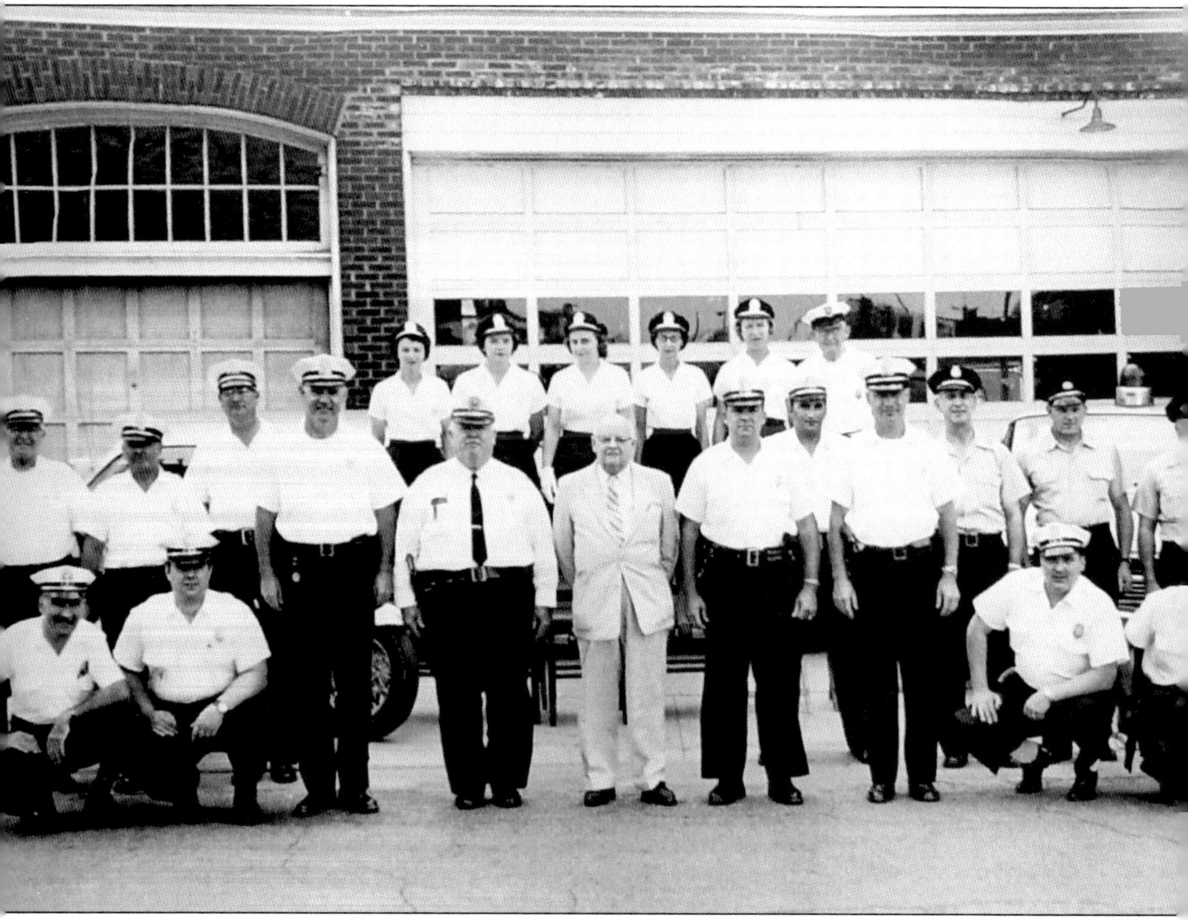

During its first years as a borough, Dormont had a constable system. Albert Ruehling was the only policeman. When another man was hired, Ruehling was made chief, the position he held until his retirement in 1930. Ralph Miller, who was then appointed, served as chief until his retirement in 1969. In the 1920s, an organized police force was instituted. It was housed in the borough building until being moved into the new municipal center in 1999. The 1960 police force is shown here outside the municipal building. Chief Ralph Miller stands to the left of Mayor James K. K. Smith.

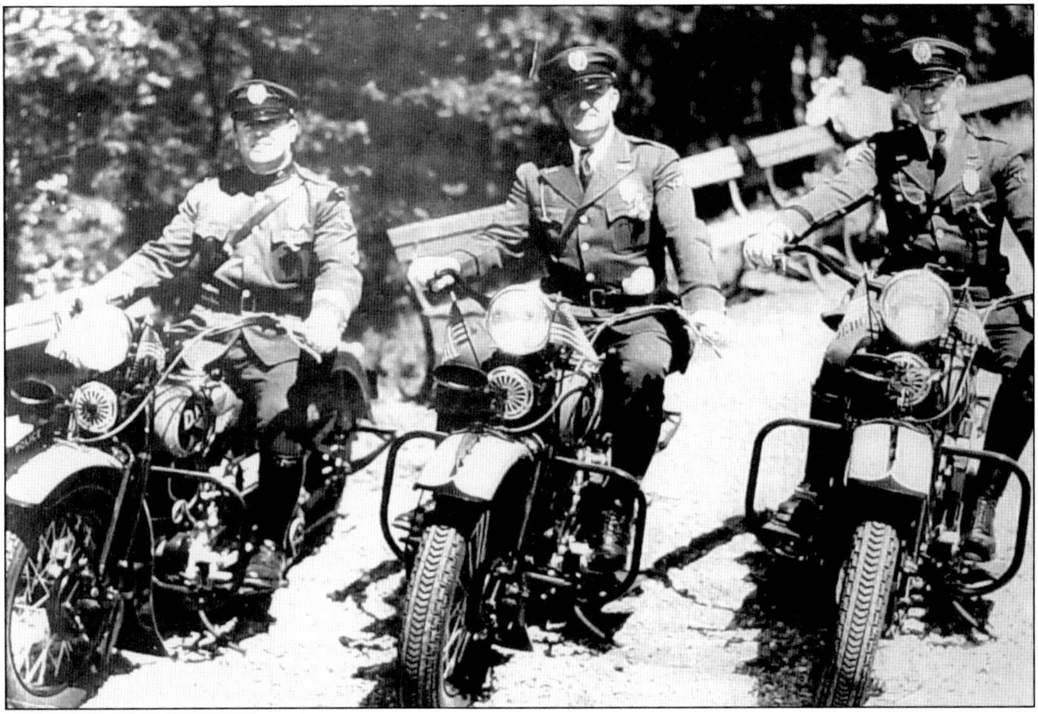

From left to right, officers Ralph Miller, Casper "Cap" Hasley, and Robert Wilson pause while riding through Dormont Park.

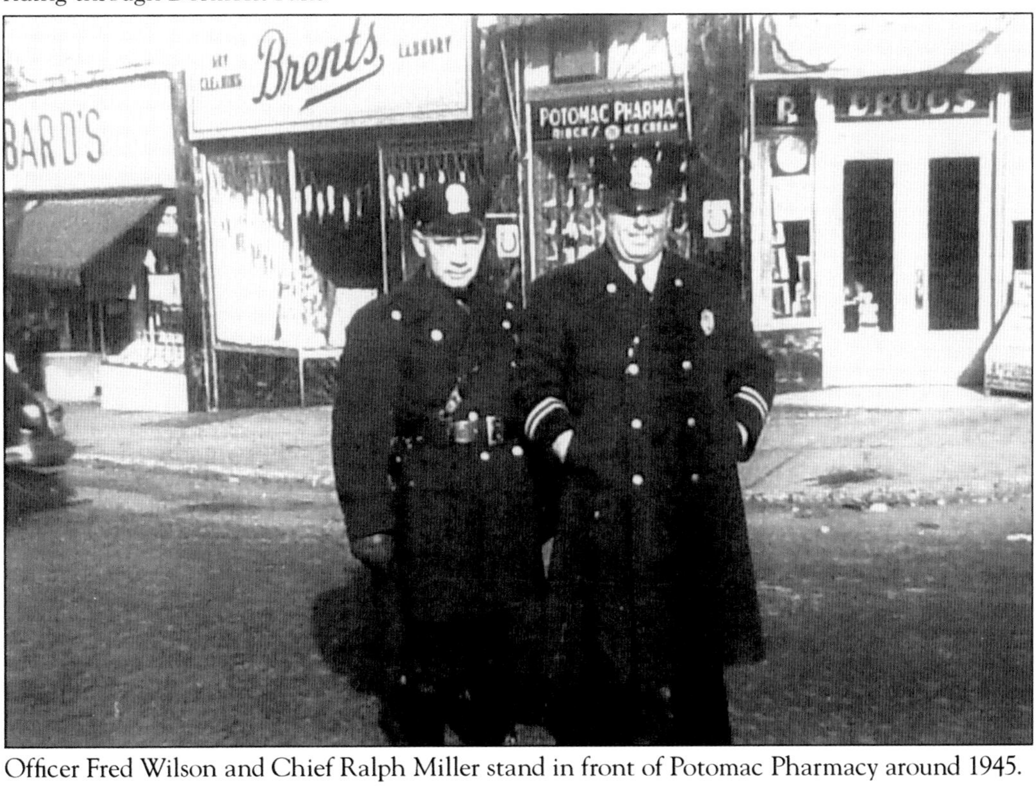

Officer Fred Wilson and Chief Ralph Miller stand in front of Potomac Pharmacy around 1945.

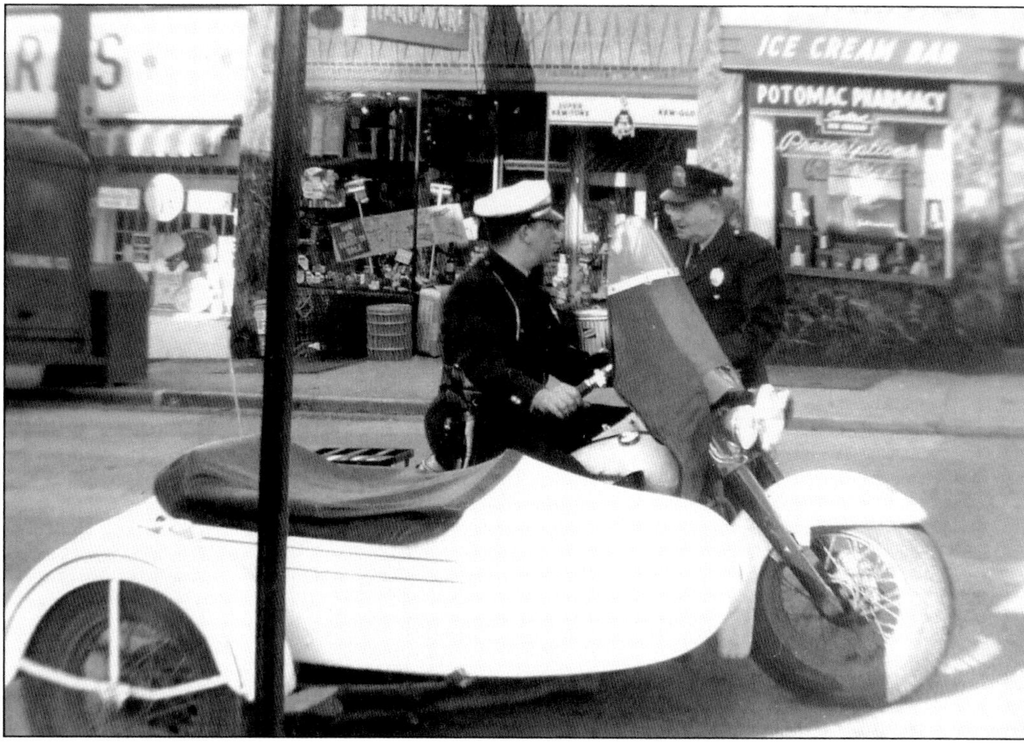

Motorcycle officer Donald Hasley confers with officer Raymond Grogan around 1955.

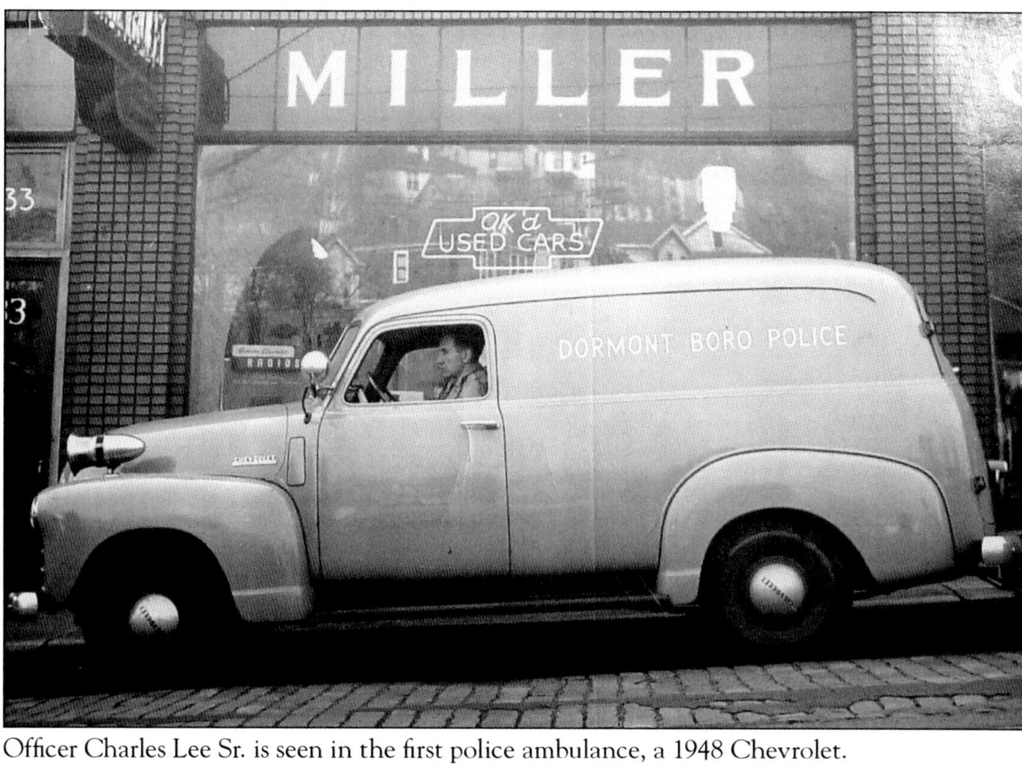

Officer Charles Lee Sr. is seen in the first police ambulance, a 1948 Chevrolet.

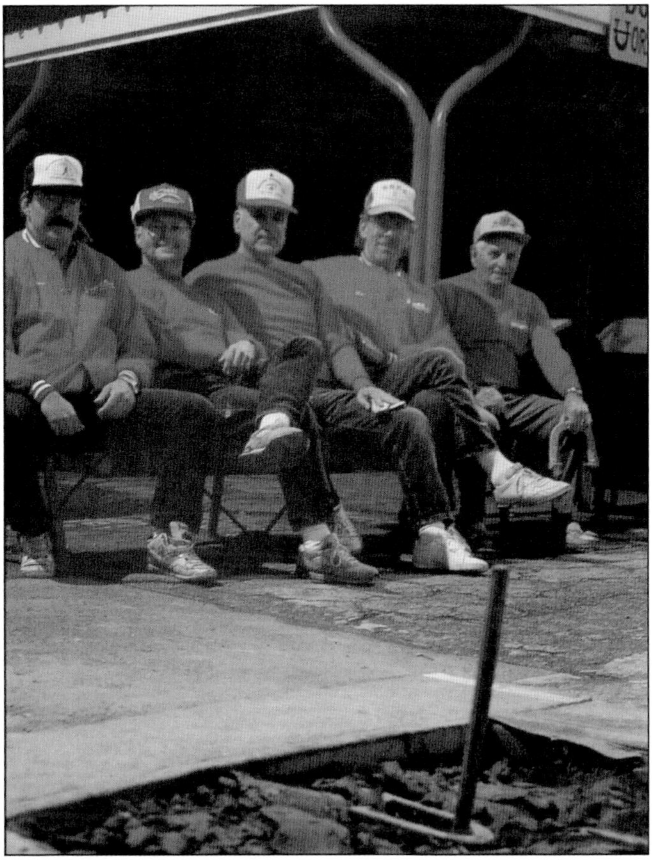

Dormont Horseshoe Club, founded in the late 1950s, is one of the oldest horseshoe clubs in western Pennsylvania. Its members compete weekly from May through September on the courts at the intersection of Dormont Avenue and Banksville Road. Affiliated with the Western Pennsylvania Horseshoe Association, the club has a long history of hosting nationally sanctioned tournaments.

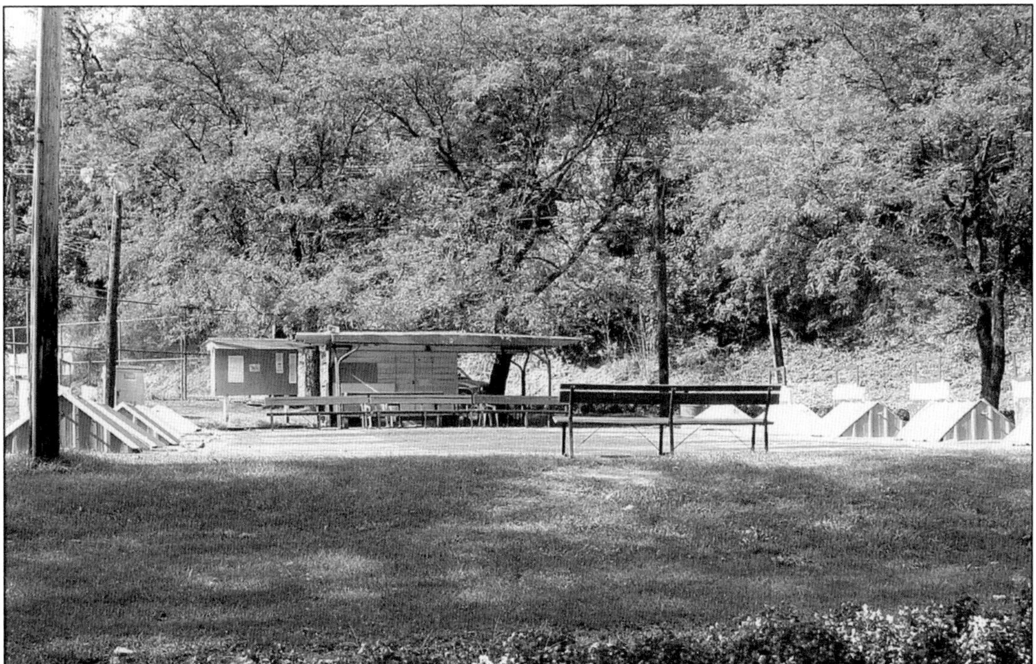

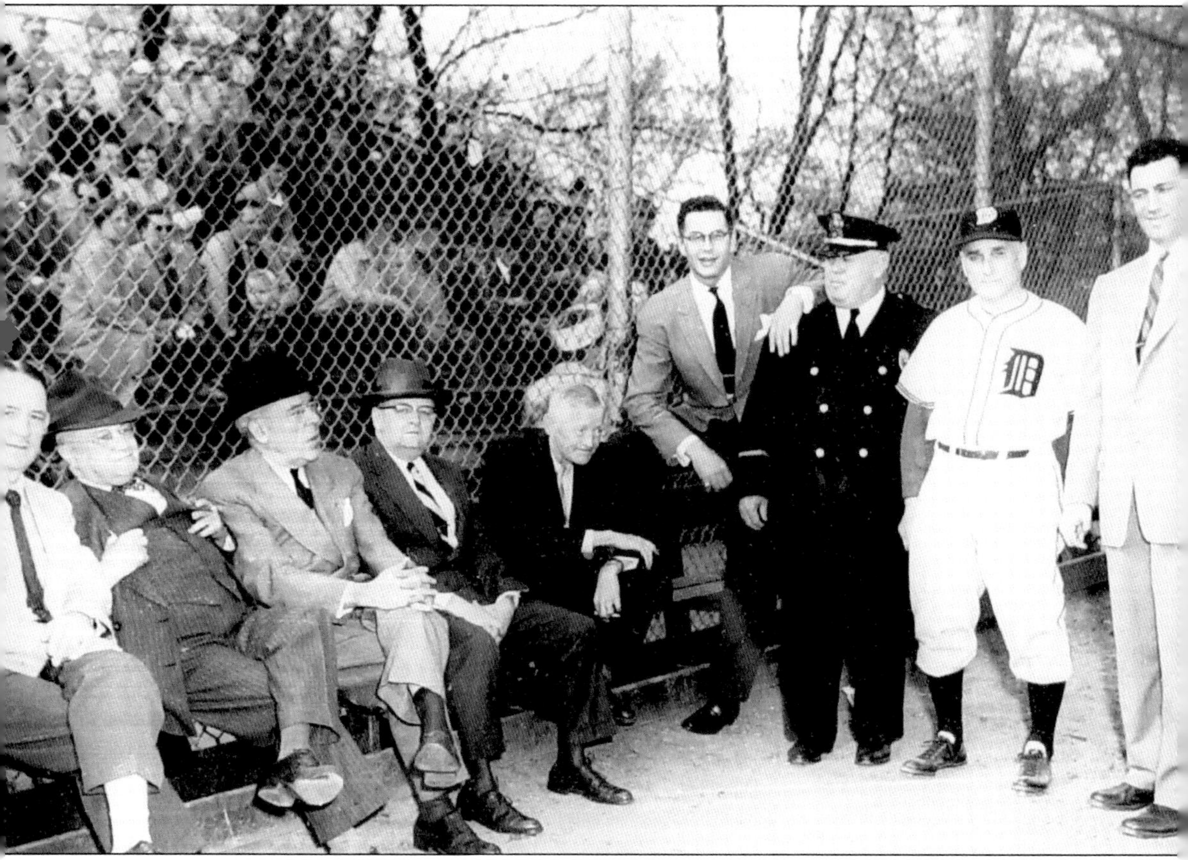

Going to the high school football field to watch the Dormont Baseball Club play other semiprofessional teams was a favorite pastime for South Hills residents during the late 1920s through the 1950s. The club, organized in 1925, traveled to such far away places as Kansas, North Dakota, and Canada. Paul Waner, Josh Gibson, Dizzy Dean, Wilbur Cooper, and Frankie Gustine are but a few of the big leaguers who appeared in Dormont's lineup. That residents from the area appreciated the team was evidenced by the capacity crowds at every game and the overflow crowds when there were special attractions such as Pittsburgh's famous Homestead Grays. Seen here attending the May 1948 opening day game are, from left to right, an unidentified man, Edwin Beck, president of borough council; David L. Lawrence, mayor of Pittsburgh; James K. K. Smith, mayor of Dormont; "Rosey" Rosewell, Pirates announcer; Robert Prince, Pirates announcer; Ralph Miller, chief of police; Billy Fuchs, team manager; and an unidentified man.

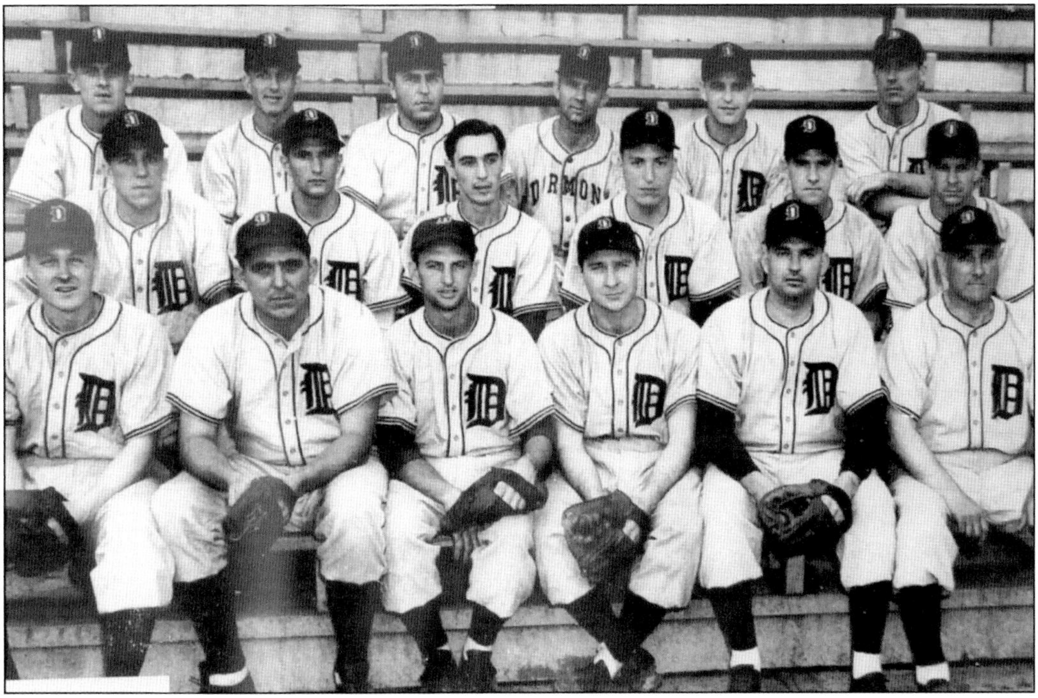

Longtime Dormont resident Elmer Grey, third from the left in the front row, was the club's second baseman from 1951 to 1960. After playing with the St. Louis Browns, he began his scouting career; he spent 13 years with the Orioles, 18 years with Cincinnati, and has been with the Pittsburgh Pirates since 1985. The baseball clubs' games were always full of action.

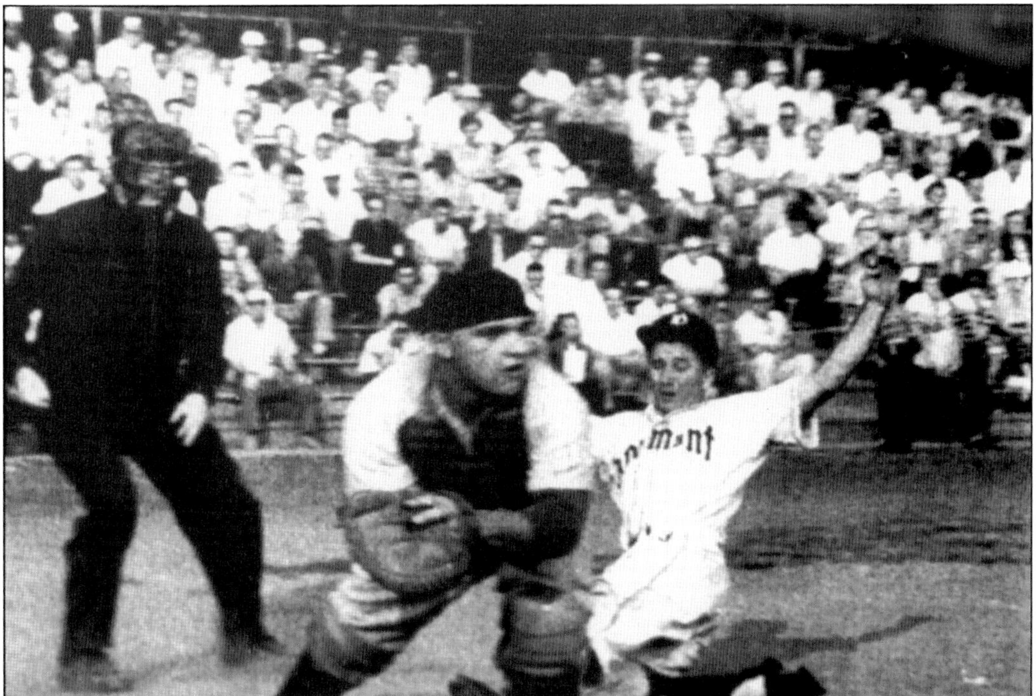

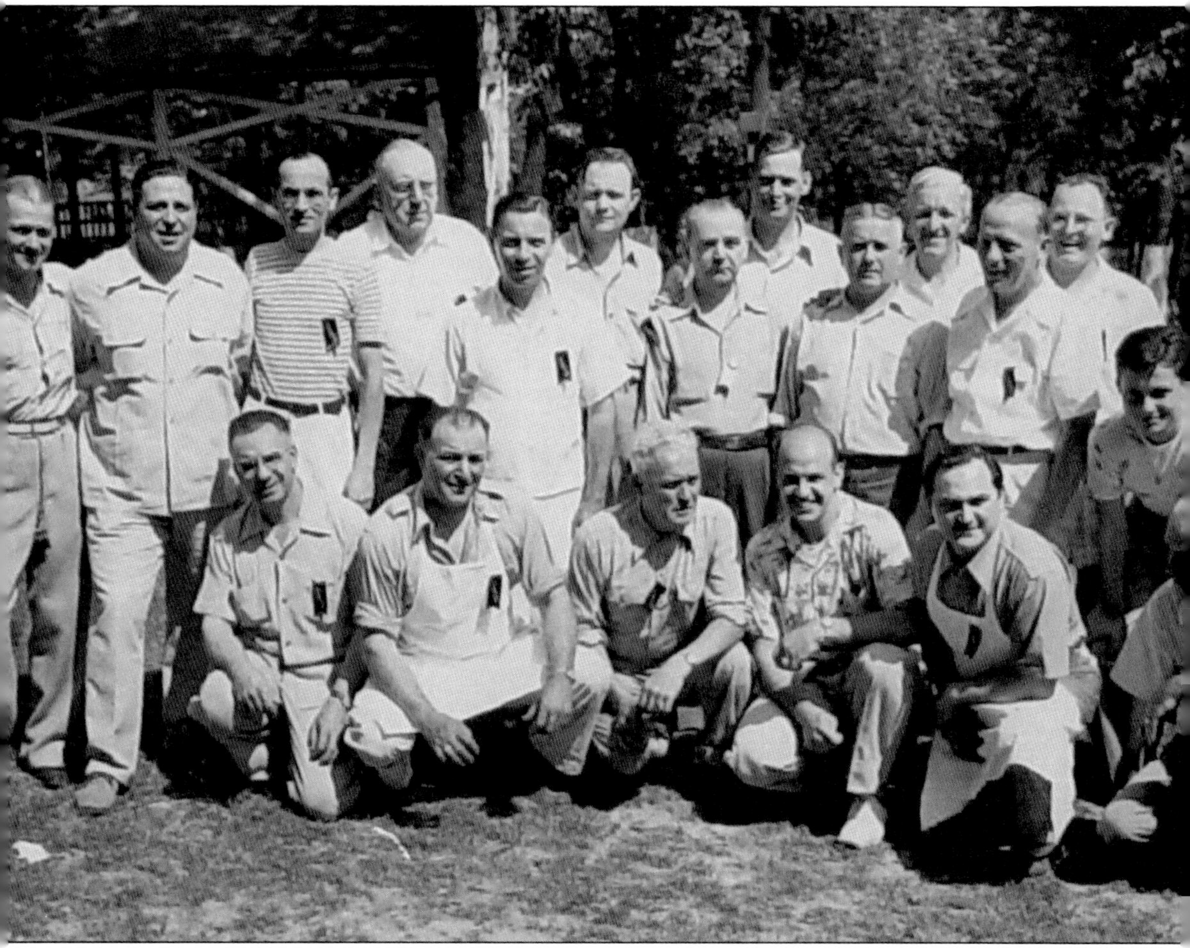

Dormont Athletic Boosters Association (DABA) was organized in 1949 by 13 sports-minded men for the purchasing of maroon and gray satin jackets to be presented annually to the seniors on the high school's sports teams. Through the years, the group has been the primary fund-raiser for many activities within the community. Its hardworking members, like the ones pictured here, have organized and sponsored multiple sports activities for Dormont and Keystone Oaks boys and girls while helping to maintain and upgrade the facilities and equipment.

In 1983, the Little League field was renamed in honor of William "Pop" Murray, who coached and managed Little League, Pony, and Colt teams for 69 years.

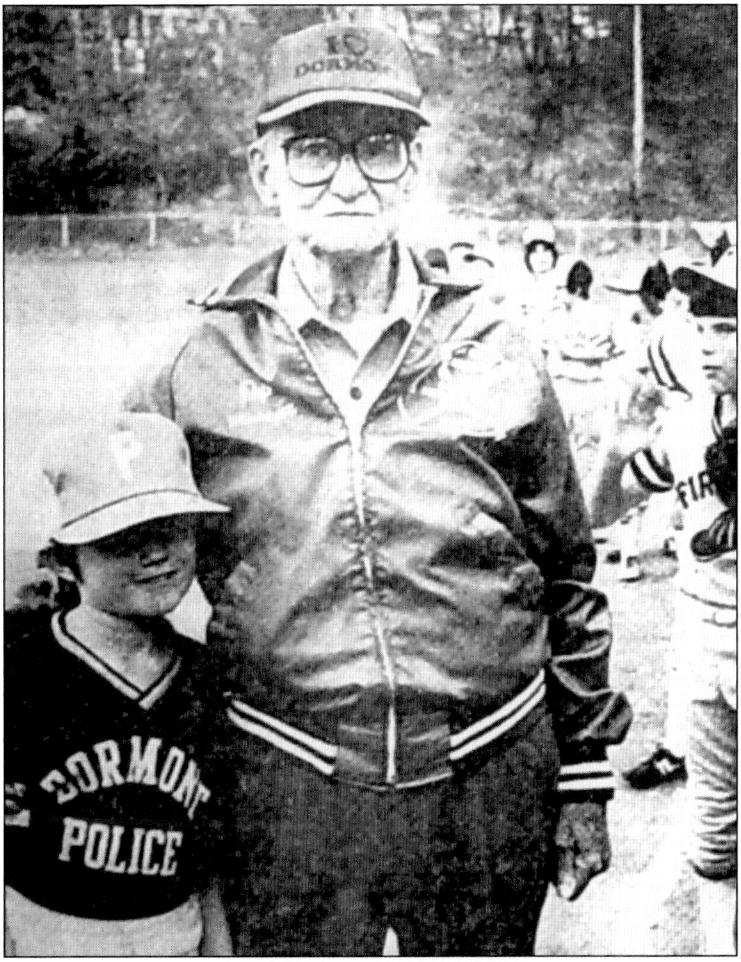

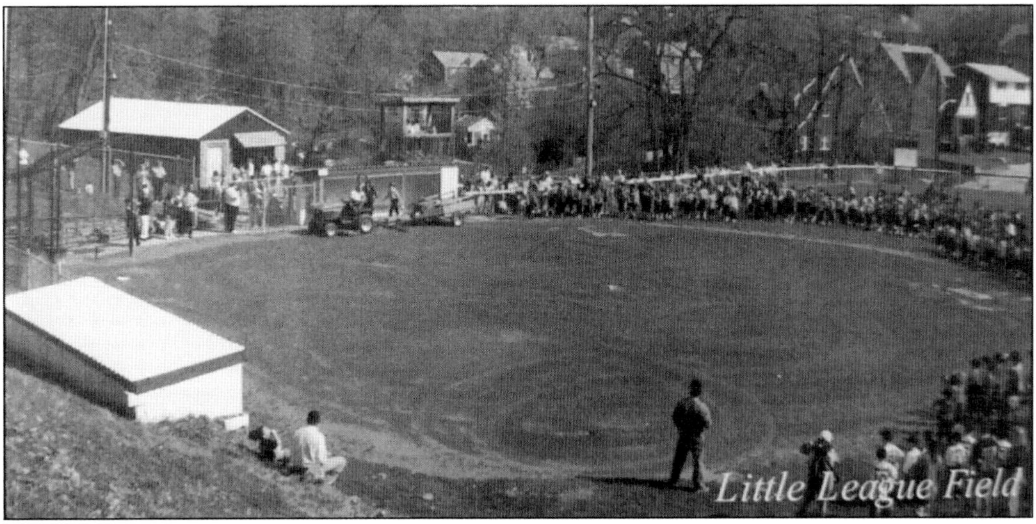

Little League, Pony League, and other games make the field a busy place during the baseball season.

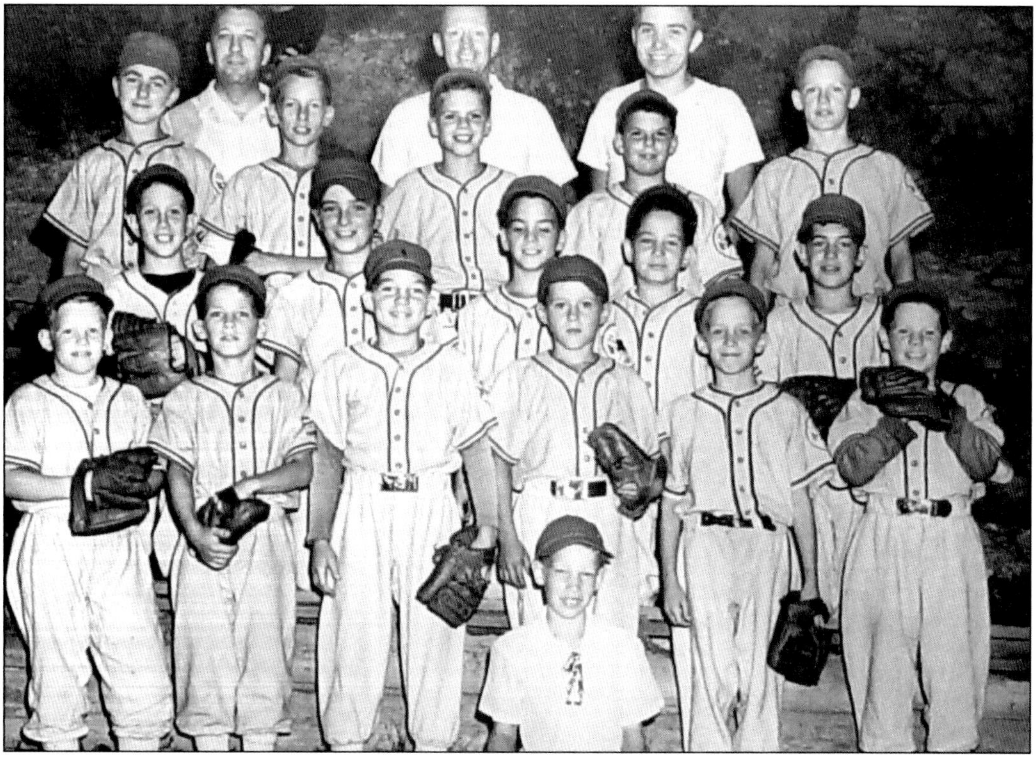

Coaches for the 1954 Firemen Little League team are (from left to right) Fred Clerihue, Gerald Bodine, and Harry Luebbe.

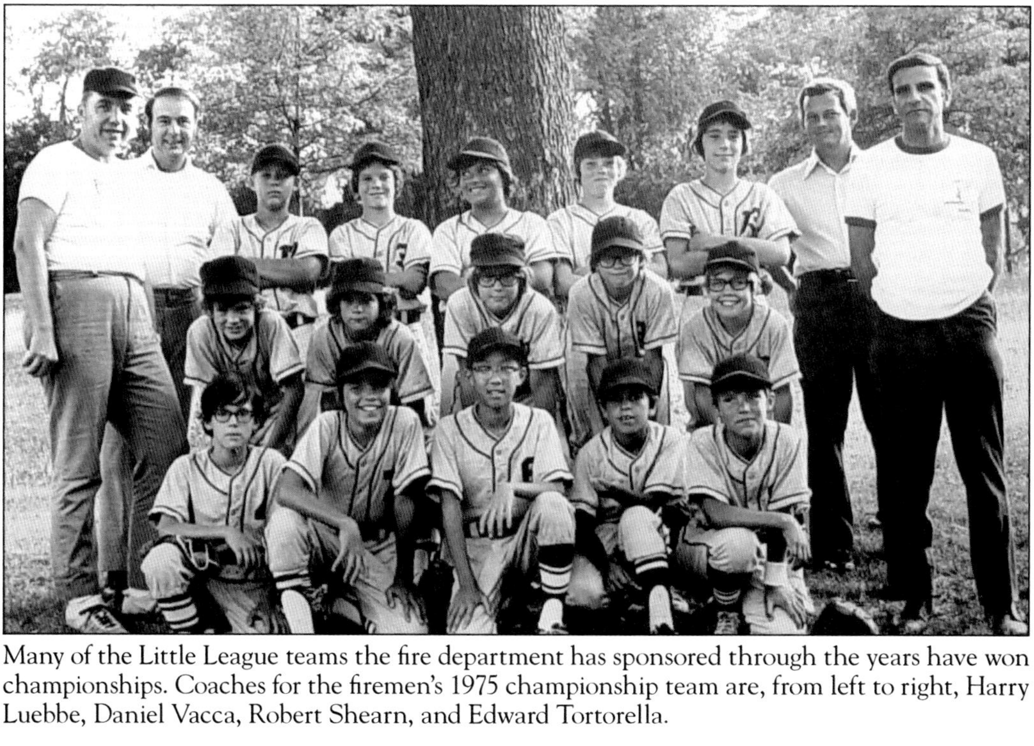

Many of the Little League teams the fire department has sponsored through the years have won championships. Coaches for the firemen's 1975 championship team are, from left to right, Harry Luebbe, Daniel Vacca, Robert Shearn, and Edward Tortorella.

This 1910 political campaign card shows the candidates who ran in the borough's second election. In the first election, in 1909, some of the officials were elected for one-year terms. One of the councilmen elected then moved away and another resigned. Fred Walling and Joseph H. Shipp, seen at top, were elected to take their places for four-year terms.

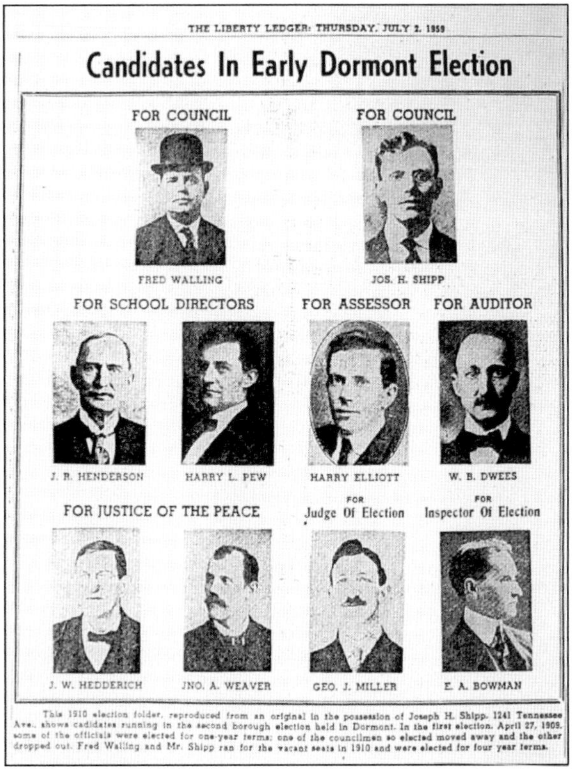
THE LIBERTY LEDGER: THURSDAY, JULY 2, 1959

Candidates In Early Dormont Election

FOR COUNCIL — FRED WALLING

FOR COUNCIL — JOS. H. SHIPP

FOR SCHOOL DIRECTORS — J. R. HENDERSON, HARRY L. PEW

FOR ASSESSOR — HARRY ELLIOTT

FOR AUDITOR — W. B. DWEES

FOR JUSTICE OF THE PEACE — J. W. HEDDERICH, JNO. A. WEAVER

FOR Judge Of Election — GEO. J. MILLER

FOR Inspector Of Election — E. A. BOWMAN

This 1910 election folder, reproduced from an original in the possession of Joseph H. Shipp, 1241 Tennessee Ave., shows cadidates running in the second borough election held in Dormont. In the first election, April 27, 1909, some of the officials were elected for one-year terms; one of the councilmen so elected moved away and the other dropped out. Fred Walling and Mr. Shipp ran for the vacant seats in 1910 and were elected for four year terms.

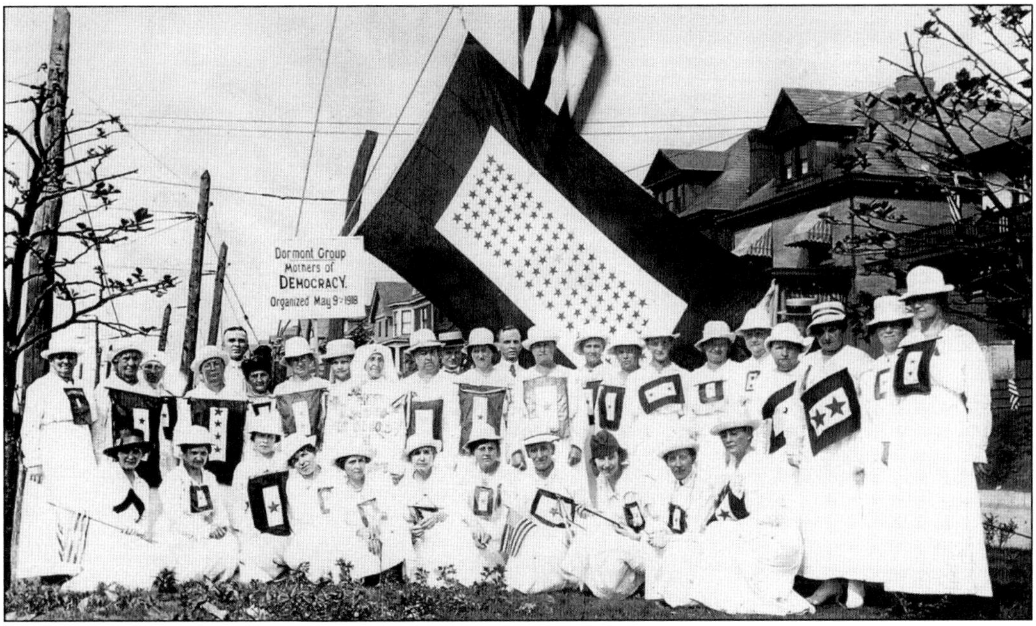

The Mothers of Democracy was organized on May 9, 1918. Here members display their service flags at the intersection of Broadway and Potomac Avenues. Each blue star represented a son or husband who served the country during World War I; gold stars represented those who lost their lives. The stars on the large flag show the total number of Dormont men who served during that war. Flags like these are displayed by some families of service personnel today.

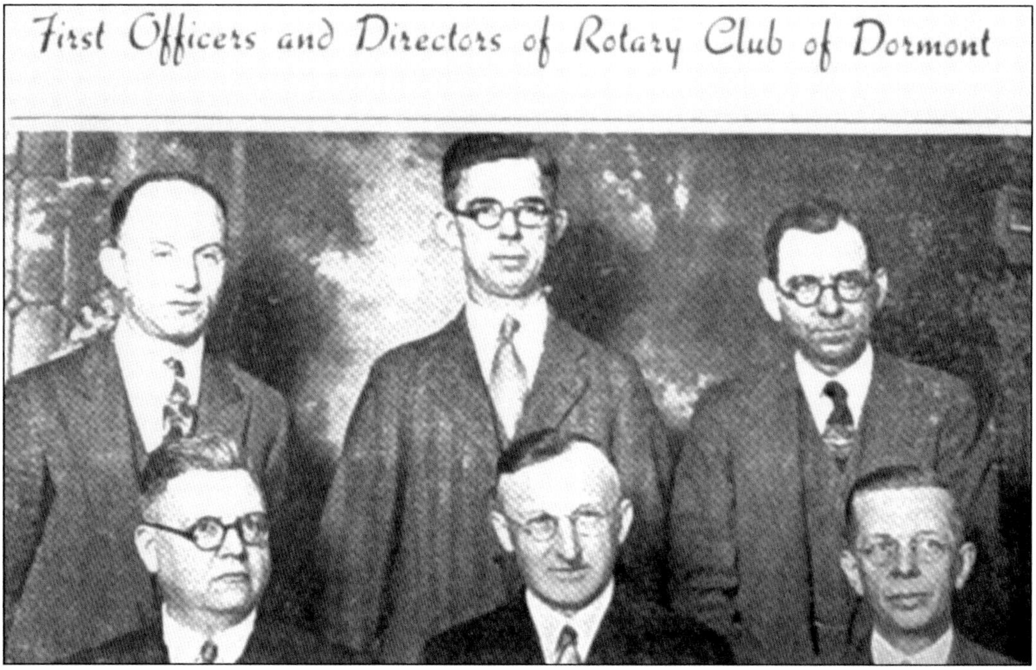

From the time of its organization in 1928, Dormont's Rotary Club was very active in community affairs and development. Three of its many projects were funding student loans, working with crippled children, and donating generously to the Red Cross for flood relief. The first officers of the club are pictured here; from left to right are (first row) William Palmer, treasurer, C. F. Lauer, president; and L. C. "Sim" Price, vice president; (second row) Charles Paull, director; James Zewe, secretary; and George Hards, director. The club later merged with Mount Lebanon Rotary.

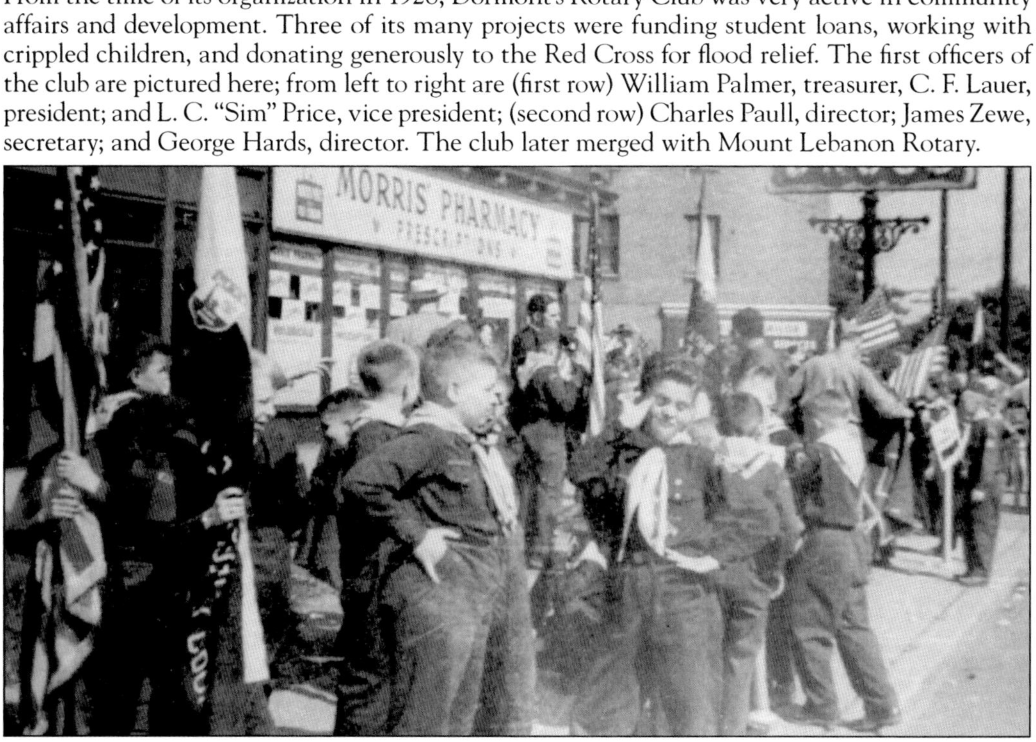

Many boys and girls have belonged to Dormont's Scout troops through the years. The boys have worked with the borough's street crew to erect the flags that are put along the Potomac and West Liberty Avenue business districts every major holiday. The troop seen here has just disbanded after one of the parades that it participated in.

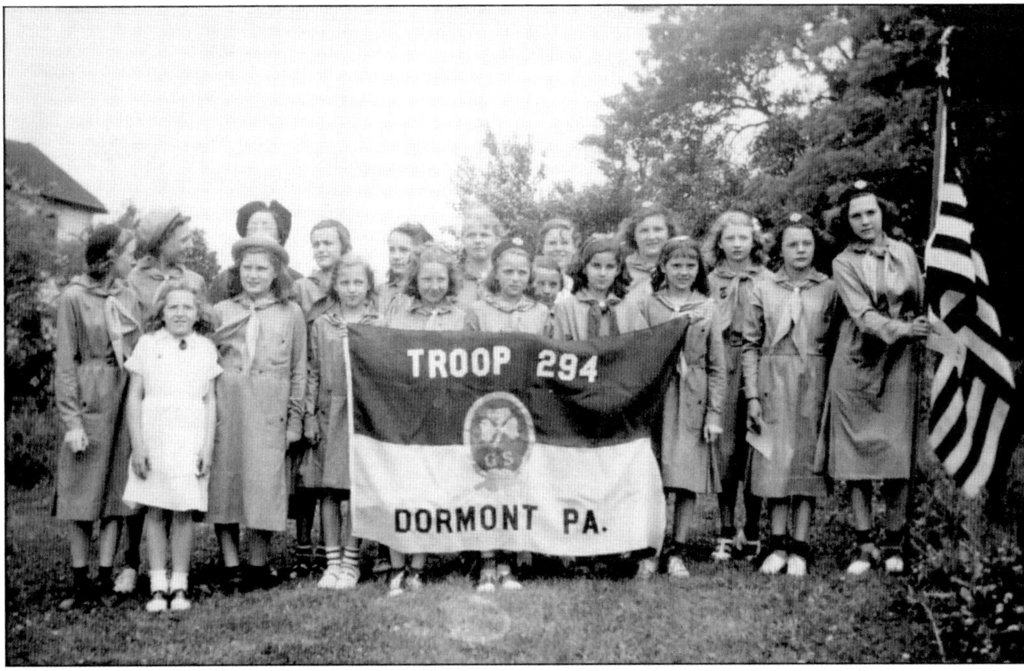

Members of this Girl Scout troop display the banner they carried in local parades around 1938.

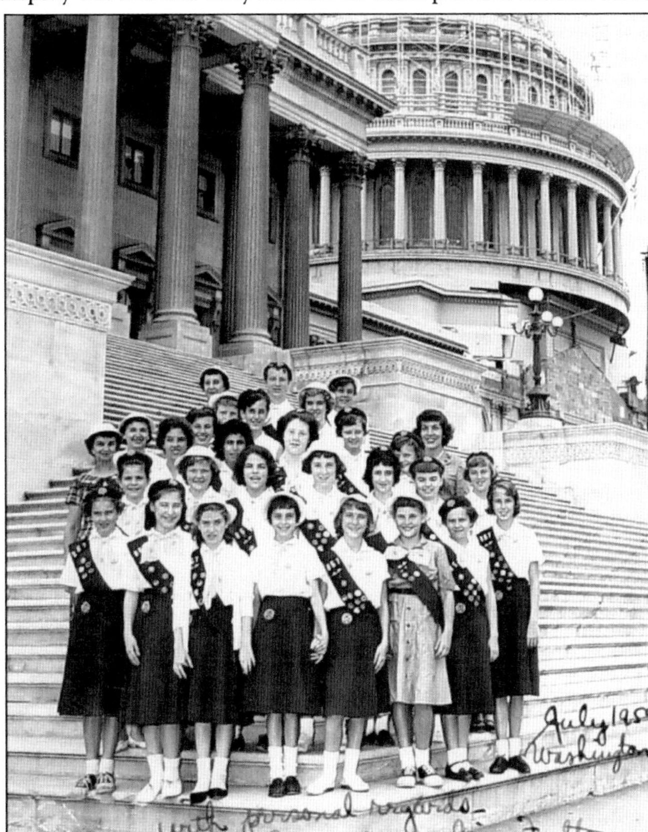

These Girl Scouts worked hard to earn their trip to Washington, D.C.

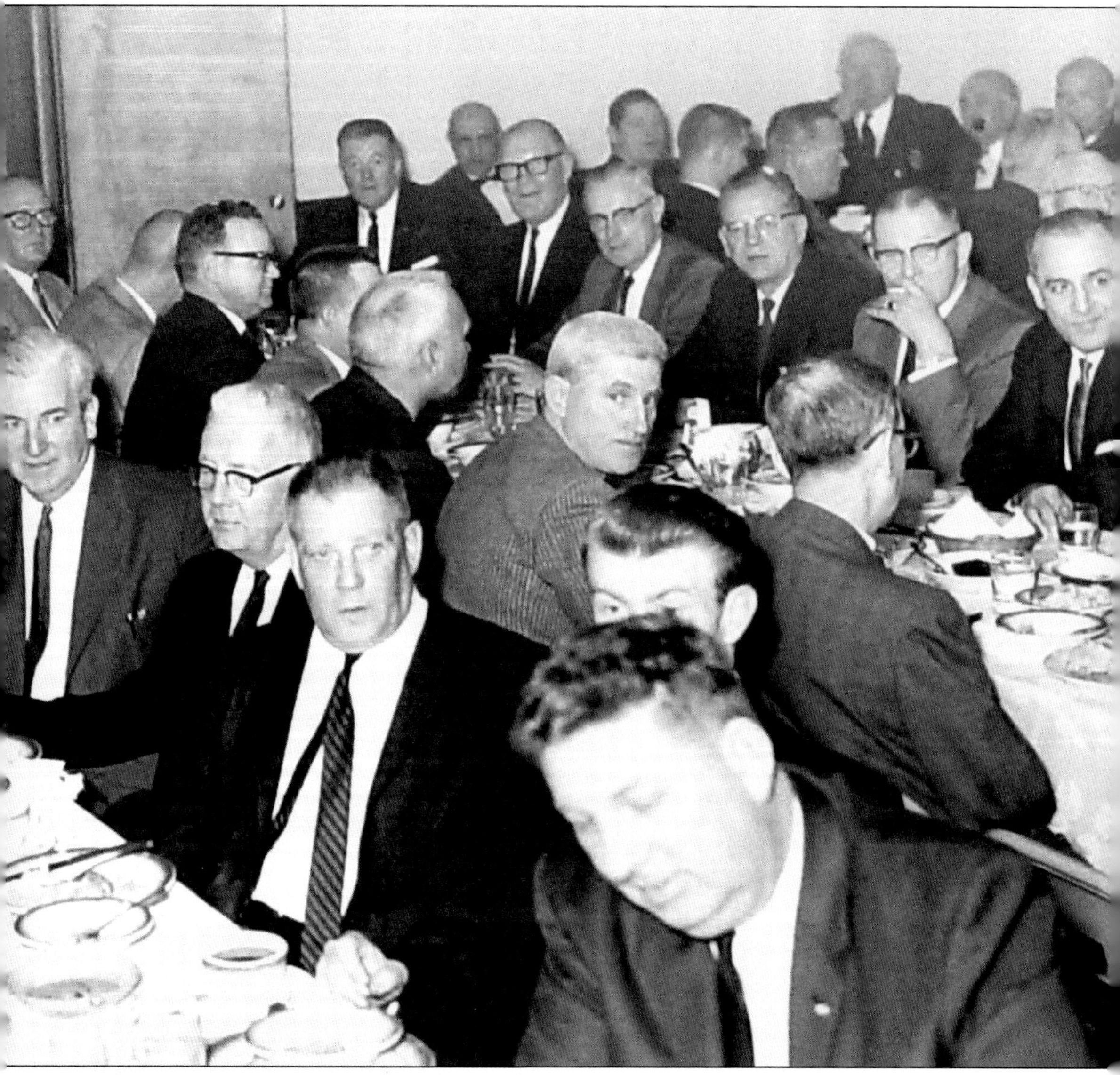

The Dormont Business and Professional Association was organized in 1957 "to foster civic spirit and to develop the commercial and trade area within the borough." That same year, its members funded the installation of Dormont's first Christmas street-lighting display. In 1969, they organized the borough's first Christmas parade, now an annual event sponsored by the fire department. The parade was but one of the many projects that they worked on during their years, but it is the one that the people who line the streets the first Saturday mornings in December always enjoy. The fire truck with Santa waving at the onlookers signals the end of the parade. These members are attending a luncheon in honor of Charles Paull.

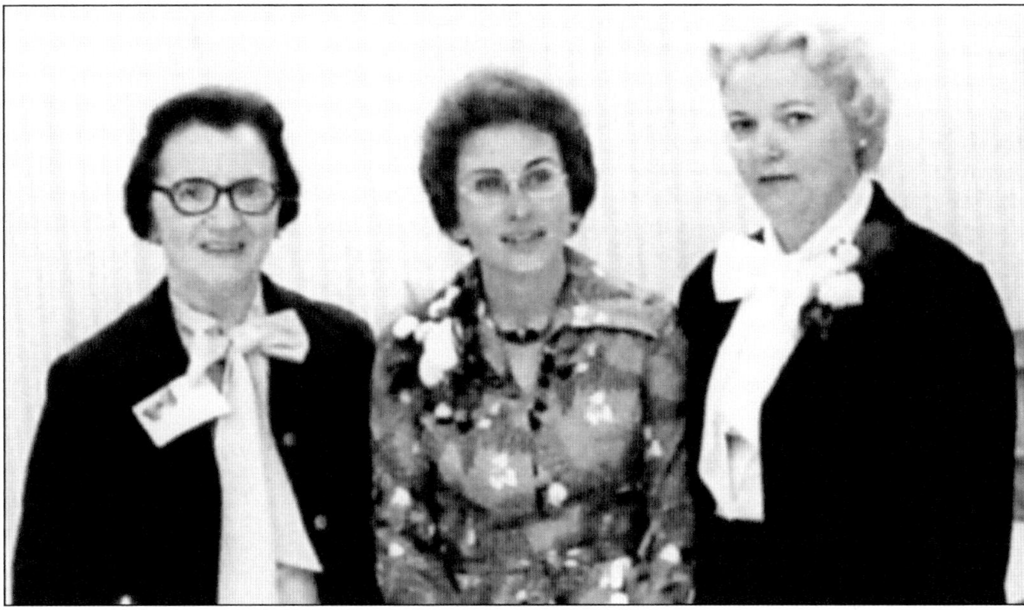

The name of the Dormont Mother's Club, founded in 1921, was changed to the Dormont Women's Club in 2007. Through the years, many groups, such as veterans, children, blind persons, Zoar Home, and the Dormont Public Library, have benefited from the club members' charitable projects. In this picture are, from left to right, Dolores Chaney, Dolores "Dee" Chaney Krugh, and Sara (Sally) Bernhart shortly after Dee was installed as president and Sally as vice president.

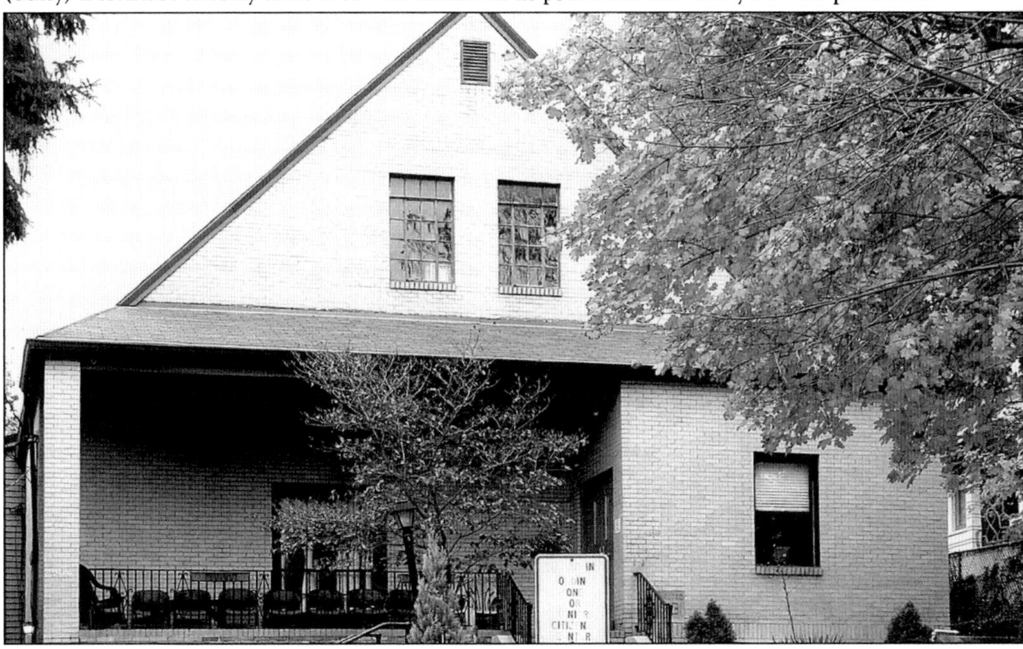

Seventeen women were awarded the charter for the Dormont New Century Club in 1914. As the membership grew, meetings were held in various locations until their clubhouse at 2866 Glenmore Avenue was dedicated on September 23, 1931. The members worked hard on projects, the profits from which were donated to countless charities and provided annual scholarships to Dormont High School students. The clubhouse was sold in 1980, and the club disbanded the next year.

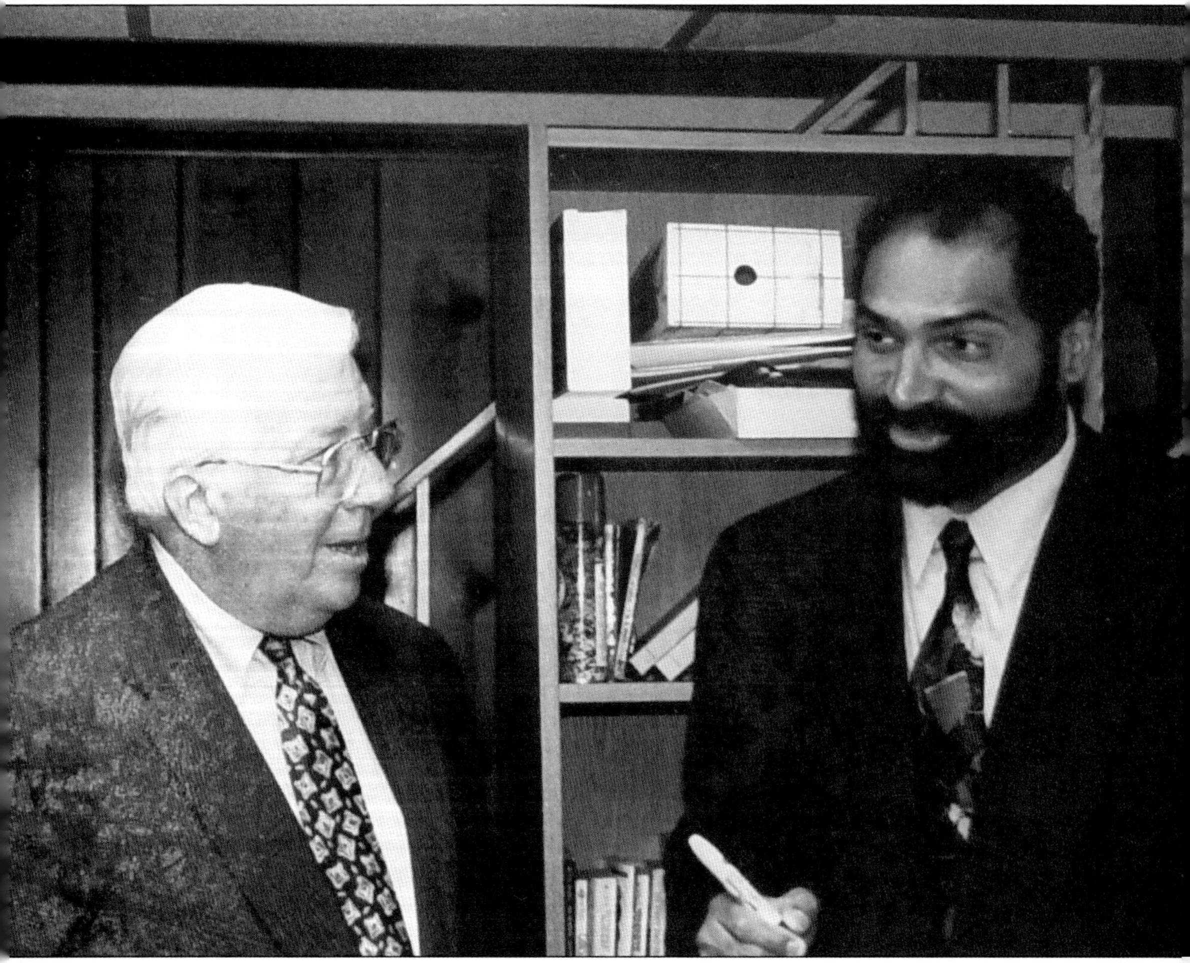

LifeSpan's history in the borough dates back to 1972, when the Dormont Senior Resource Center moved into the former Dormont New Century Club building on Glenmore Avenue. In 1974, this service provider became Southwest Services. It merged with New Heritage to officially become LifeSpan, Inc., on January 1, 1999. The center moved into the Dormont Municipal Center in 2000. The director oversees a wide variety of programs, classes, activities, and the home-delivered meals weekly Monday through Friday. Some of the opportunities offered area seniors 60 and older are painting classes, bridge, bingo, interesting trips, a summer picnic, and exercise classes. Mayor Thomas Lloyd is pictured with former Pittsburgh Steelers great Franco Harris, a guest speaker.

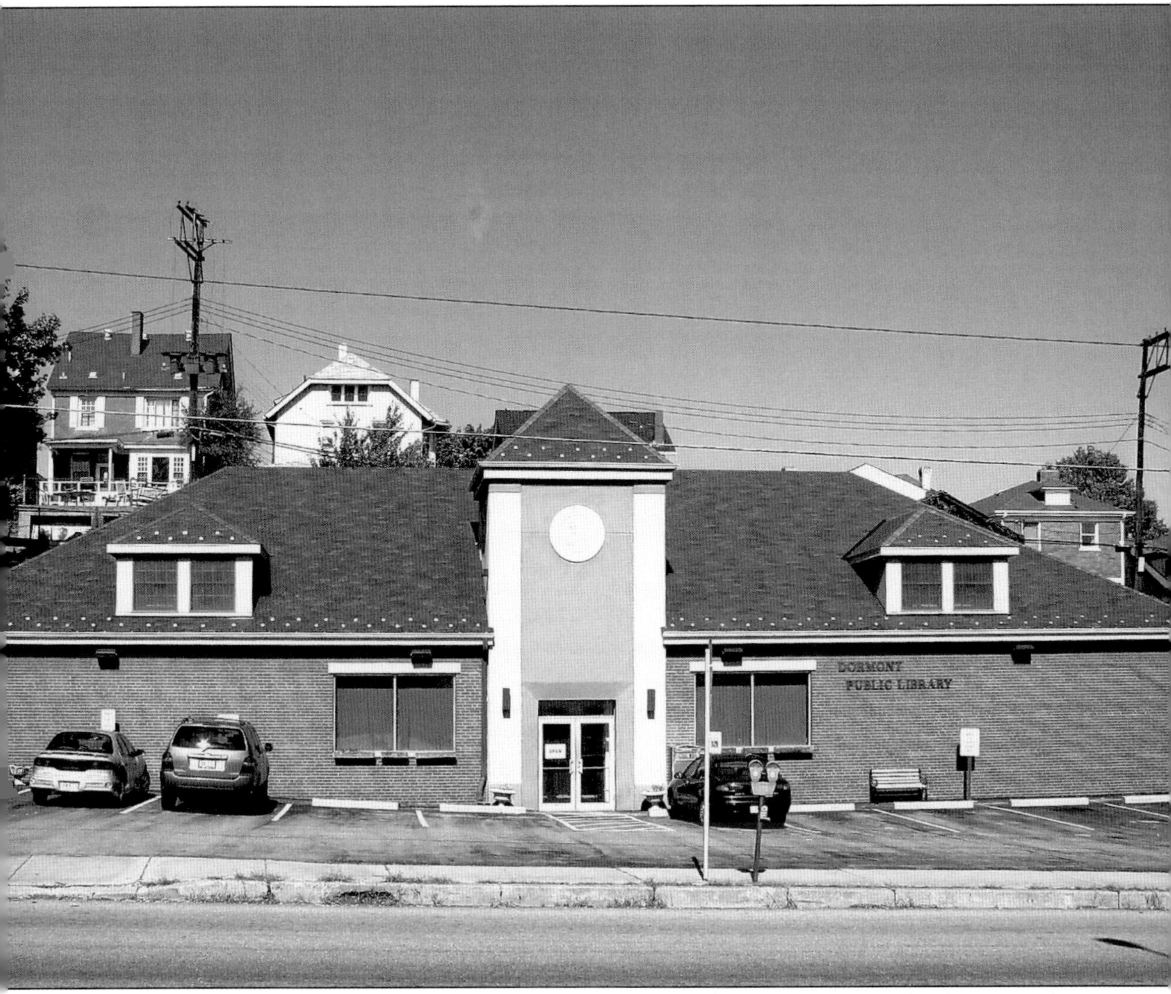

In 1936, Kelton School's Parent-Teacher Association set aside $25 to buy the books that were the start of the Dormont Public Library. The collection grew rapidly because of dedicated leadership and support from the borough officials and the community. After the library was housed in various locations, ground was broken in 1962 for its own building at 2950 West Liberty Avenue. A second story was added in 1989 to provide a computer laboratory, offices, and a large public meeting room. Besides its book collections and research facilities, the library offers a wide range of activities. Story times, book discussion groups, computer lessons, poetry contests, and evenings with speakers are some of the opportunities available to the public. The library has something for all ages all year round.

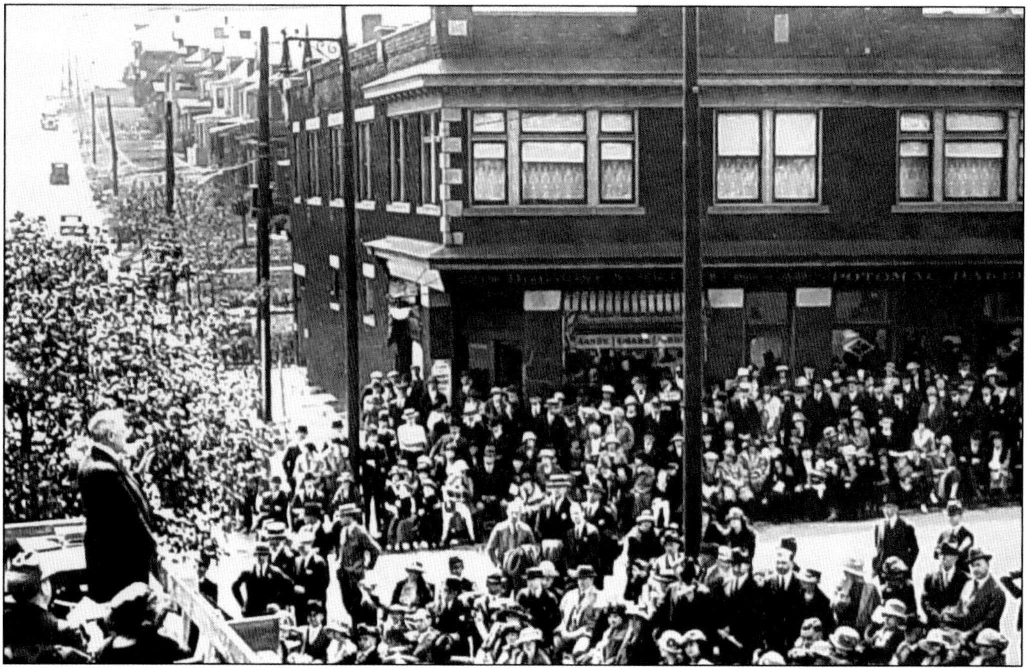

A large crowd gathers at the corner of Potomac and Glenmore Avenues for the dedication of Dormont Presbyterian Church's new building in 1924. The original brownstone building was incorporated into this sanctuary.

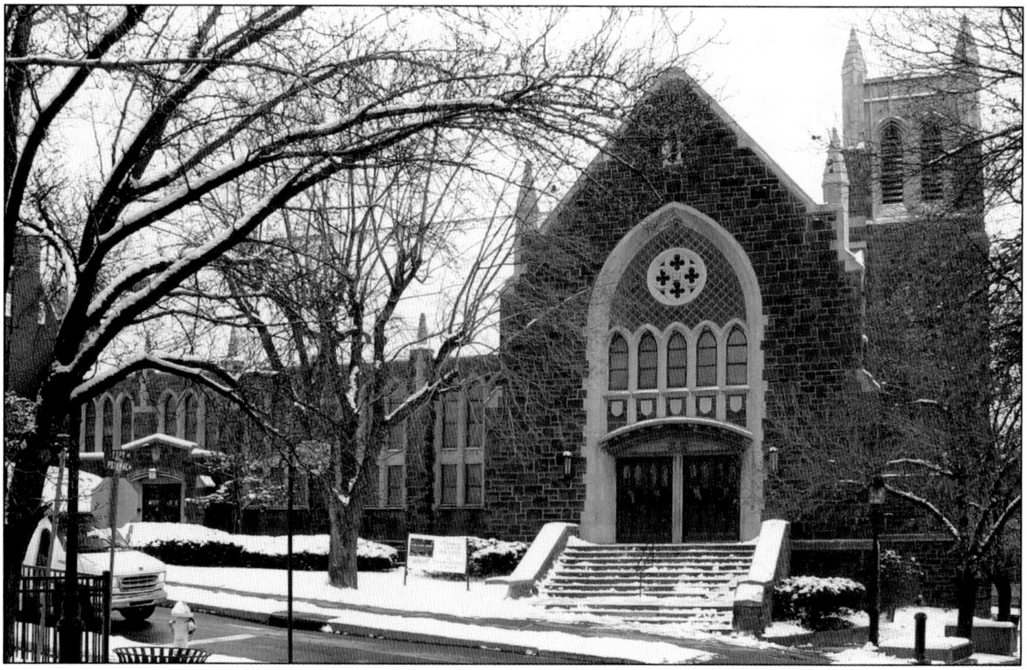

Dormont Presbyterian Church began as a Sunday school that was organized in 1905. After the church was chartered in 1907, land was purchased at Potomac and Espy Avenues. A brownstone building was dedicated there in 1909. This was incorporated into the current sanctuary that was erected in 1924. The Christian education wing was added in 1952.

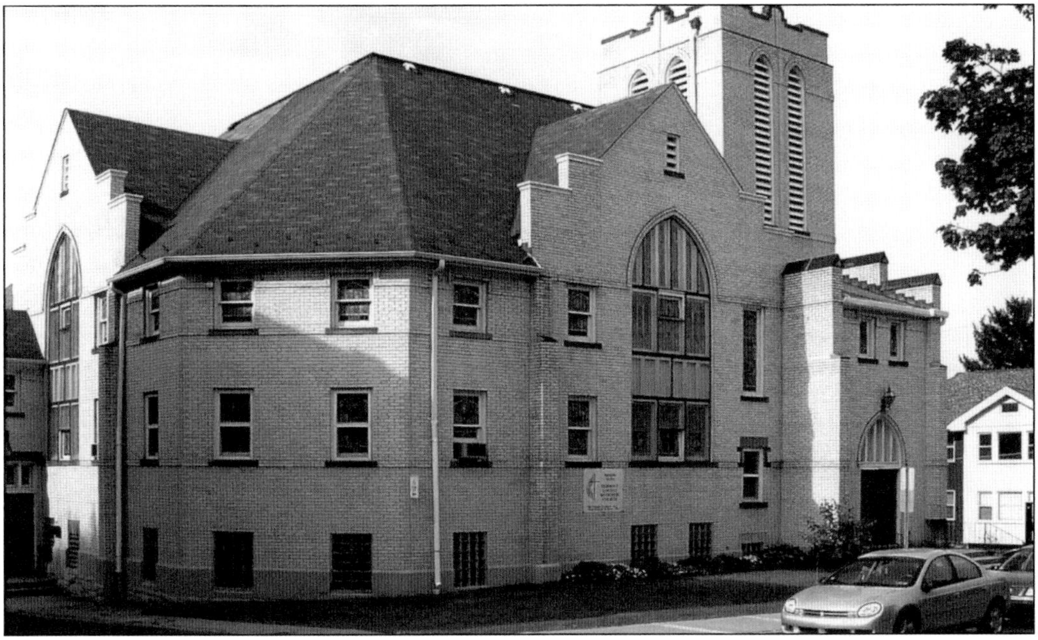

The first service of the Dormont Methodist Episcopal Church was held in the Dormont Masonic Hall on July 8, 1917. The cornerstone of the present church was laid at Potomac and Mattern Avenues in 1920, and the building was dedicated in 1922. In 1945, the name of the church was changed to Dormont Methodist Church and then changed again in 1969 to Dormont United Methodist Church.

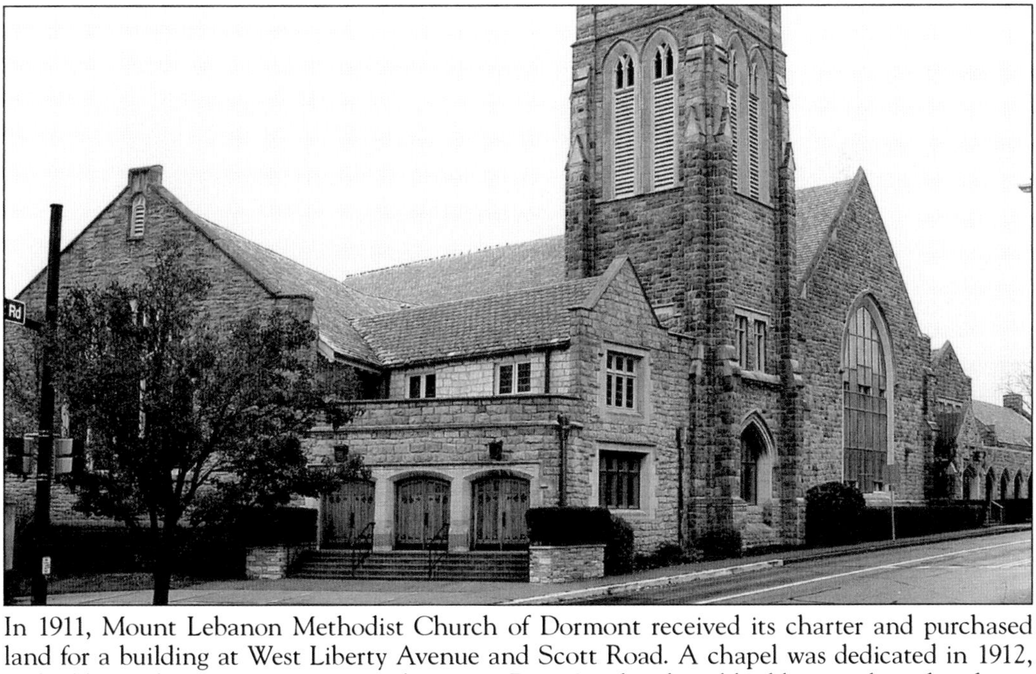

In 1911, Mount Lebanon Methodist Church of Dormont received its charter and purchased land for a building at West Liberty Avenue and Scott Road. A chapel was dedicated in 1912, and additional property was acquired in 1914. By 1924, the chapel had been enlarged and new facilities, including an auditorium, had been added. Vice Pres. Richard Cheney and his wife, Lynne, attended a service there in 2003 while visiting Pittsburgh.

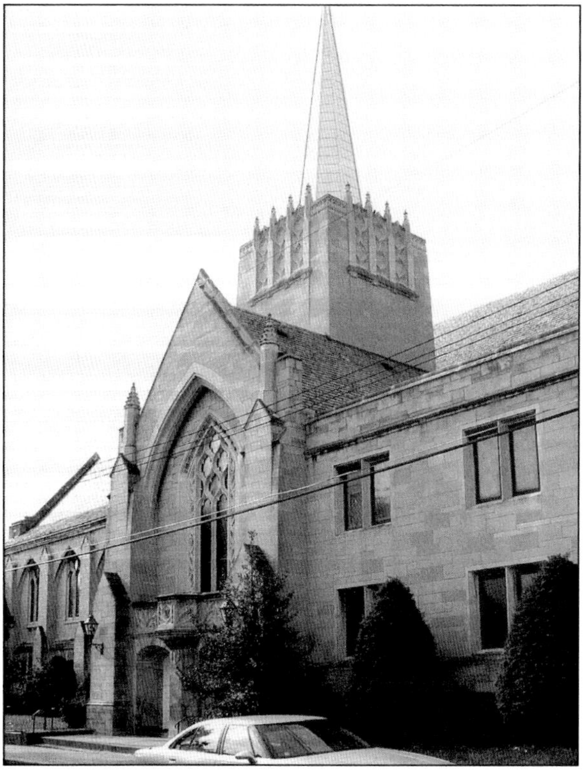

Mount Lebanon Baptist Church traces its beginning to 1907, when cottage prayers were held and a Sunday school was started. The church was organized in 1915, and in October 1917, ground was broken for the building on Alabama Avenue. Growth in membership meant a larger church was needed. The new building, dedicated in 1930, included an auditorium and fellowship hall.

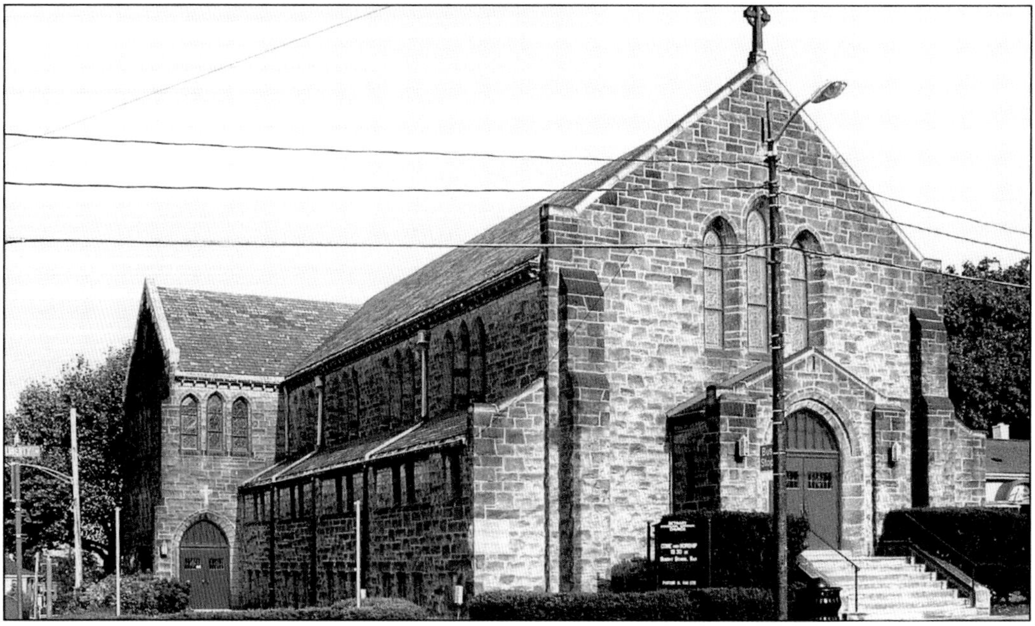

Bethany Evangelical Lutheran Church started with a meeting held in the home of David Barker, at the corner of West Liberty and Tennessee Avenues, in 1917. After its first service was held in the Dormont Public School, a Sunday school was organized. The frame chapel erected in 1919 at the corner of West Liberty Avenue and Park Boulevard was replaced by the current stone structure in 1924.

Five

Events and Recreation

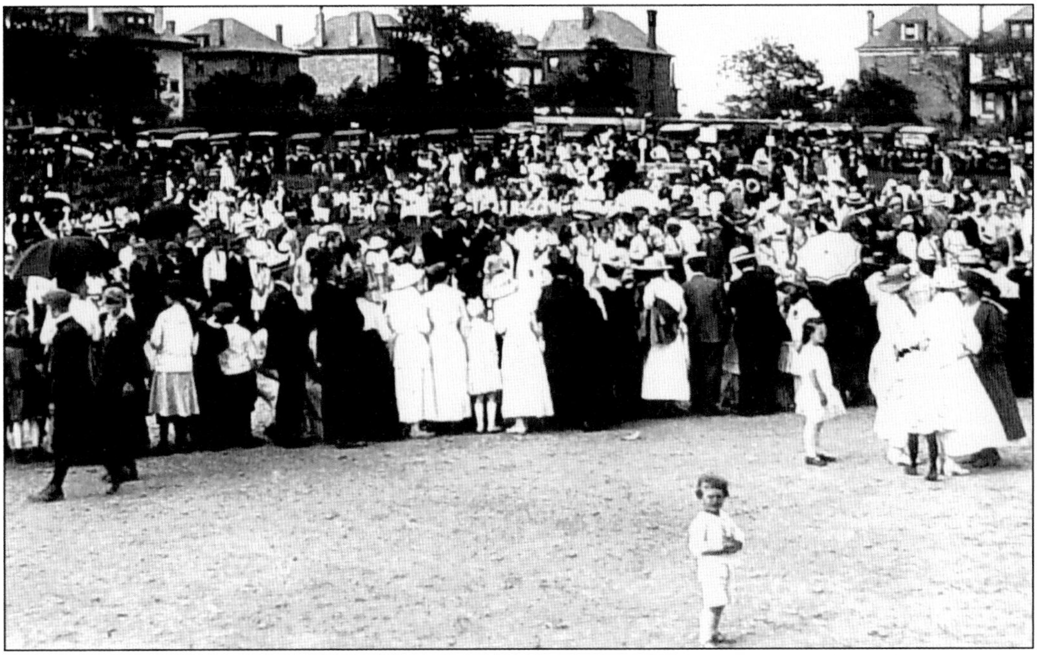

July 4 may be called Independence Day in many places, but since 1912, it has been Dormont Day in this park. These folks gathered at Bailey Field on Annapolis Avenue for the 1917 celebration. The schedule of daylong events for the first Dormont Day included a parade, clay pigeon shoot, banquet, movie, and dancing. Now that annual day is filled with more family-oriented activities until the families spread their blankets on the hillside to watch the fireworks display that begins at dusk.

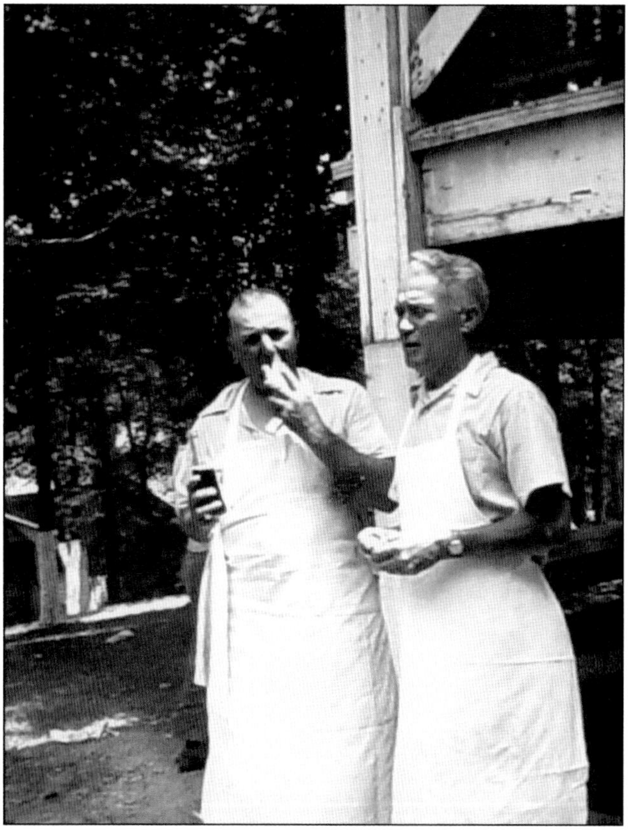

Harold "Beggs" Snyder, seen on the right, worked with the Dormont Day Committee for more than 40 years. He also helped organized the DABA; organized and managed the old Dormont Fraziers baseball team; was a staunch supporter of the Dormont Baseball Club; officiated basketball, baseball, and football; and was an official in a Sugar Bowl Tournament.

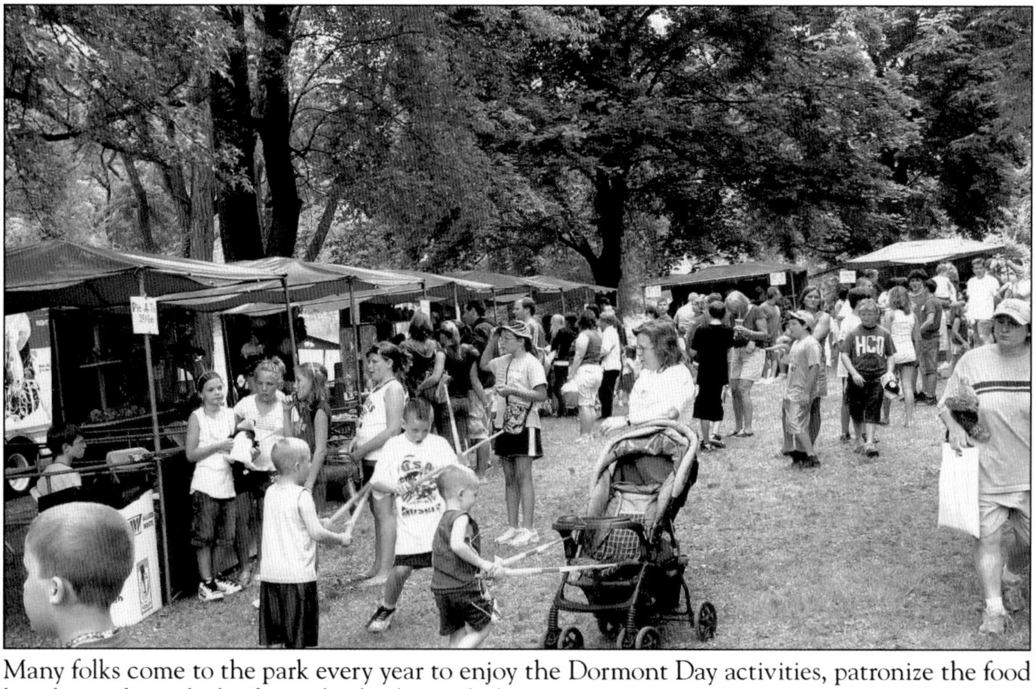

Many folks come to the park every year to enjoy the Dormont Day activities, patronize the food booths, and watch the fireworks display at dusk.

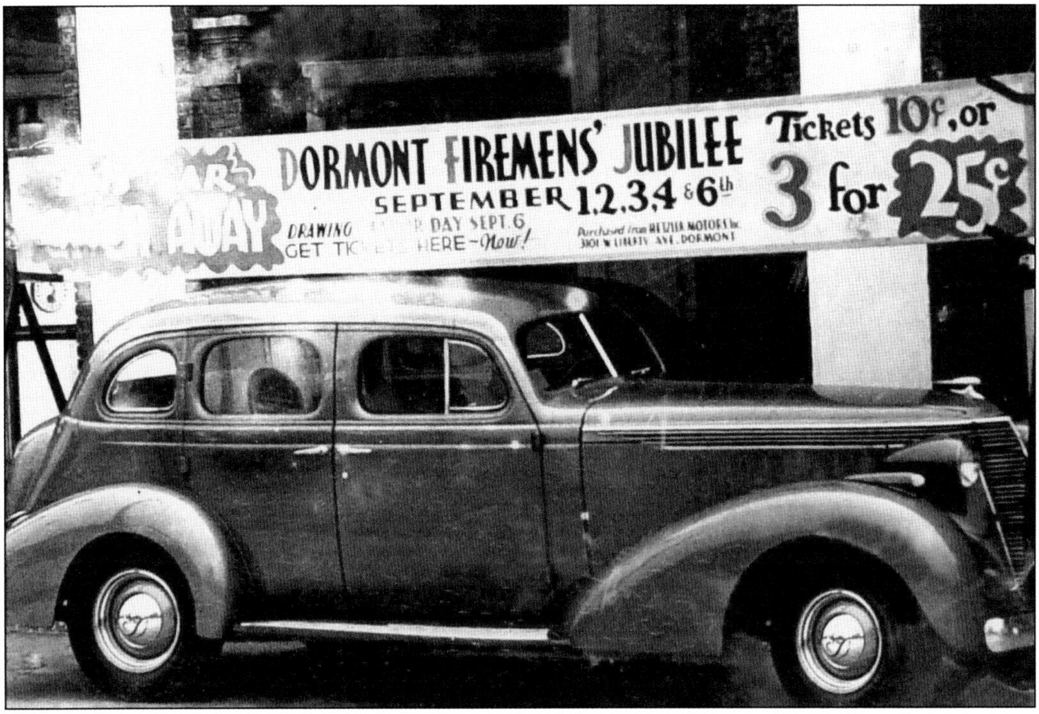

The price of a ticket in the fire department's 1937 jubilee car raffle was 10¢, or three for a quarter. The lucky ticket holder won this 1938 Studebaker.

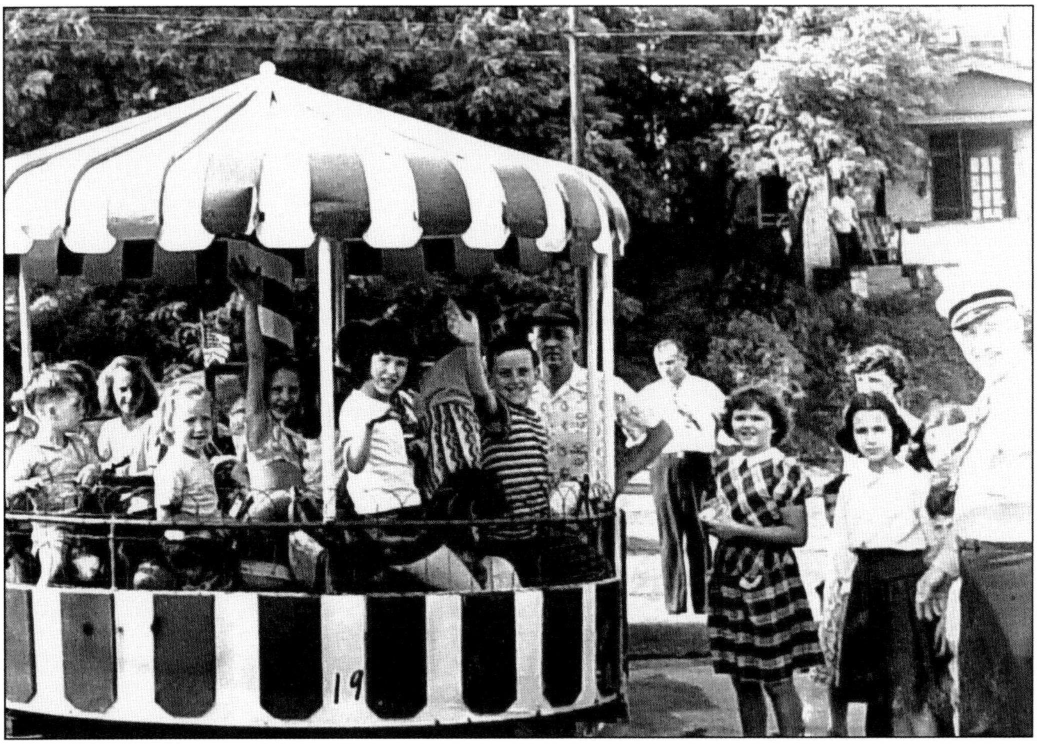

This carousel was one of the attractions at the Firemen's Jubilee in the mid-1940s.

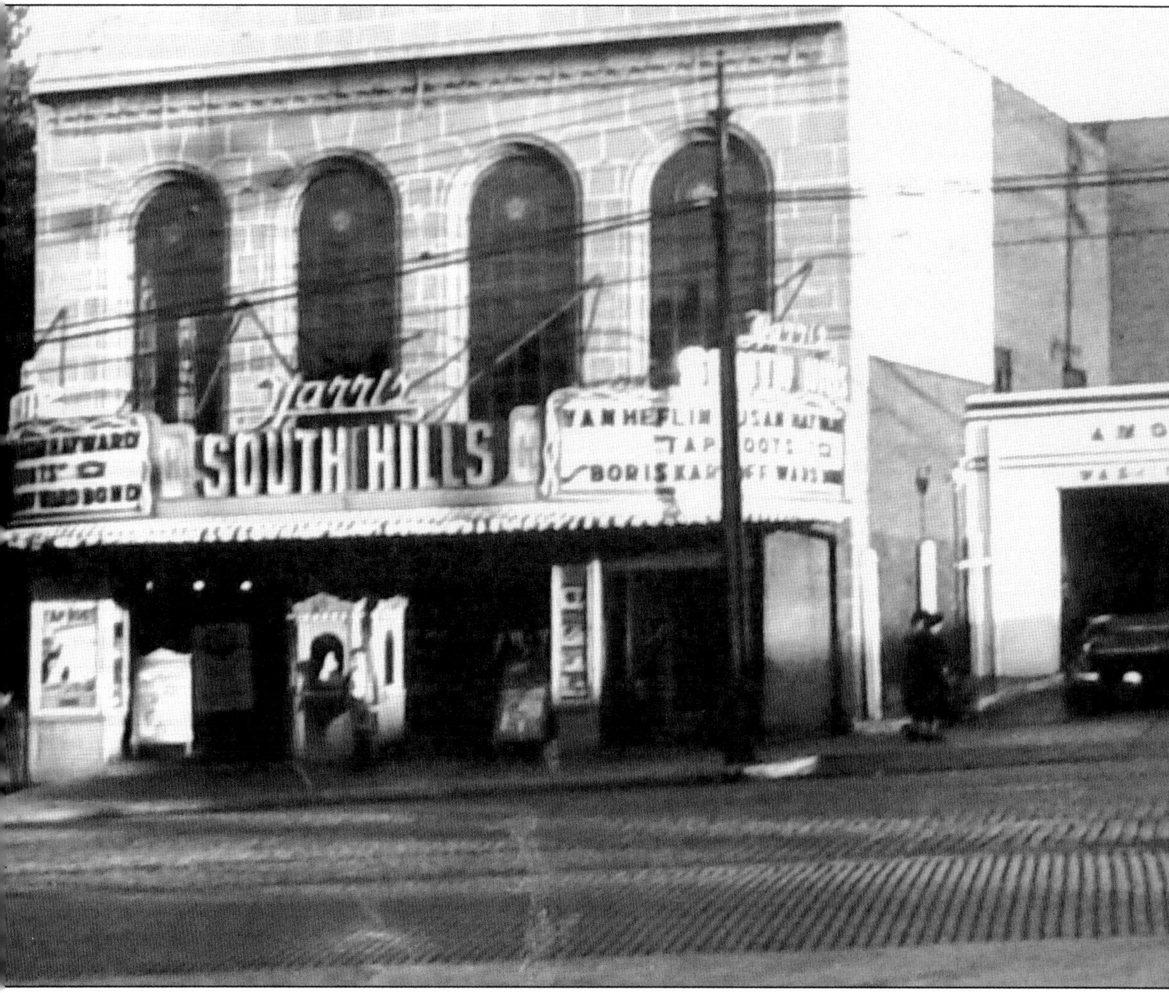

The South Hills Harris Theatre, built by prominent Pittsburgher James Harris in honor of Sen. James Harris, opened at 3975 West Liberty Avenue in 1927 to host vaudeville and silent movies. One of the first local places to be air-conditioned, it was opulent in every way. Uniformed ushers greeted the patrons as they entered. Thick carpets, beautiful chandeliers, and lovely draperies were some of the lavish furnishings. When talkies came into vogue, they were accompanied by a 2/6 Mighty WurliTzer organ. Innovative promotions such as Bank Night and Dish Night and live entertainment were popular. After James Baker bought the building, he used the upper floors for producing Mode-Art Pictures, industrial and defense films, and to house his studio players. The theater was closed in 1983, sold in 1988, and, in 1994, split into small theaters, which led to its demise within a few years.

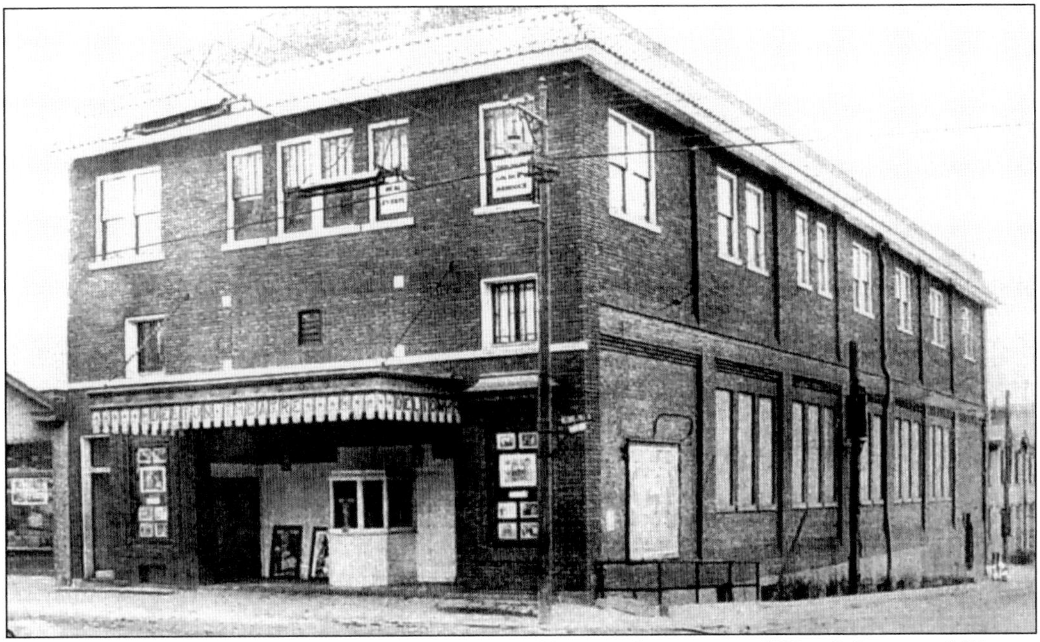

The Delton Theater opened in the Alderdice Building at the corner of West Liberty and Illinois Avenues in 1914 and closed in 1928. One of its advertisements states that it is "open-air with roof, cool, comfortable, and sanitary." The steps down the side of the building used to lead to a bowling alley and then a poolroom. Wilkie's Inn is now located there.

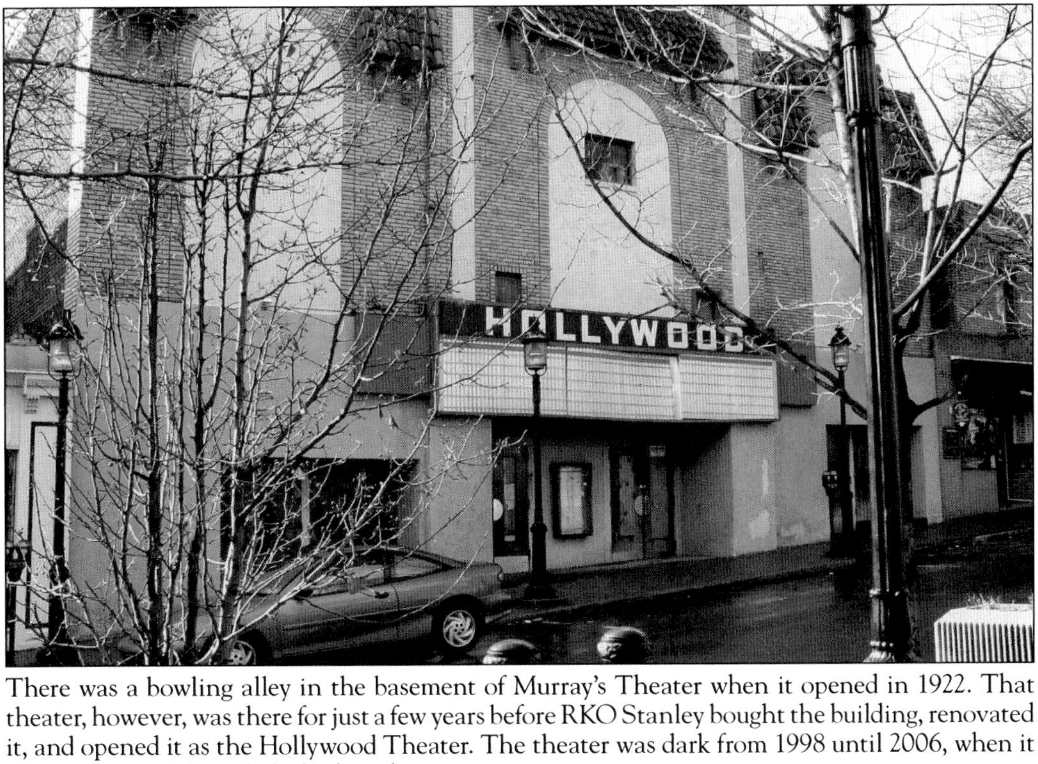

There was a bowling alley in the basement of Murray's Theater when it opened in 1922. That theater, however, was there for just a few years before RKO Stanley bought the building, renovated it, and opened it as the Hollywood Theater. The theater was dark from 1998 until 2006, when it opened, beautifully refurbished, under new management.

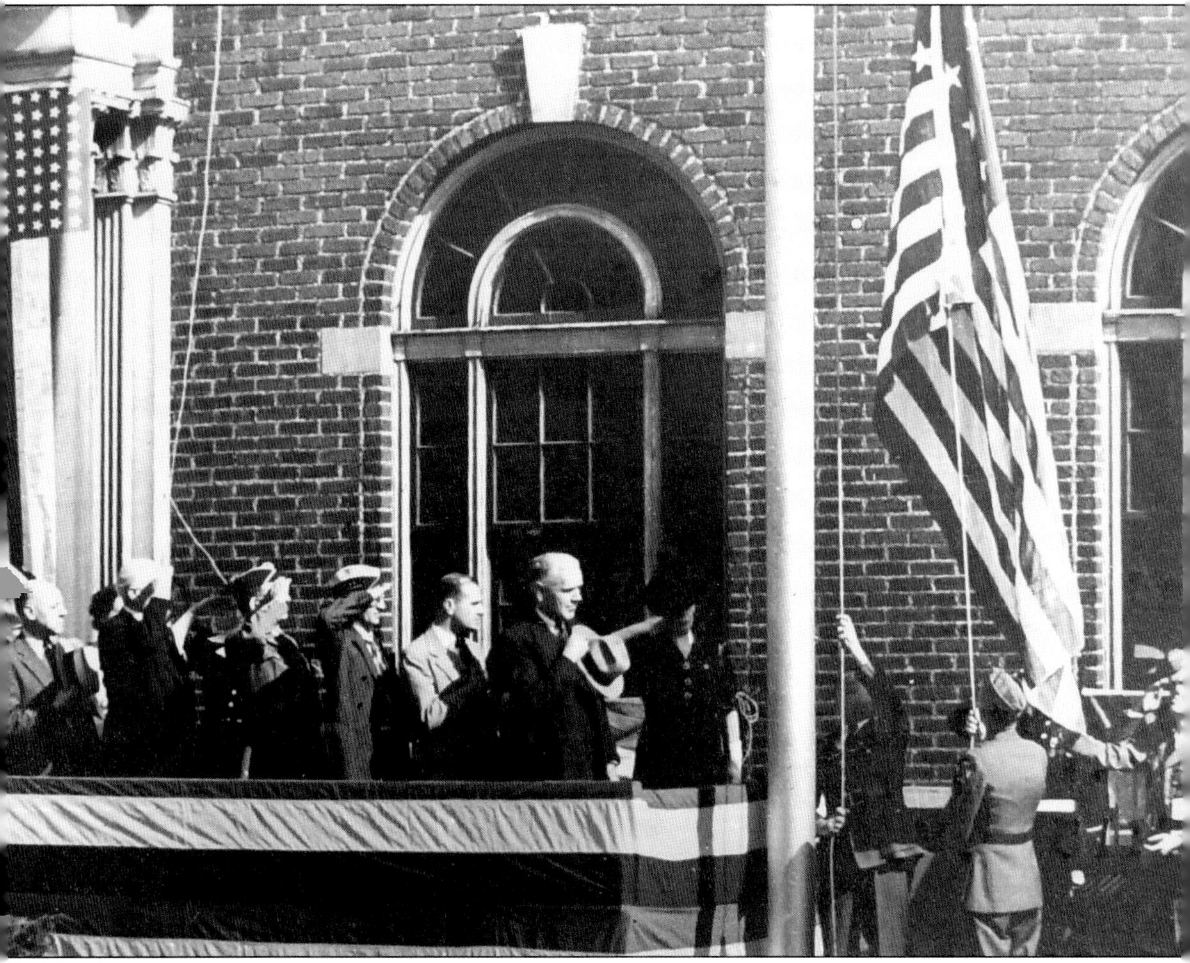

On September 13, 1941, members of McCormick-Dorman Post No. 694, Veterans of Foreign Wars, conducted their fifth annual ceremony honoring National Anthem Day in front of the borough building. The post, established by a charter on November 9, 1933, on a petition signed by 57 World War I veterans, was dedicated to George McCormick and F. H. Dorman, local men who lost their lives in that war. The members work hard to raise money for charitable causes, and they take an active part in borough activities.

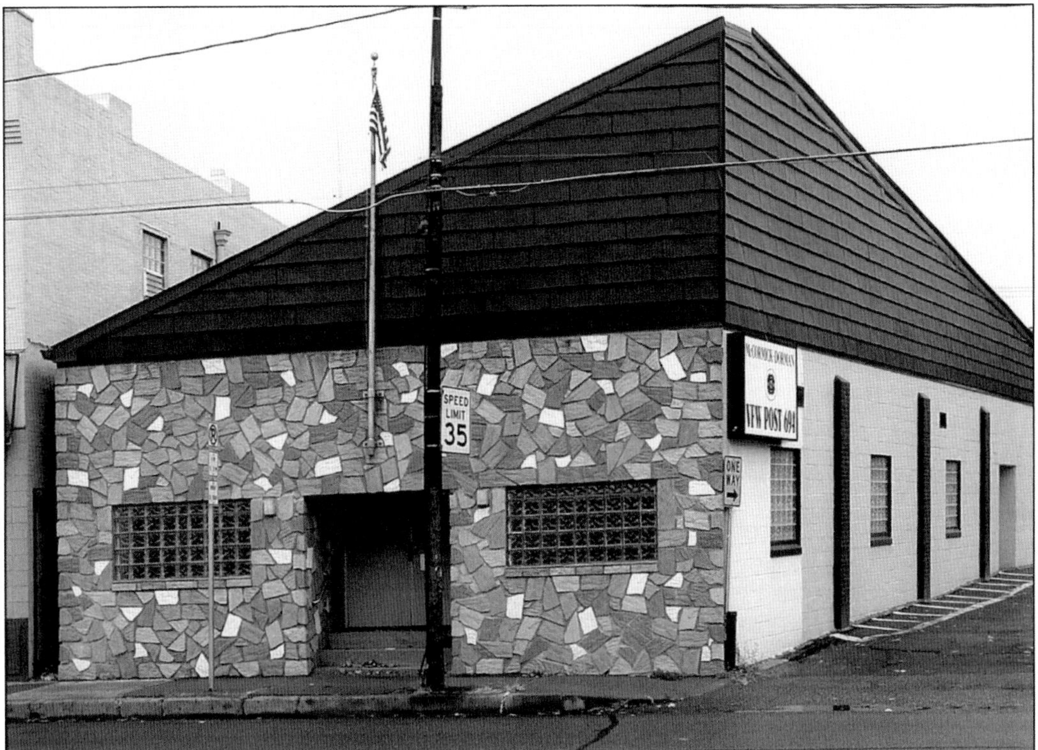

Originally housed on Tennessee Avenue near West Liberty Avenue, the post needed larger headquarters when veterans returned home after World War II. Dedication of its building at 3014 West Liberty Avenue was held on January 1, 1955

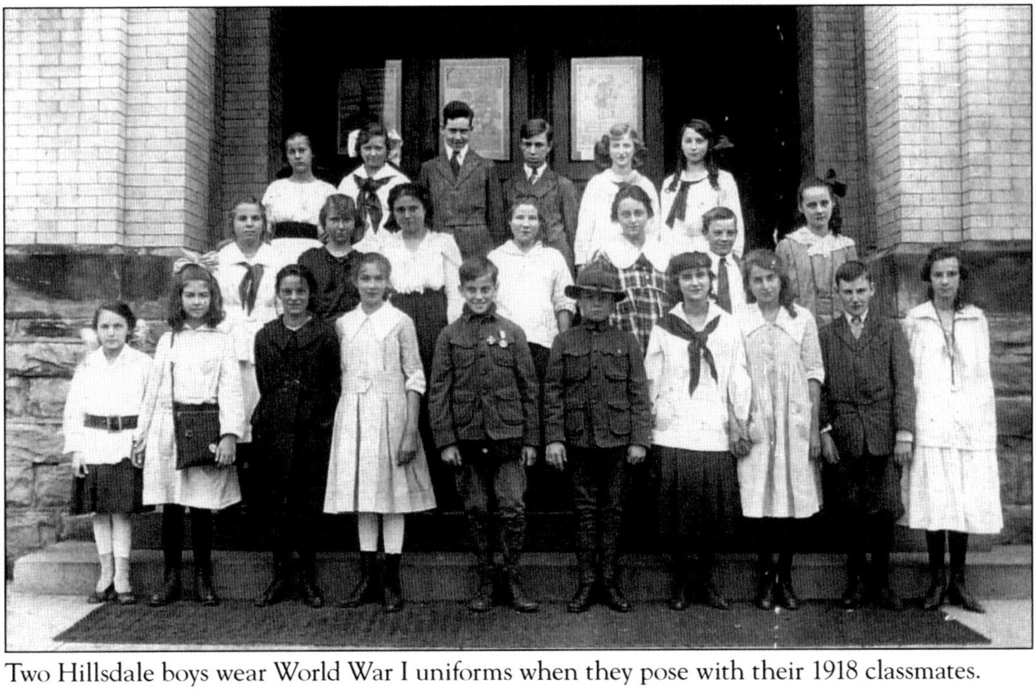

Two Hillsdale boys wear World War I uniforms when they pose with their 1918 classmates.

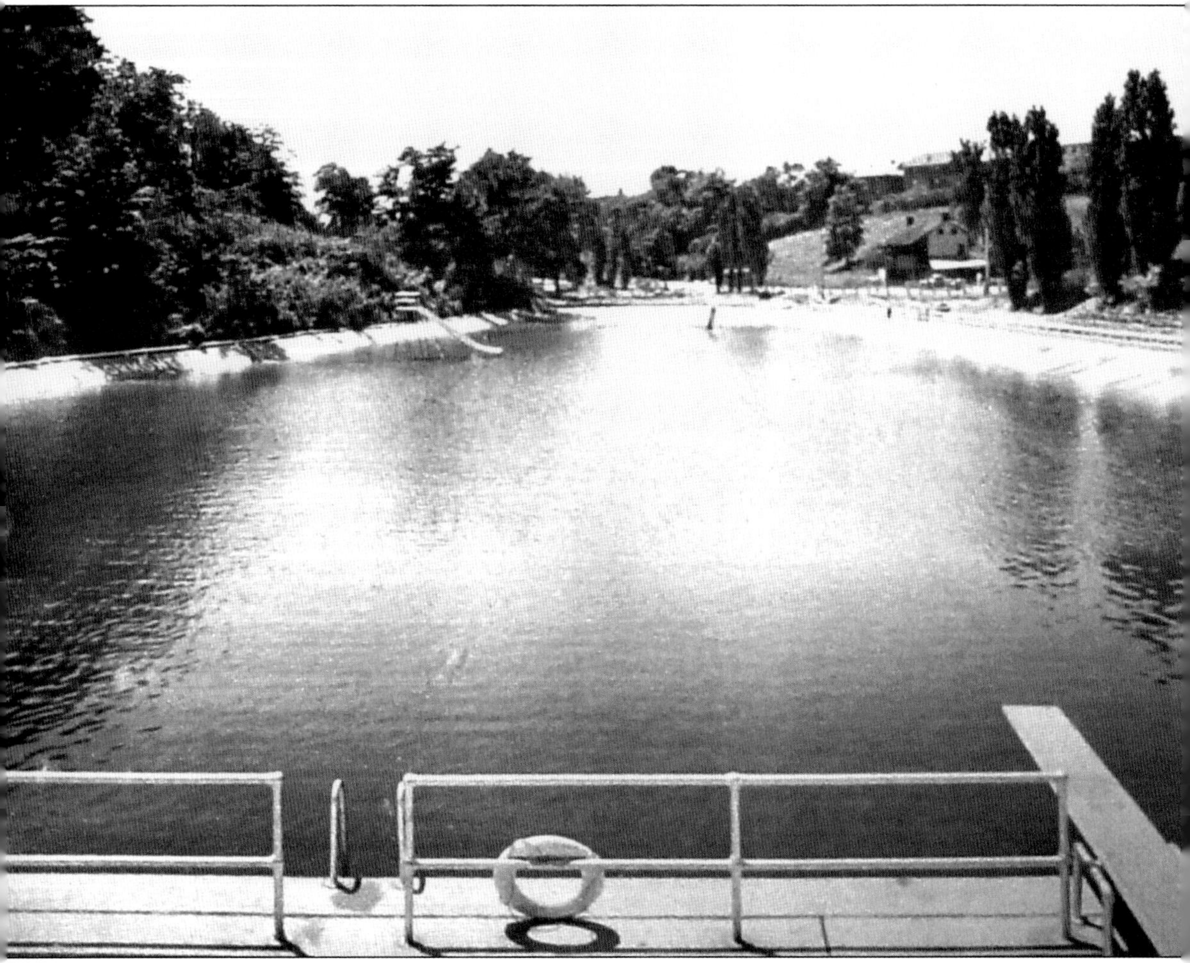

For decades, the favorite recreational place of borough residents has been its municipal pool, one of the largest in Pennsylvania. Its beginning is accredited to a local man who dammed a stream to make a wading pool for his children. In 1922, the borough contracted for the building of a bigger dam to make a swimming area. Its slanted sides and gently sloping shallow end make it enjoyable for swimmers of all ages and ability. The diving boards had to be removed, but a waterslide and large mushroom sprinkler have been added for the children.

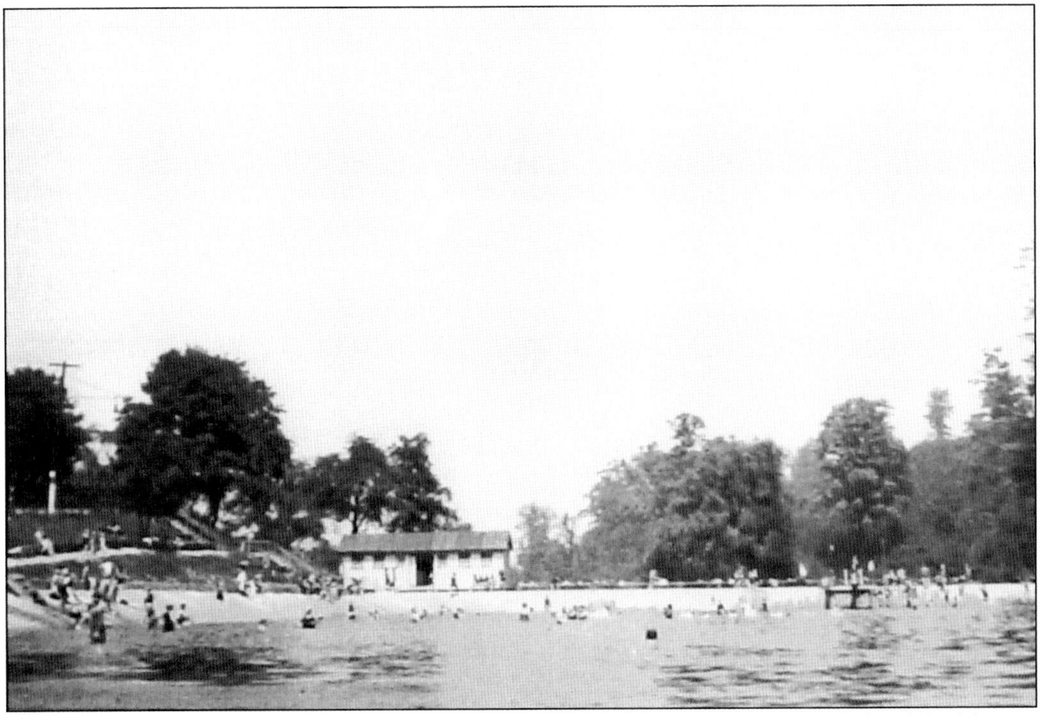

The building seen in the background is the wooden bathhouse built in 1926. A brick bathhouse replaced it in 1936 when the pool was concreted.

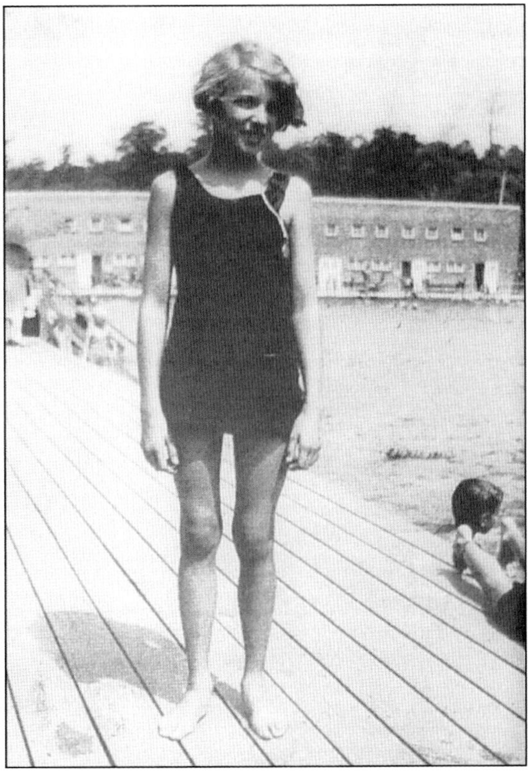

This picture taken on Labor Day 1930 shows the boardwalk that ran down one side of the pool for a few years.

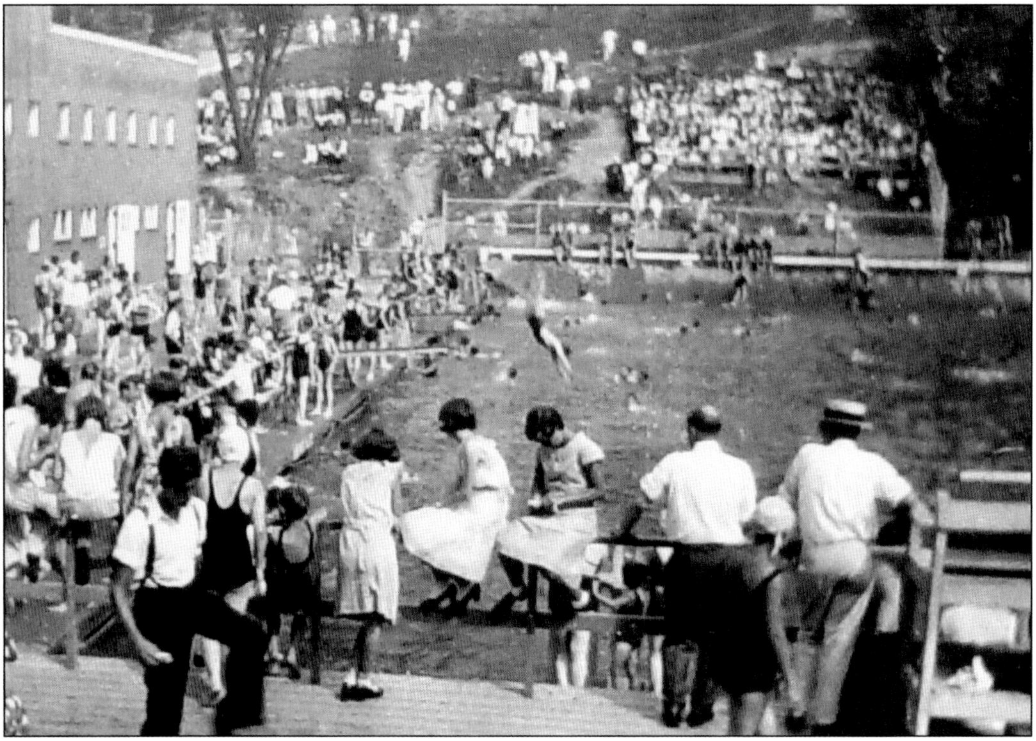

Diving exhibitions, like this one on a Dormont Day in the 1930s, always attracted a crowd.

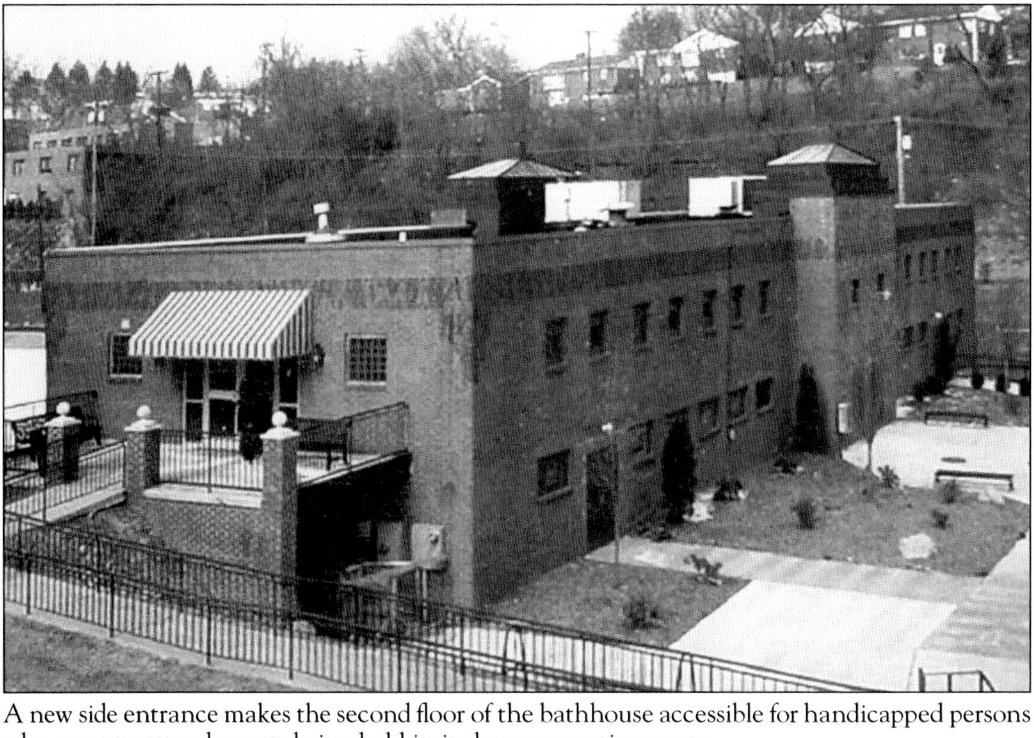

A new side entrance makes the second floor of the bathhouse accessible for handicapped persons who want to attend events being held in its large recreation room.

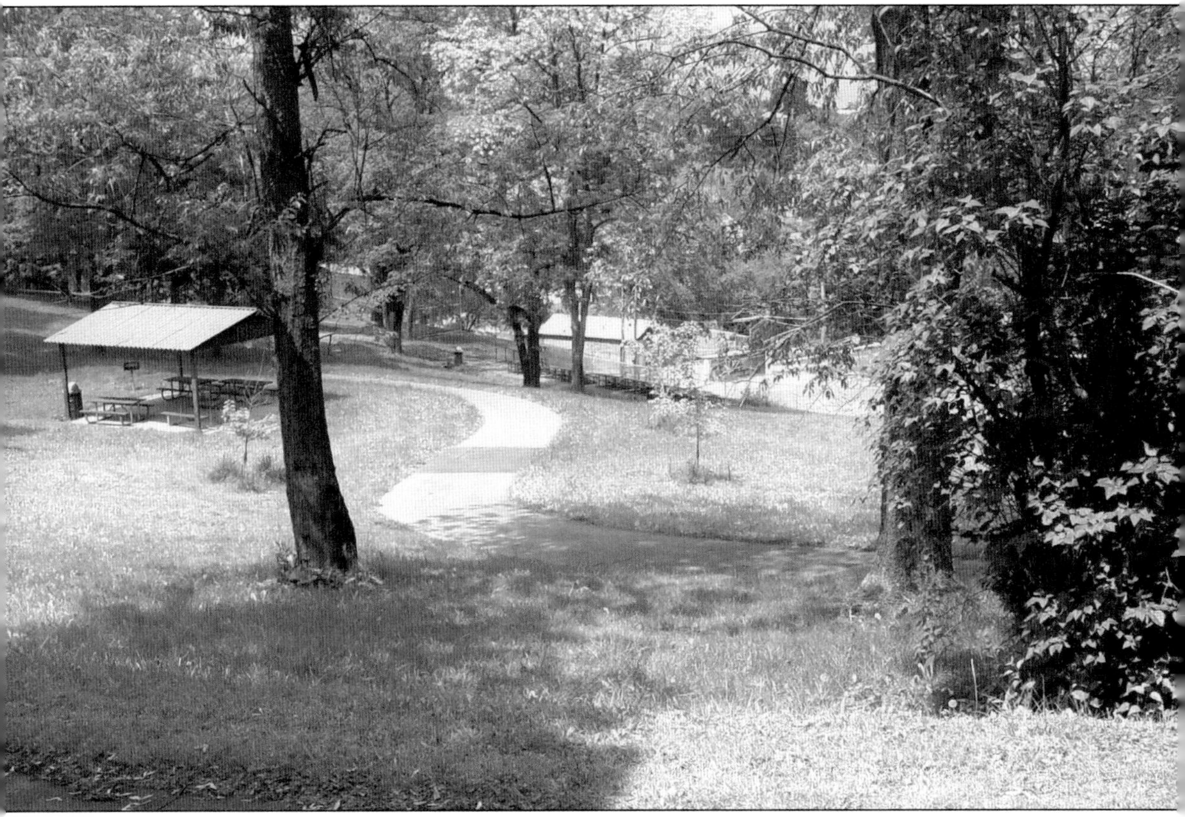

Dormont Park is located at the intersection of Banksville Road and Dormont Avenue, the main entrance to the borough. Fashioned from 22 acres of what had been Bailey Field, it offers many types of activities. Upon entering Dormont, people pass the William H. Moreland Jr. Memorial Garden, veterans monument, and horseshoe courts. Beyond those, to the right, are the basketball and tennis courts that line the parking lot at Dormont Pool. Continuing up the hill, they pass the Castle Playground, at the intersection of Dormont Avenue and Memorial Drive. The "Pop" Murray Little League Field is seen before the top of the park, at the intersection with Annapolis Avenue, is reached. Bicycle and walking trails run through the main body of the park, passing its pavilion and picnic tables.

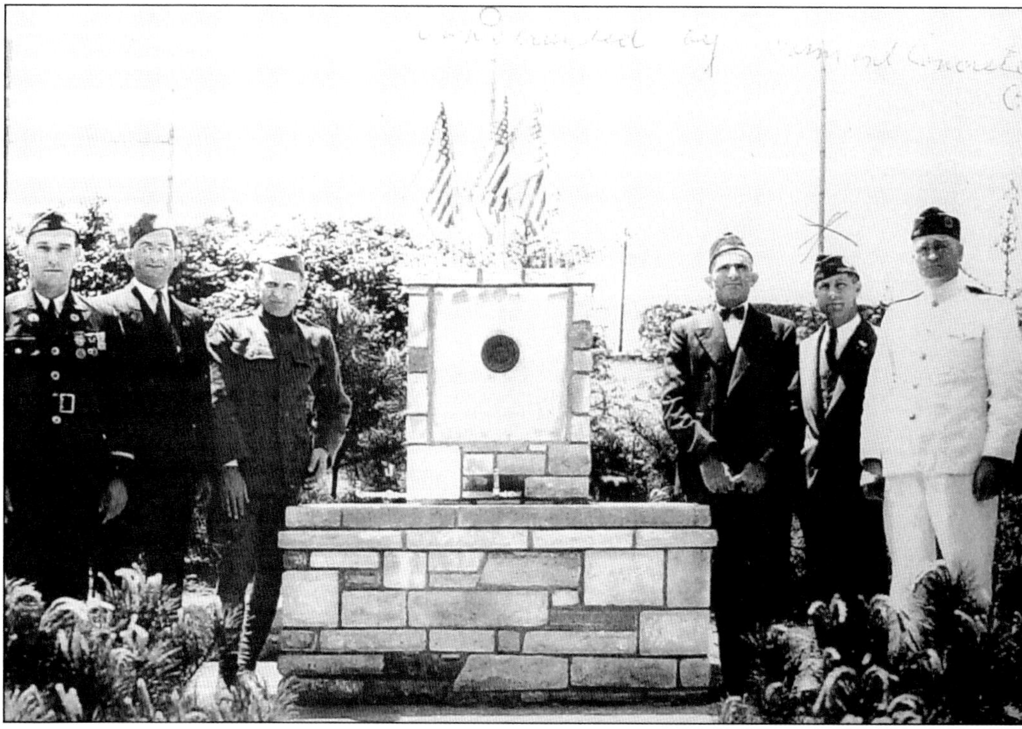

These World War I veterans participate in the dedication of the fountain that had been located near the Annapolis Avenue entrance to the park. Albert Schoenefeldt (fifth from the left) was the owner of Dormont Concrete Company, which constructed it. Although the fountain is no longer there, the cannon remains.

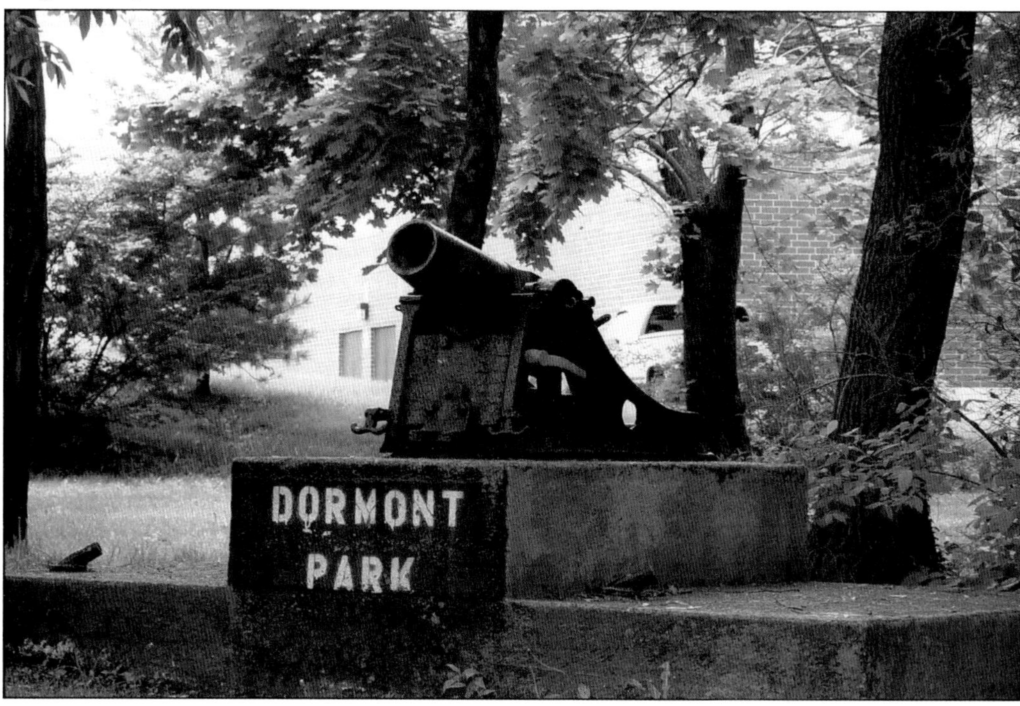

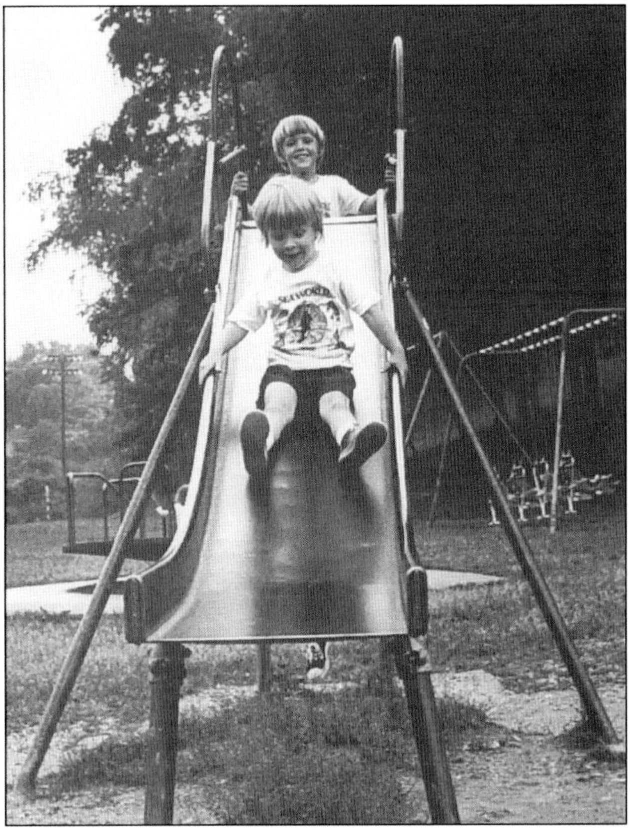

For years different pieces of playground equipment, like the slides and merry-go-round in these pictures, were features that children enjoyed while in the park. The younger children's area has different equipment today.

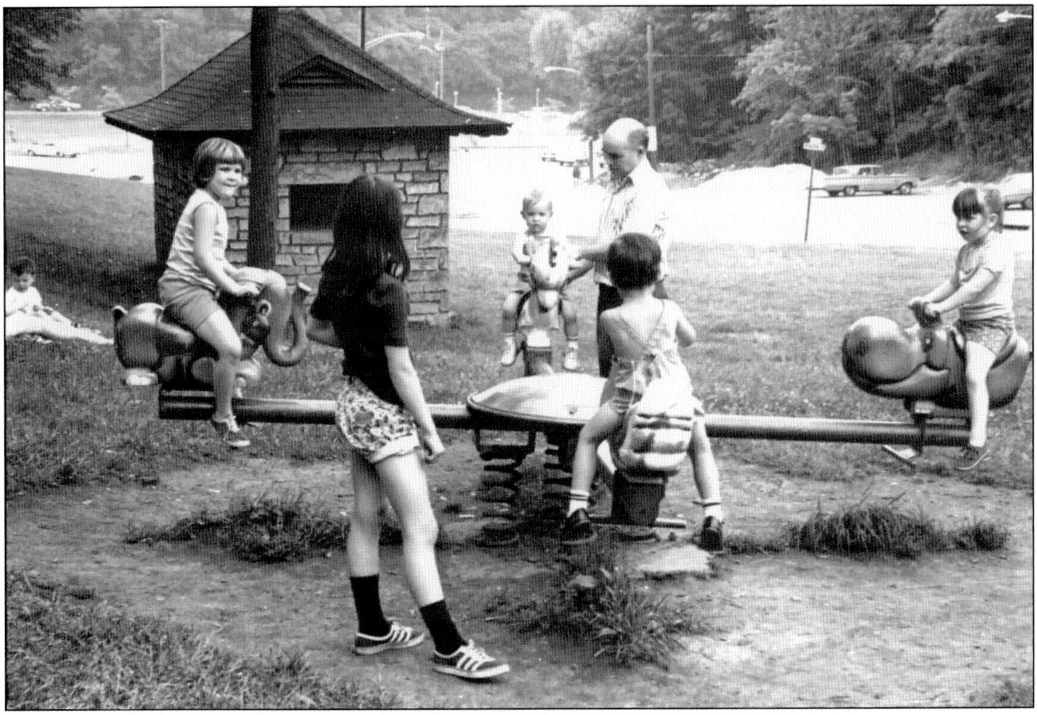

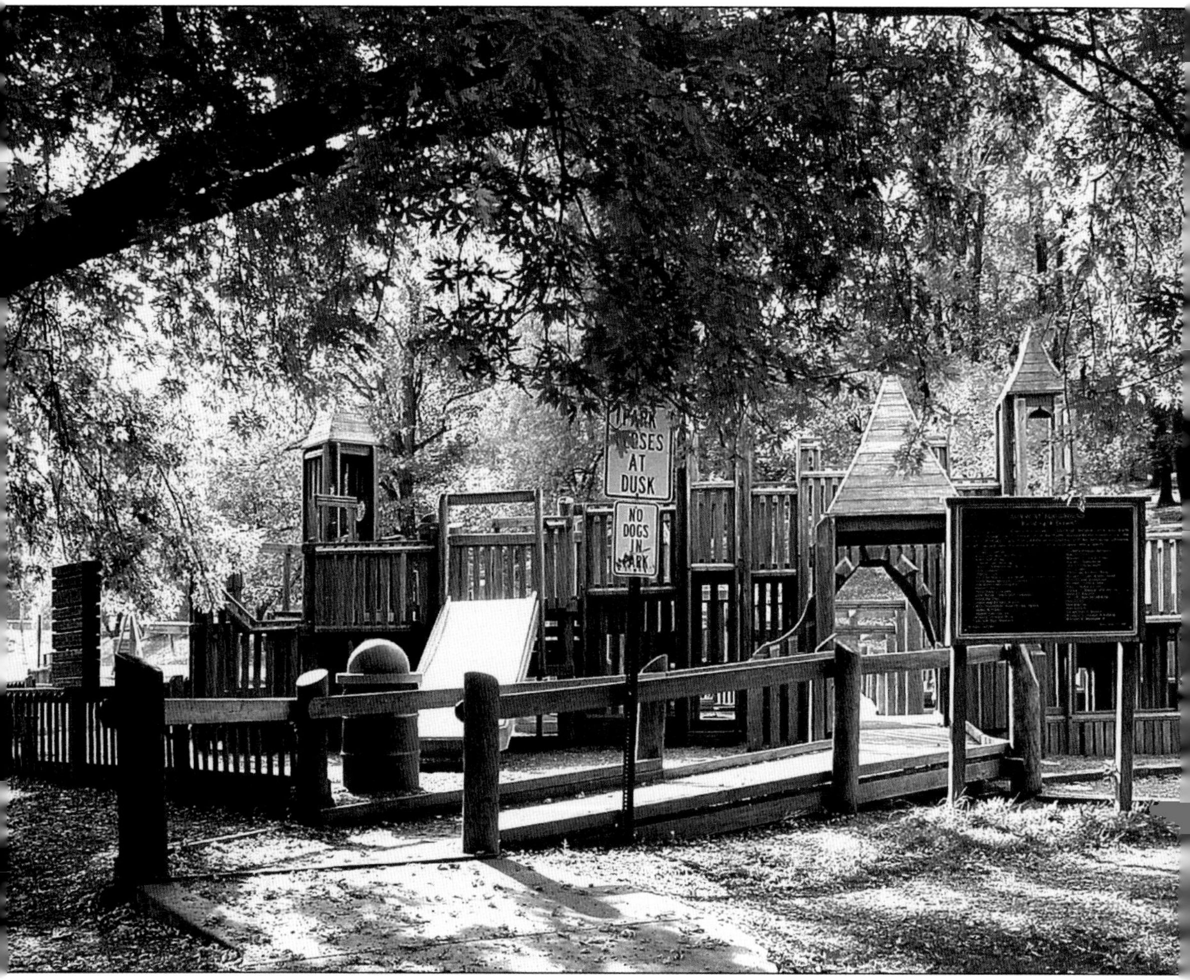

The borough's super playground, usually called the Castle Playground, opened in June 1991 at the corner of Dormont Avenue and Memorial Drive. The 9,600-square-foot pine structure is the product of five days of construction, $40,000 in donations, and hours of work by more than 1,000 volunteers. The swinging bridge and climbing tower are but two of the features that make it a special place for children.

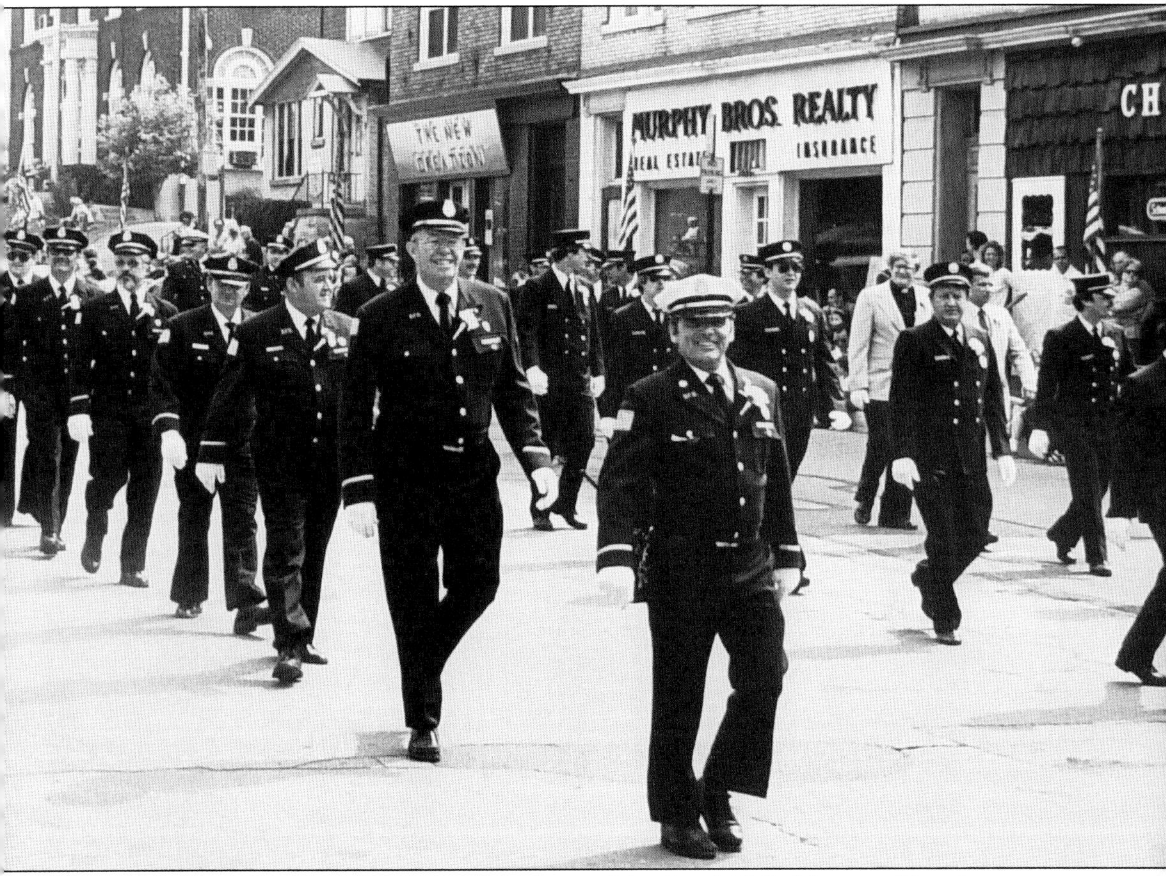

Memorial Day parades have been an annual event of the South Hills Memorial Day Association since 1920. Originally starting in the adjoining Pittsburgh suburb of Beechview, the two-mile route now begins on the city's Brookline Boulevard, comes into Dormont on Pioneer Avenue, turns onto West Liberty Avenue, and ends with a ceremony in Mount Lebanon Cemetery. Hundreds watch about 50 units, including local fire and police equipment, veterans' organizations, Scout troops, bands, Shriners units, school groups, and local historical societies pay homage to those who have served and are serving their country. Mount Lebanon and Dormont firemen are shown marching in the 2900 block of West Liberty Avenue in the 1980 parade. The Dormont firemen, in the foreground, are led by Capt. Donald James. He is followed by fellow fireman Mayor William Moreland Jr.

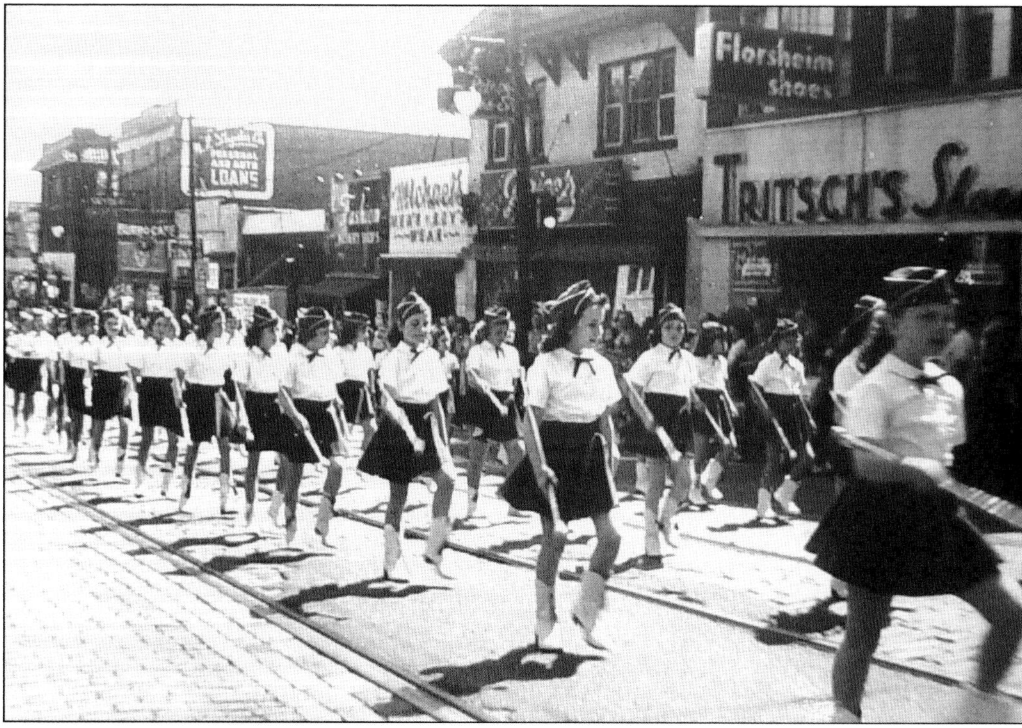

DABA's Boosterettes march near the intersection of West Liberty and Potomac Avenues in the 1958 Memorial Day parade.

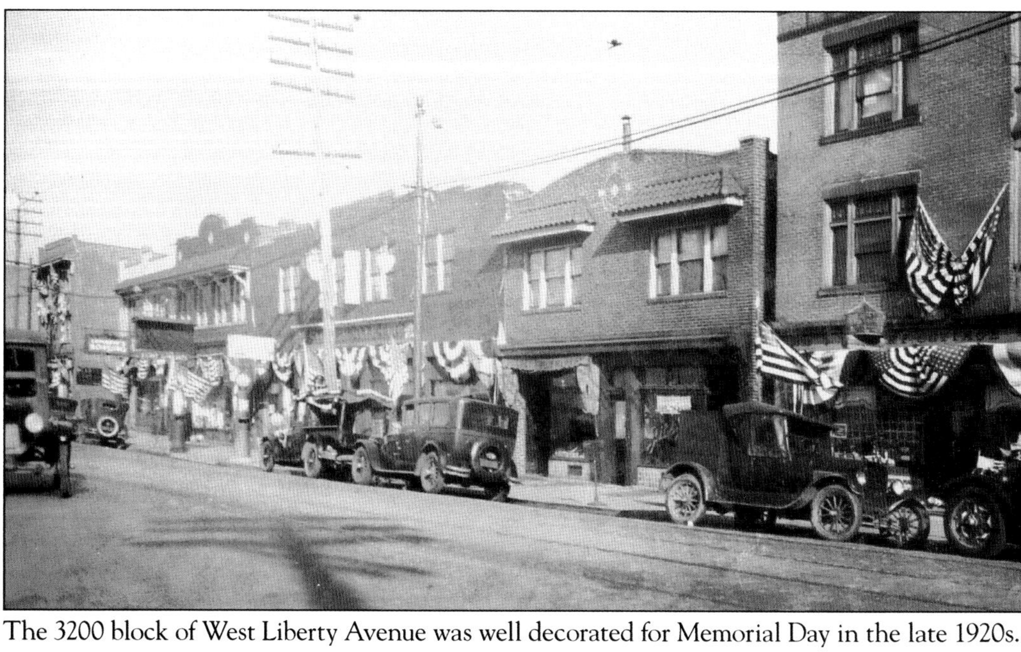

The 3200 block of West Liberty Avenue was well decorated for Memorial Day in the late 1920s.

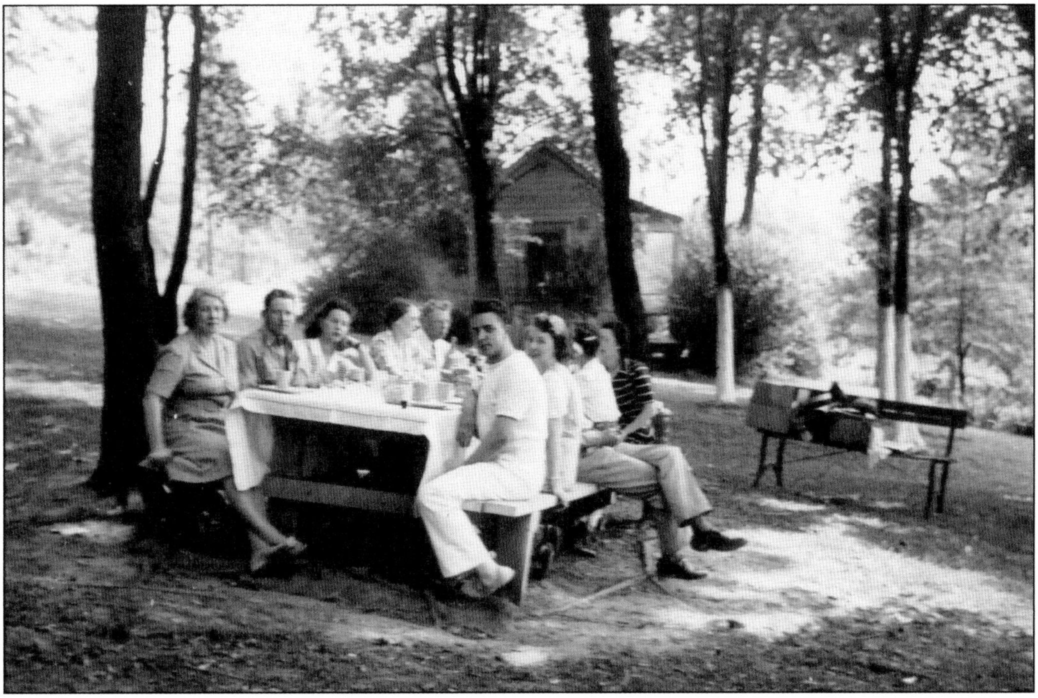

Dormont Park has always been a fine place for a picnic.

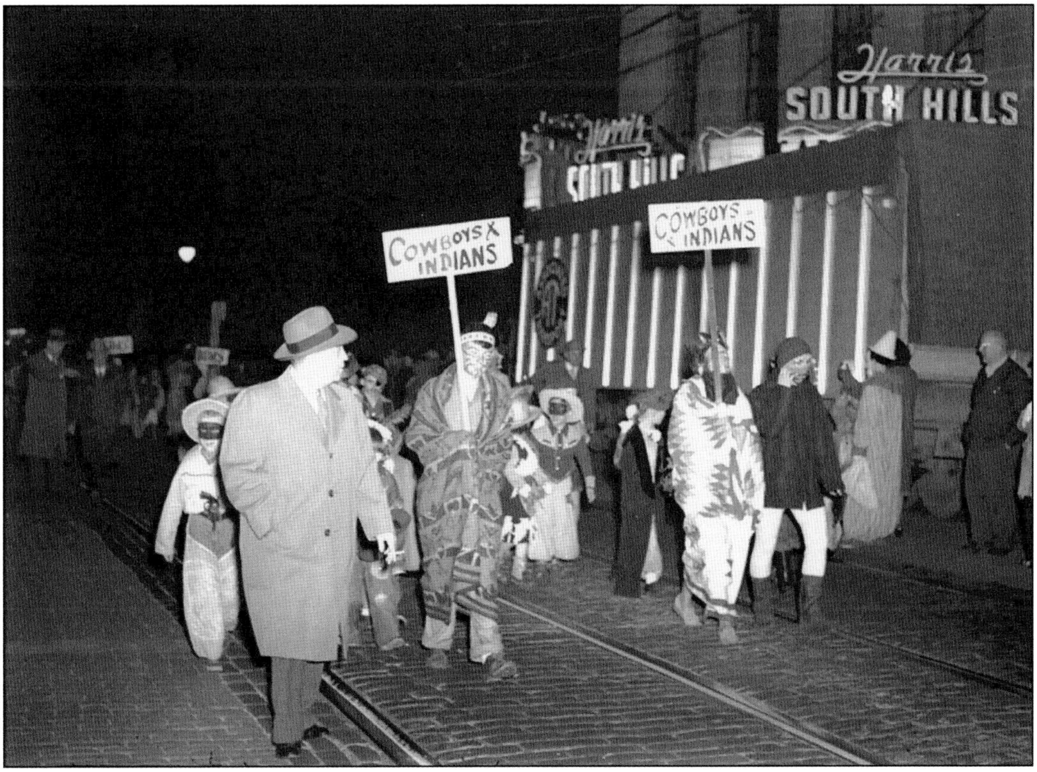

Halloween parades have been an annual event in the borough for many years.

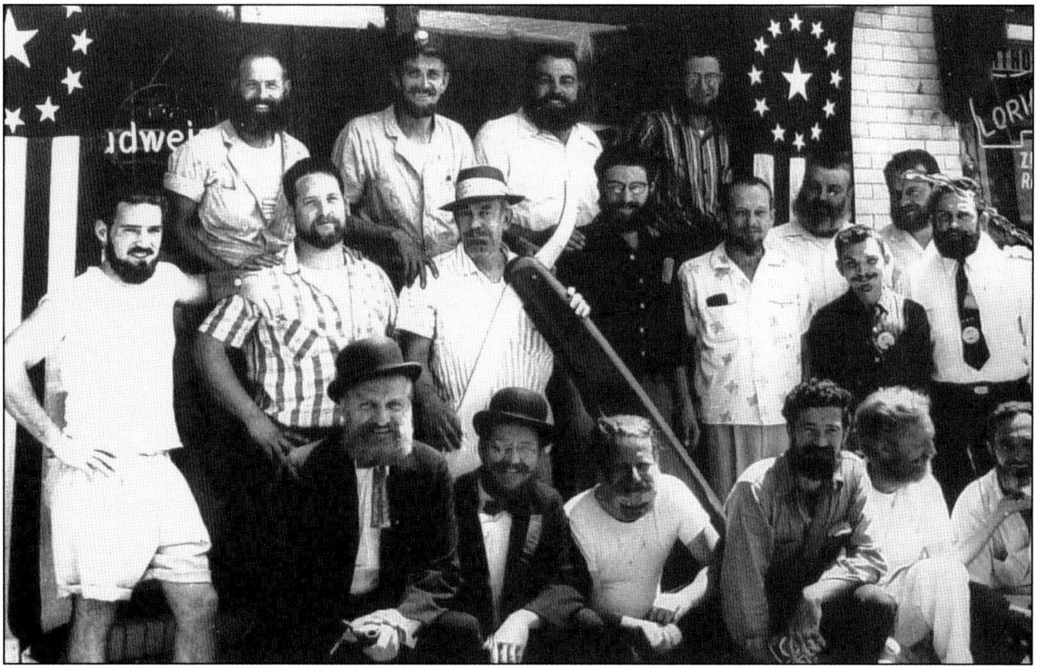

The borough's 50th anniversary celebration opened with a grand parade in April to give the men who were entering the beard-growing contest plenty of time before the judging would be held in July. After the parade, the symbolic six-foot razor seen in this picture was buried. Men who did not grow beards for the anniversary were required to buy $1 shaving permit pins.

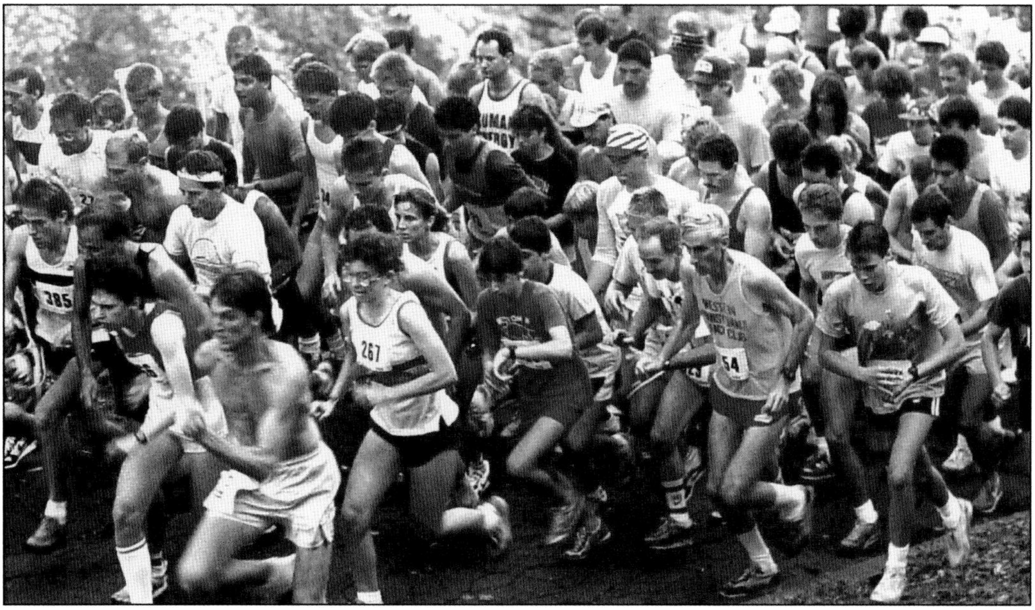

From 1983 to 1988, the Dormont Dash was a popular summer event. Its course covered three miles of residential and business streets termed "mildly rolling hills" by its organizer, Sgt. Gus Melis of the Dormont Police Department. Contestants were grouped by sex and ages from 12 to over 60. Monetary prizes were awarded to the three top winners in each group. This event is planned to be revived as part of the borough's centennial celebration in 2009.

The borough's hilly terrain has kept sled riding a popular winter pastime. Snowy days find many in the park enjoying the thrill of coasting from Memorial Drive into the pool parking lot while others coast closer to their homes.

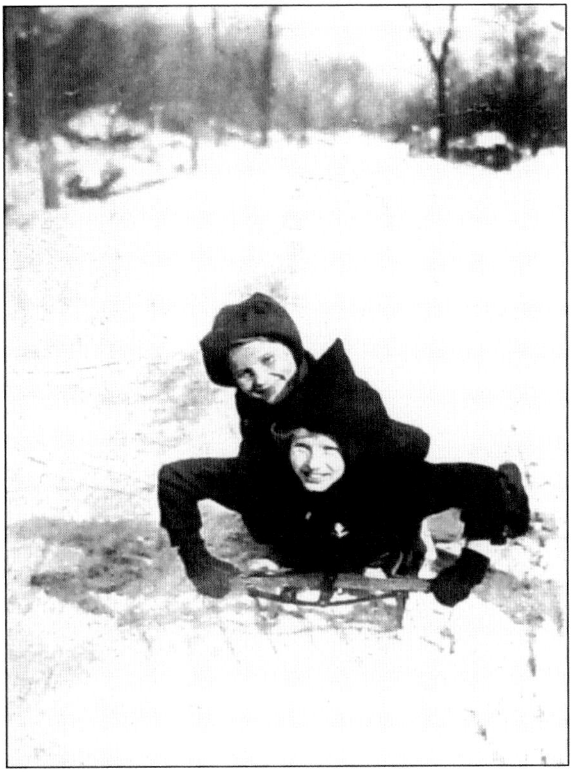

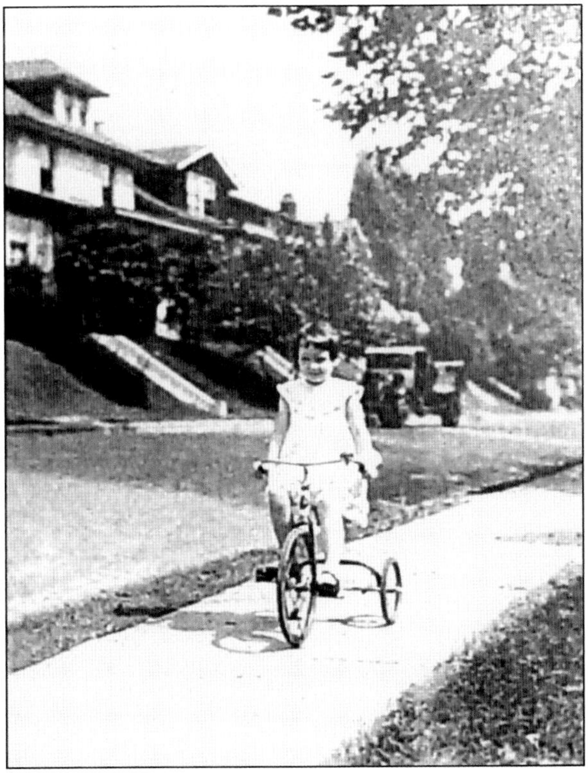

Riding tricycles and bicycles was more popular with borough children in former years than it is now, as was roller-skating. One early resident wrote of her neighbors complaining about the noise when she and her friends spent afternoons skating up and down the sidewalk.

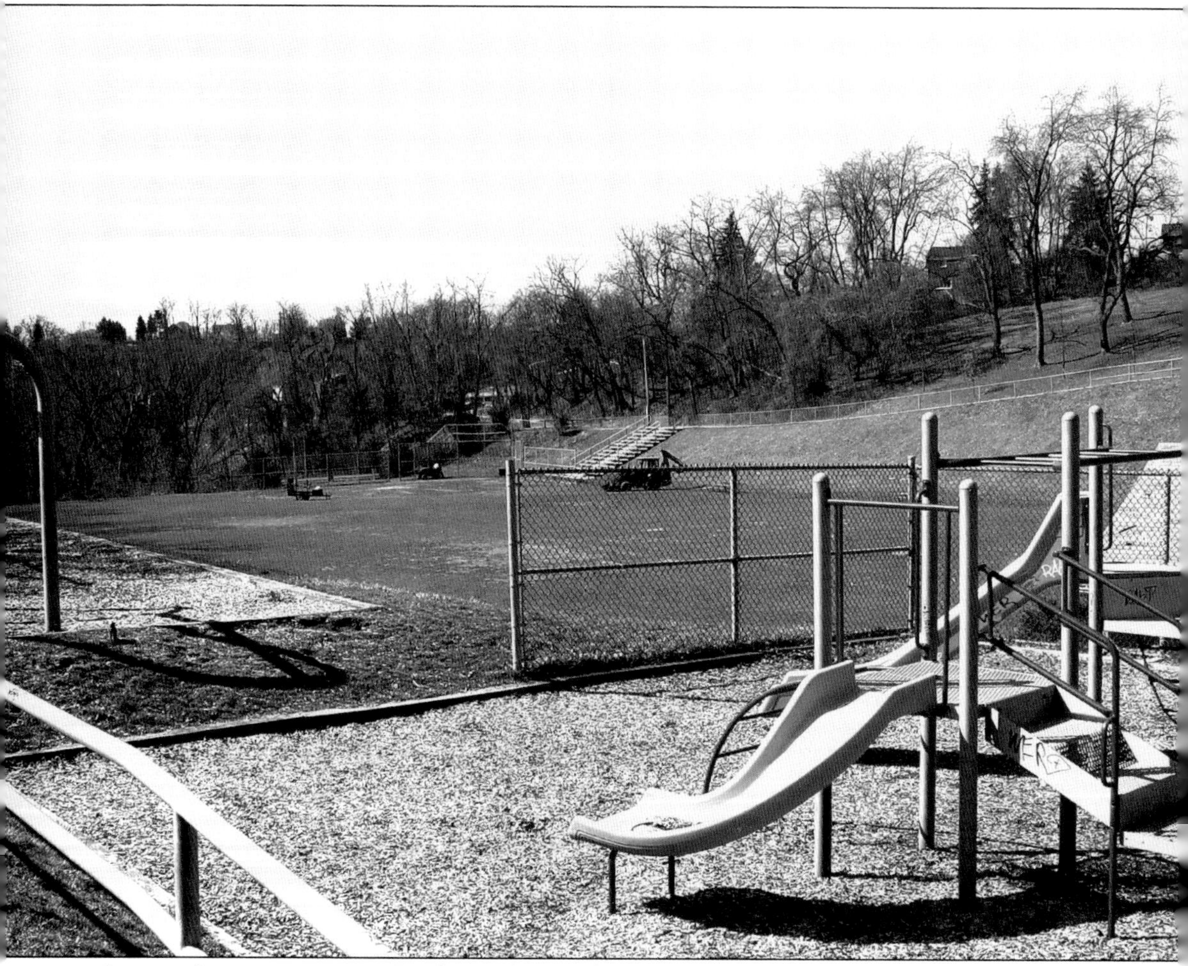

A second recreation area, Snyder Park, was developed at the end of Tennessee, Illinois, and Arkansas Avenues in the early 1980s. A granite monument near the entrance was erected when the park was dedicated in memory of Harold "Beggs" Snyder. Beggs devoted many years of his life to the organizing and promoting of sports activities for the youth of the borough. A ball field, playground equipment, and picnic facilities have been installed there.

Six

Then and Now

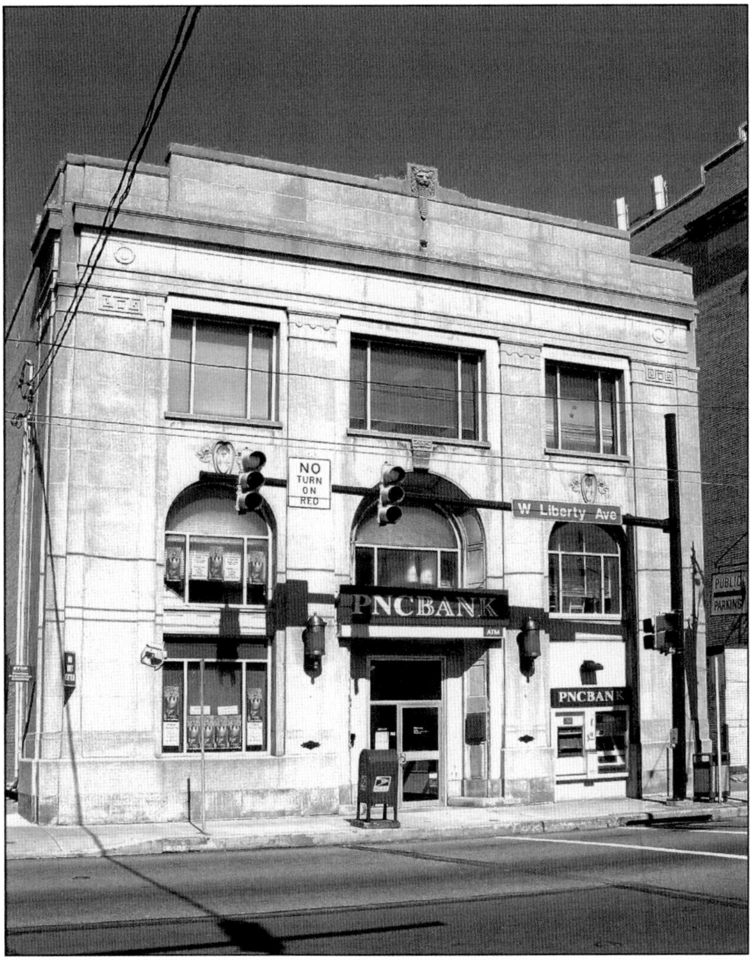

Dormont Bank opened in the Dormont Masonic Hall, 2880 West Liberty Avenue, in 1917. Its advertisements stated that "the location was very central and convenient to serve residents and businessmen of the entire South Hills district." In 1926, the bank, named Dormont Savings and Trust at that time, erected this fine building on the adjacent property at 2882. After a few name changes through the years, the bank is now a branch of Pittsburgh National Corporation.

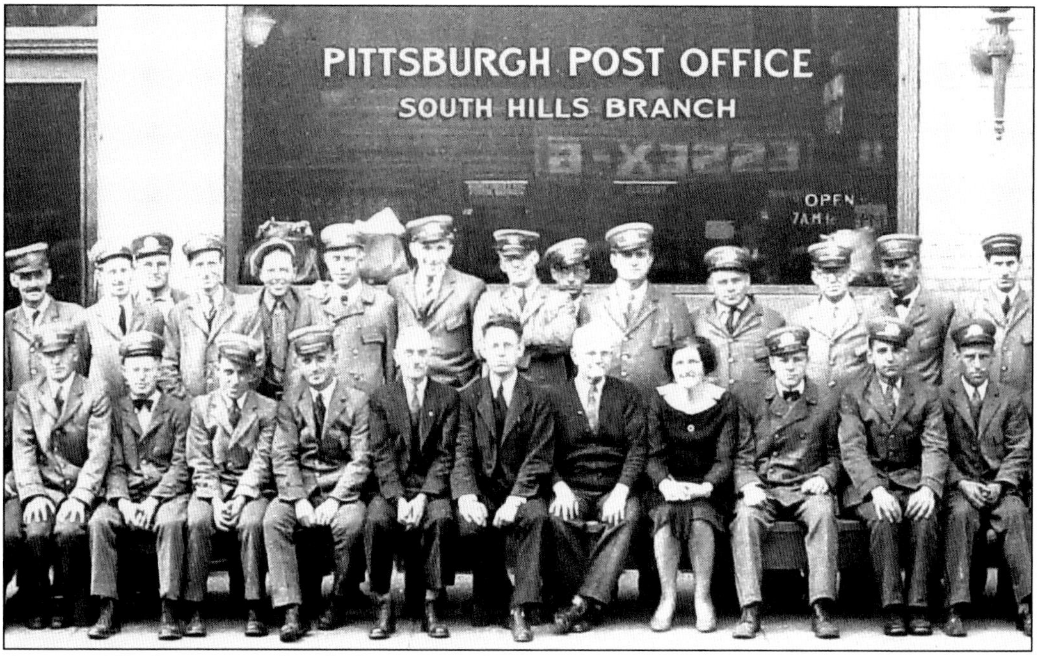

August Wilhelm, owner of Wilhelm's General Store at the corner of Tennessee and West Liberty Avenues, was the area's postmaster from August 15, 1907, until the opening of the South Hills Post Office on August 19, 1916. Located in the Dormont Masonic Hall at 2882 West Liberty Avenue, it served Dormont, Beechview, Brookline, Banksville, and West Liberty with its staff of 6 clerks and 14 carriers. Ceremonies dedicating the South Hills Post Office building at 3038 West Liberty Avenue were held on January 20, 1937. Assistant postmaster and Dormont resident Stephen Bodkin, who years later developed the zip code, was one of the main speakers. A ceremony renaming the building for Dormont's late congressman James G. Fulton was held in 2006.

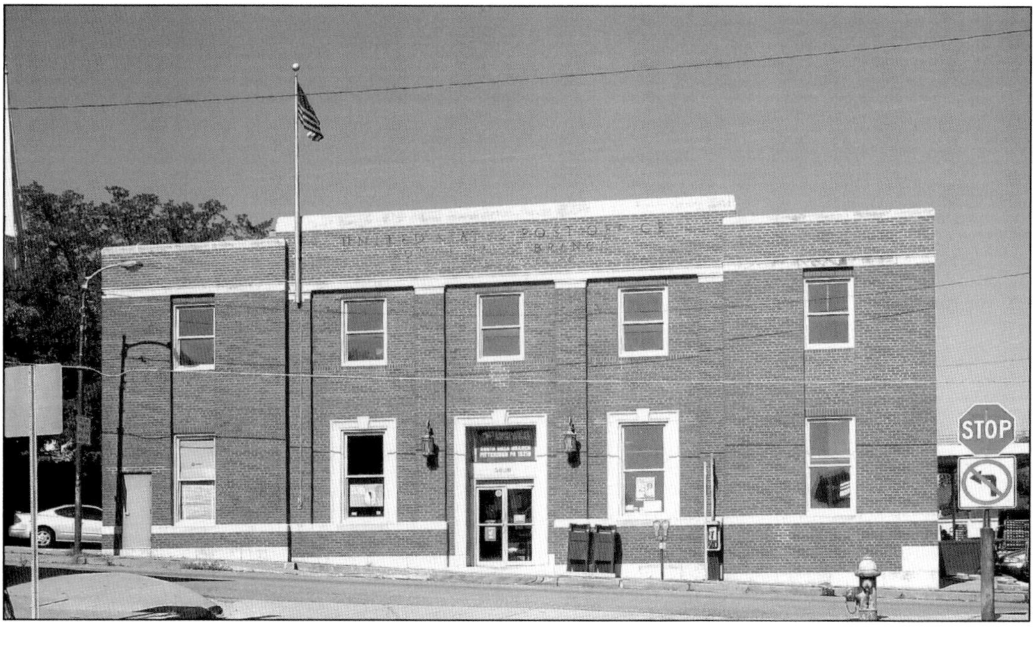

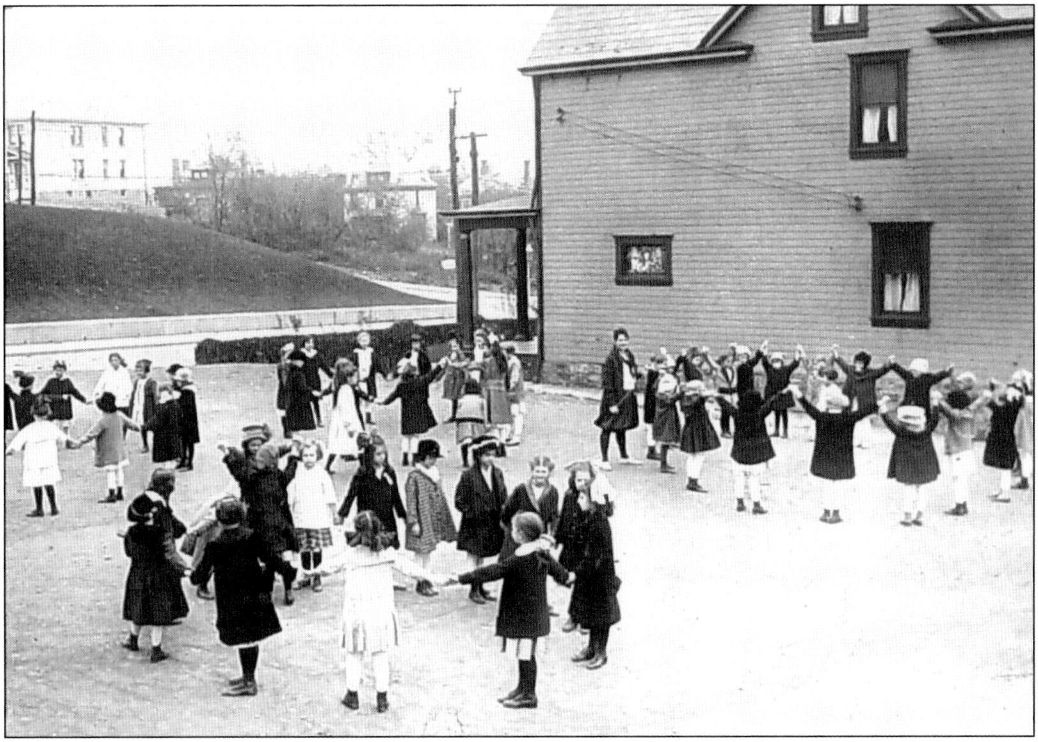

After Snyder School was razed, its site became a playground that was used by the school and the public until the firemen opened their new station there in 2003. Perhaps these little girls were playing games during recess between their classes in Dormont Public School across the street.

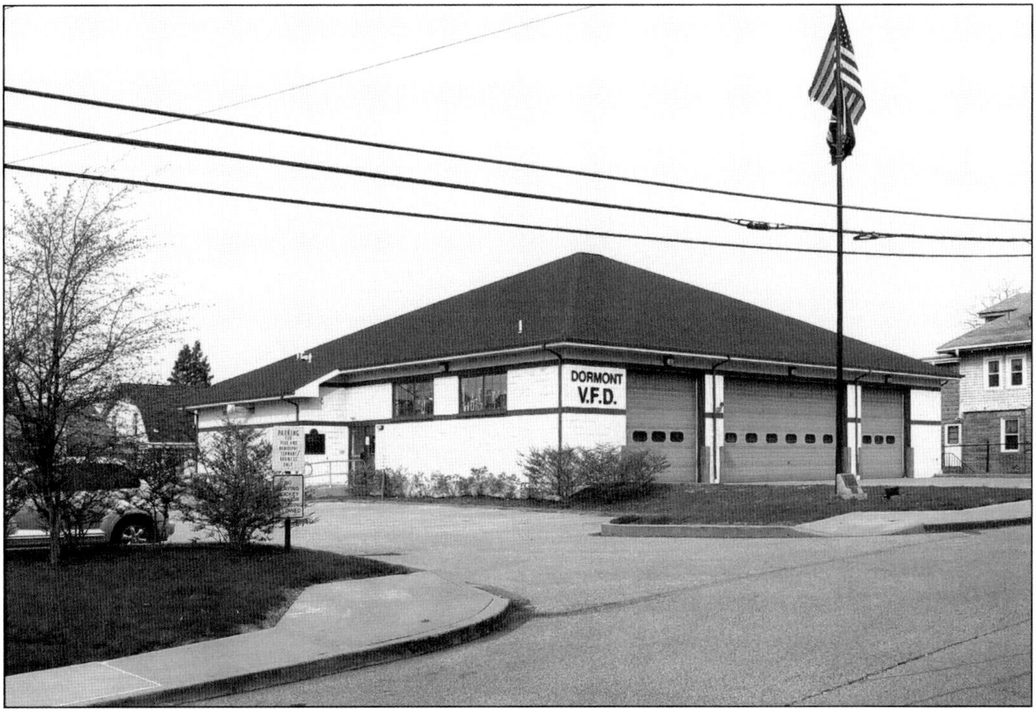

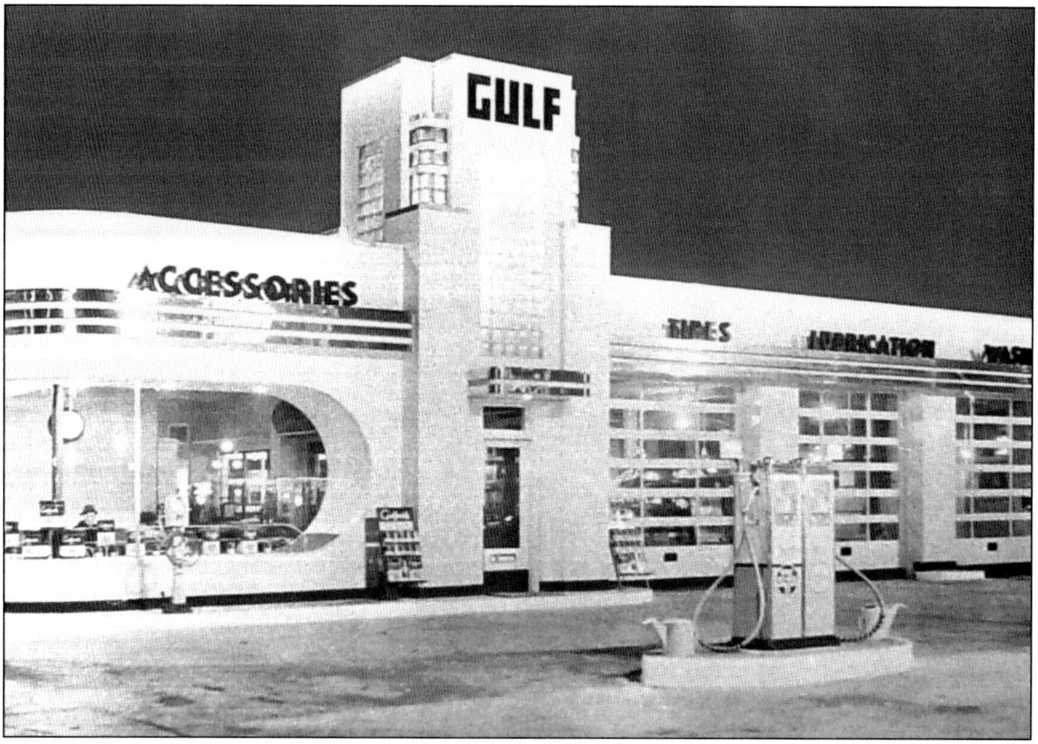

The Gulf signs on this art deco gas station, at the intersection of West Liberty and Pioneer Avenues, now are a bit of nostalgia left from the years Rectenwalds' was at that location. Ruffings service station has been there since April 1, 1962.

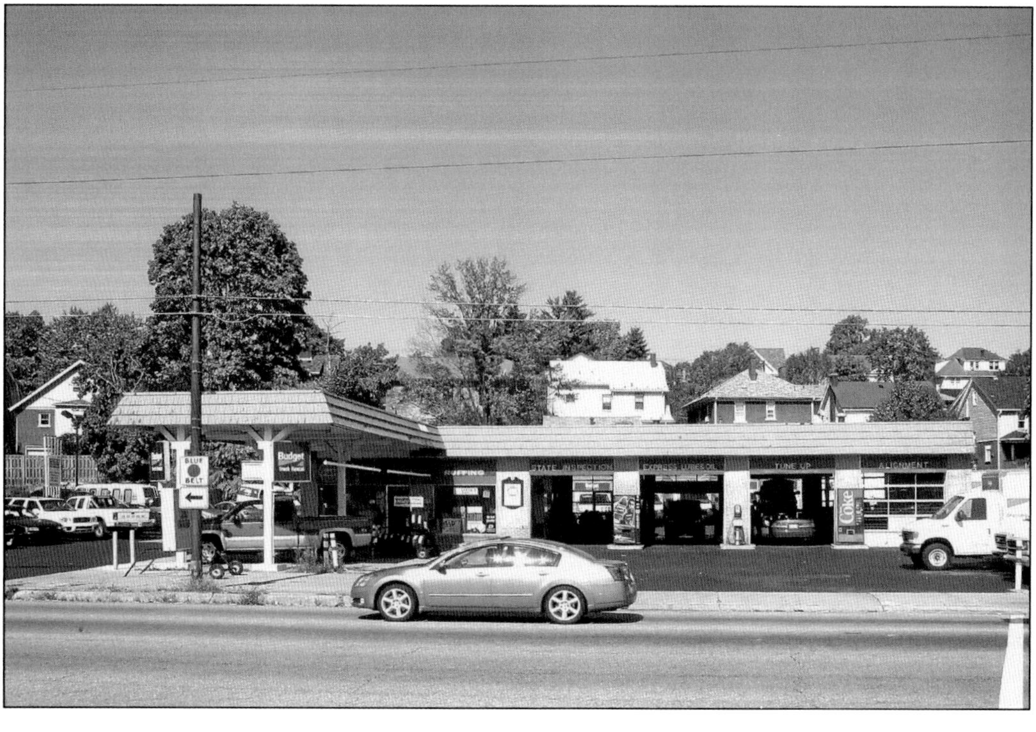

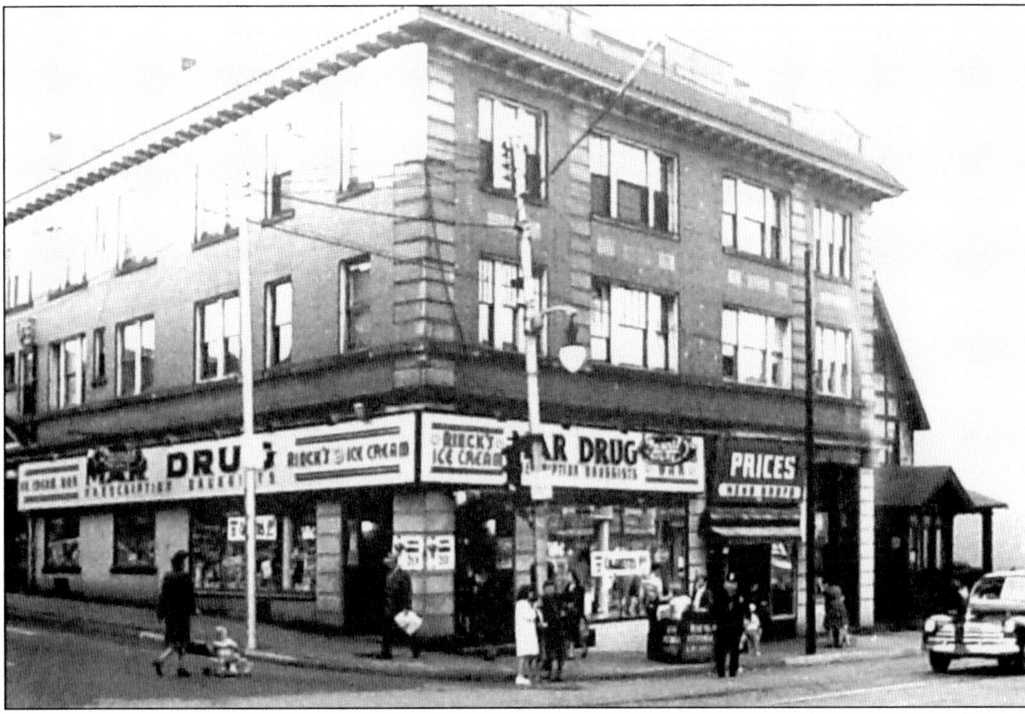

Mar Drug Store was at the corner of West Liberty and Potomac Avenues from 1923 until 1978. Some folks still remember the large pennyweight scale that stood outside its front door, while others remember the jumbo banana splits that could be bought for 21¢ with a coupon from a *Dormonitor*, the high school's newspaper. That corner looks very different today.

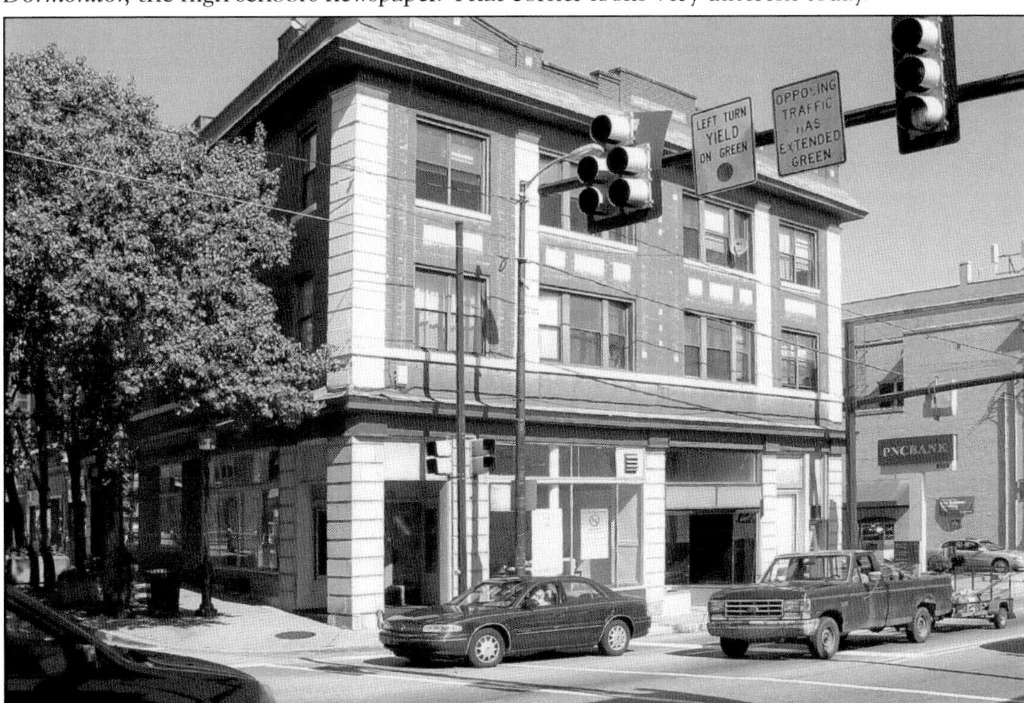

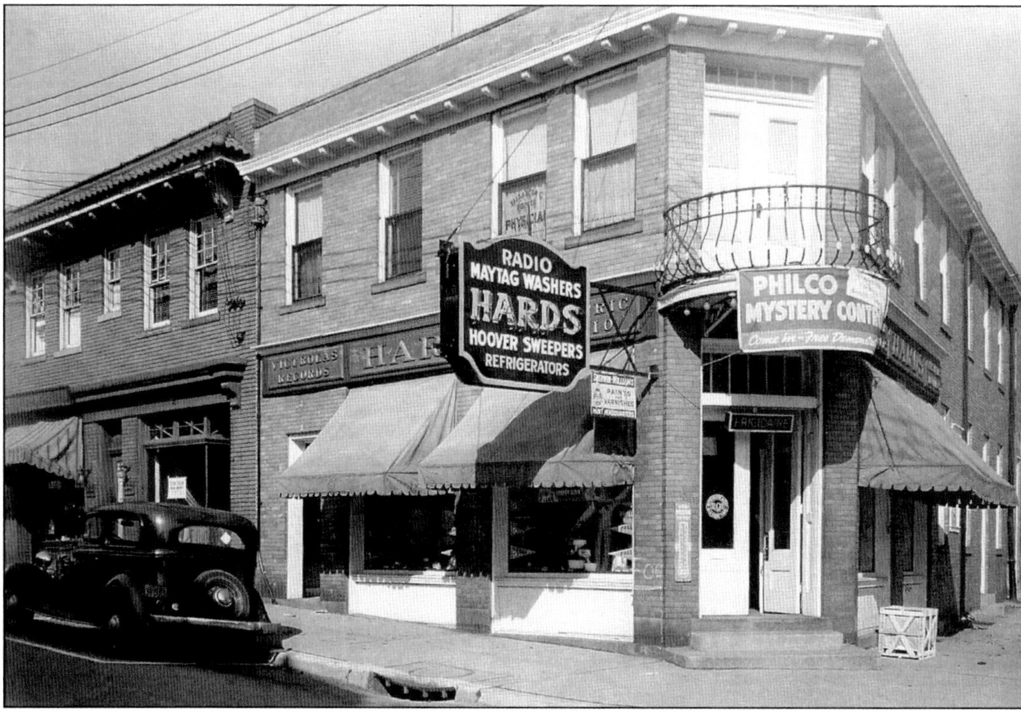

Through the years, this building at the corner of Potomac and Glenmore Avenues housed George Hards's Victrolas and appliance store, Harman Appliances, and Johnston the Florist. In 2006, the owners of the Dor-Stop Restaurant, which had been farther down Potomac Avenue for 25 years, bought the building, remodeled its interior, and moved their business into it.

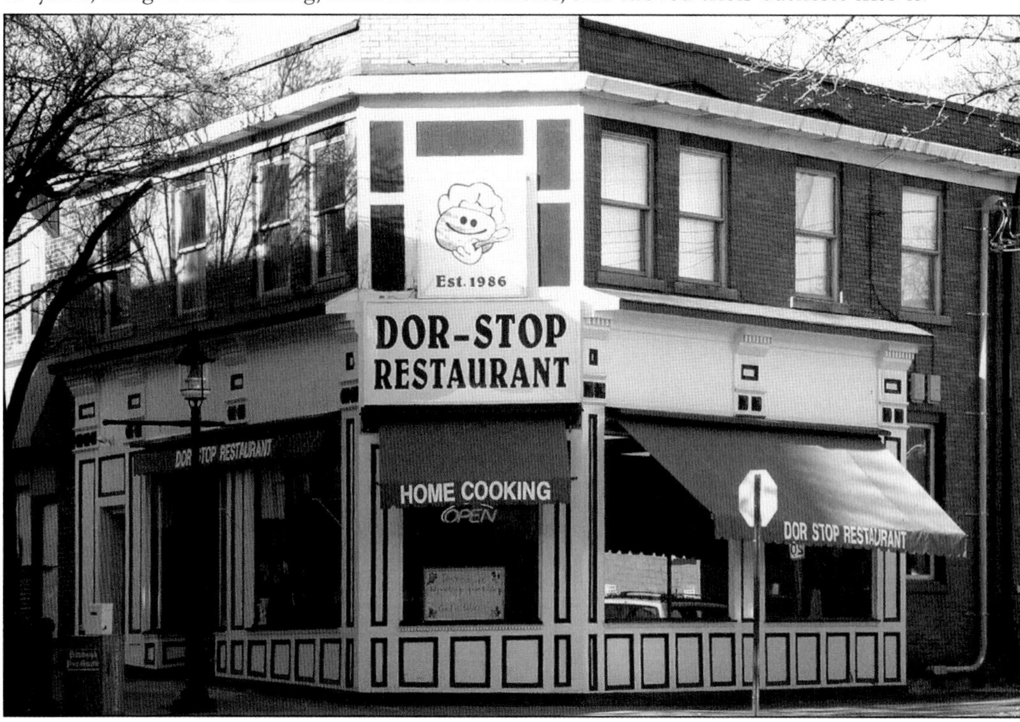

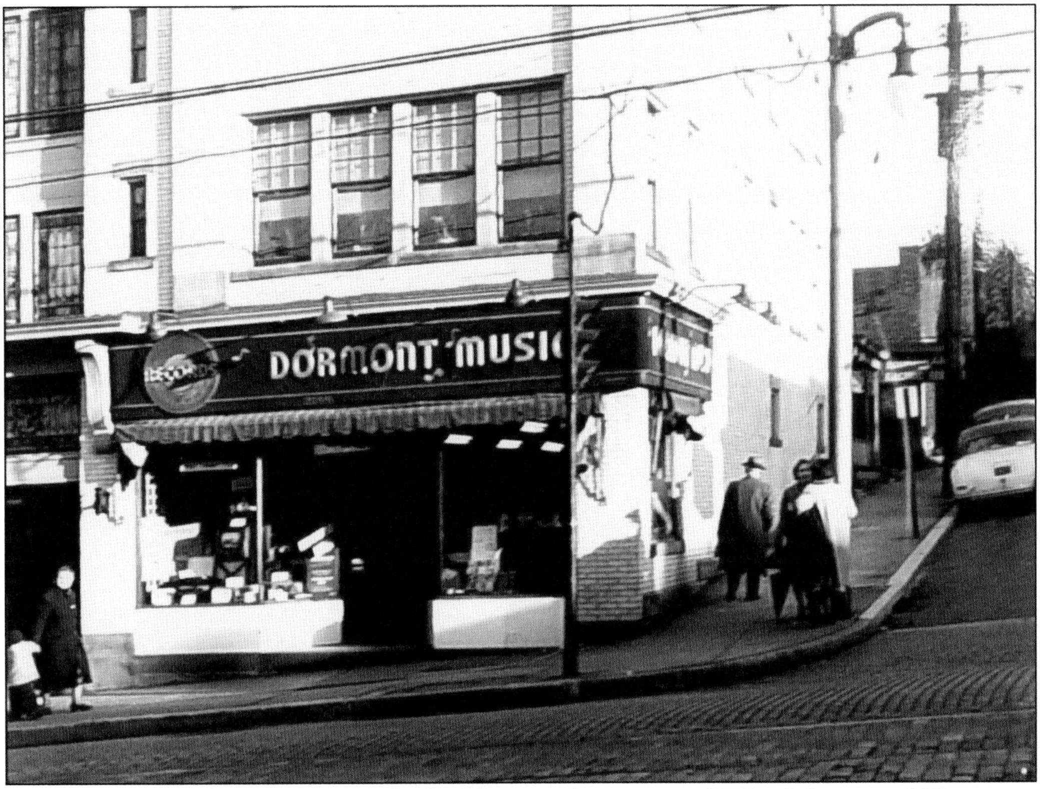

Ultimate Hair and Tan occupies the building at the corner of West Liberty and Tennessee Avenues where William and Betty Haseman had their music store in the 1950s.

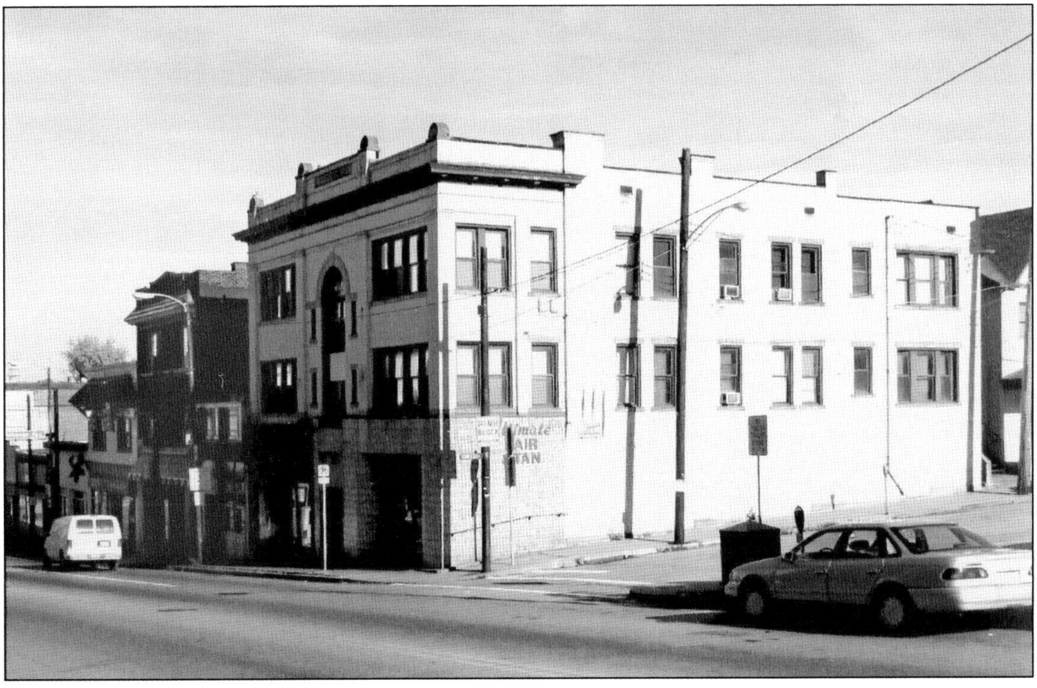

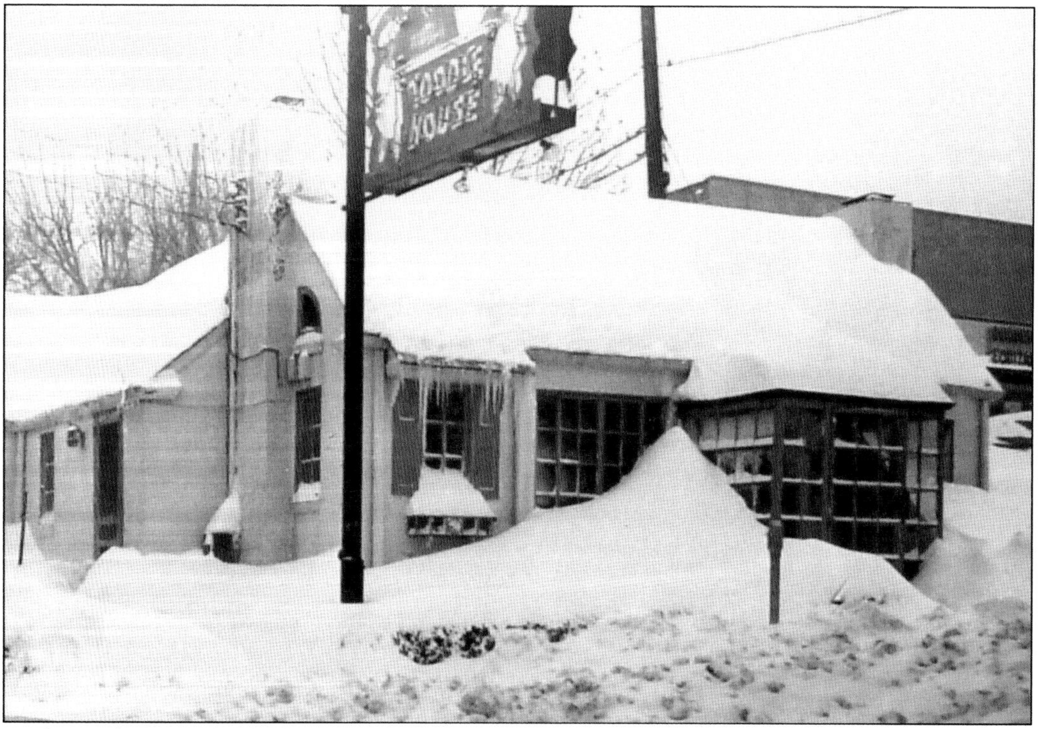

In the mid-1940s, the building that housed the Toddle House restaurant was moved from its location in the Pittsburgh section of West Liberty Avenue to the corner of West Liberty and Mississippi Avenues. It is almost buried by the big snow that covered this area at Thanksgiving 1950. Tom's Diner has been at that corner since 1983.

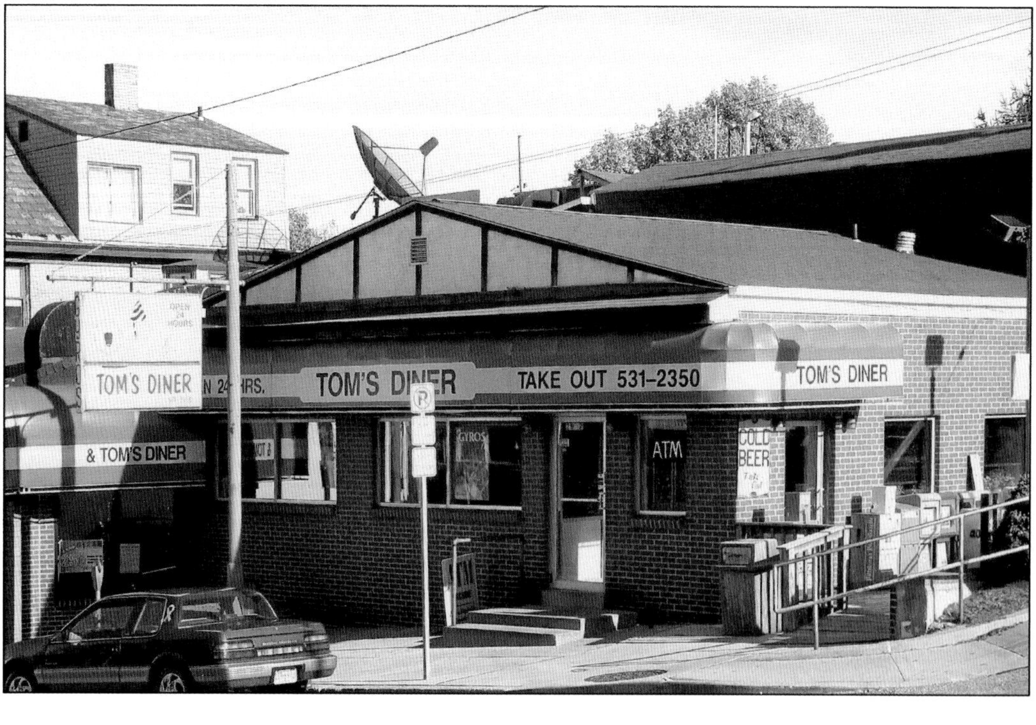

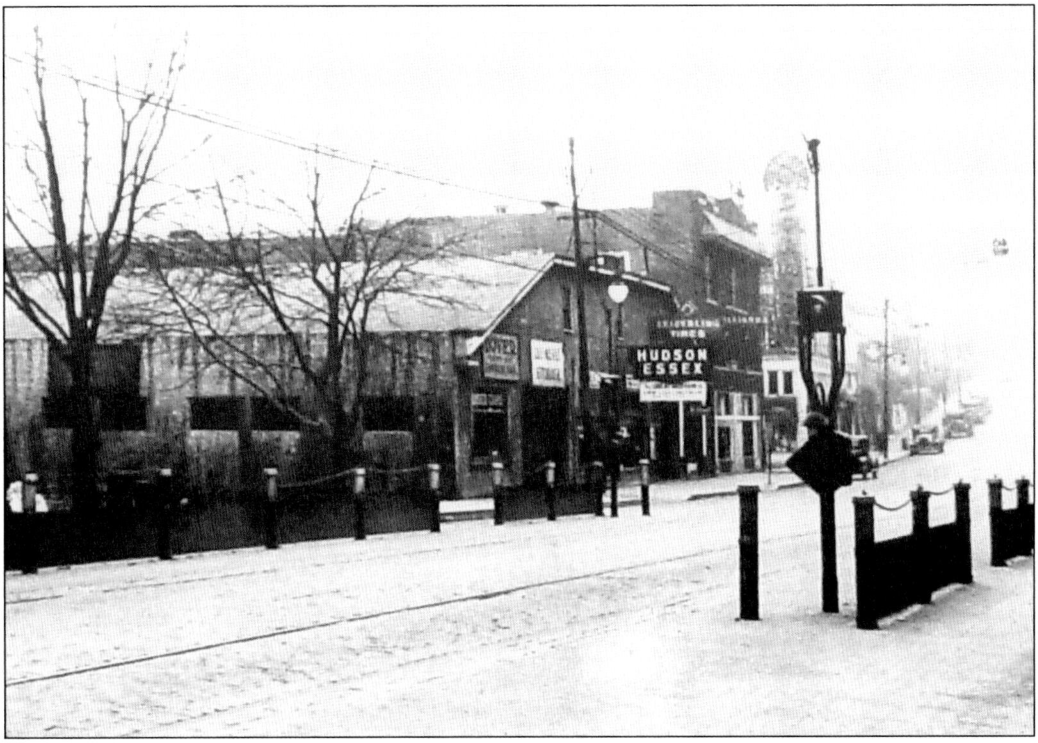

For many of the borough's early years, Hahn's Nursery was at the corner of West Liberty and Pioneer Avenues. This Exxon gas station is now at that location. Looking closely at the picture above, one may be able to make out the sign for the Dormont Theater that preceded the Delton Theater in the 1920s.

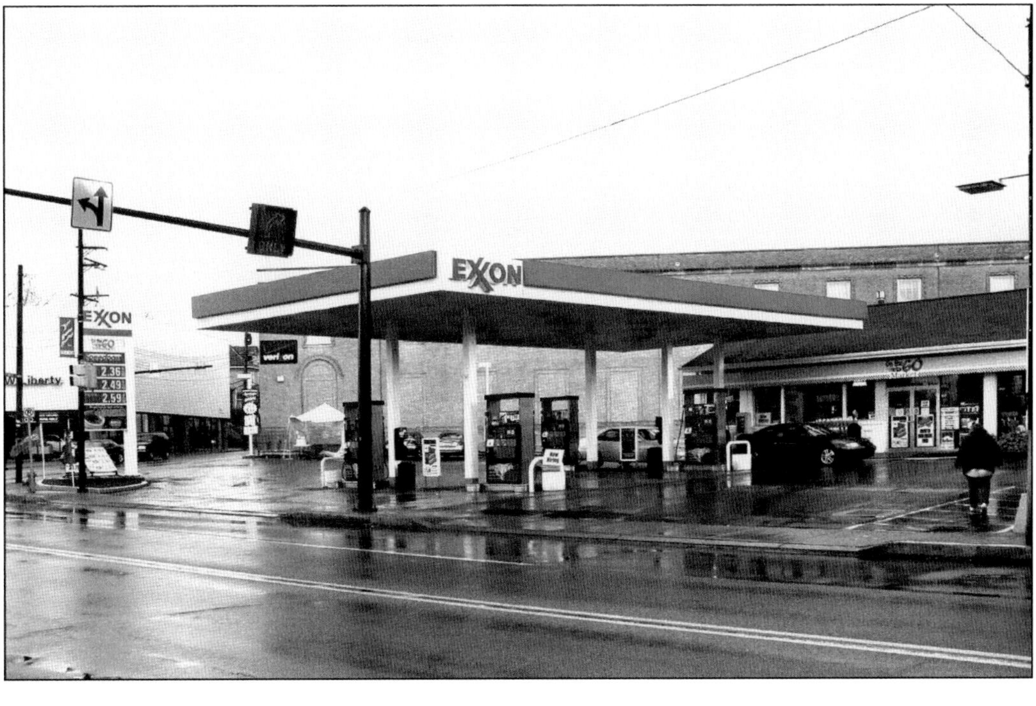

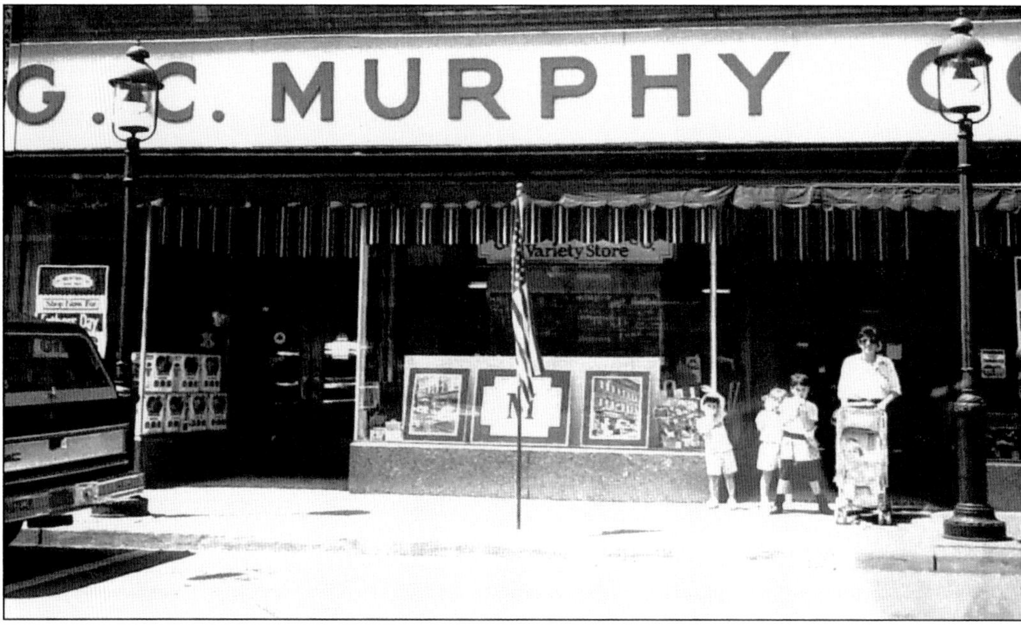

G. C. Murphy Company closed its Potomac Avenue store in July 1989. For almost 70 years, shoppers walked its wooden floors to buy sewing items, window blinds, school supplies, candy, and everything else that was sold in five-and-tens. The building is now occupied by Breakers, a billiard parlor.

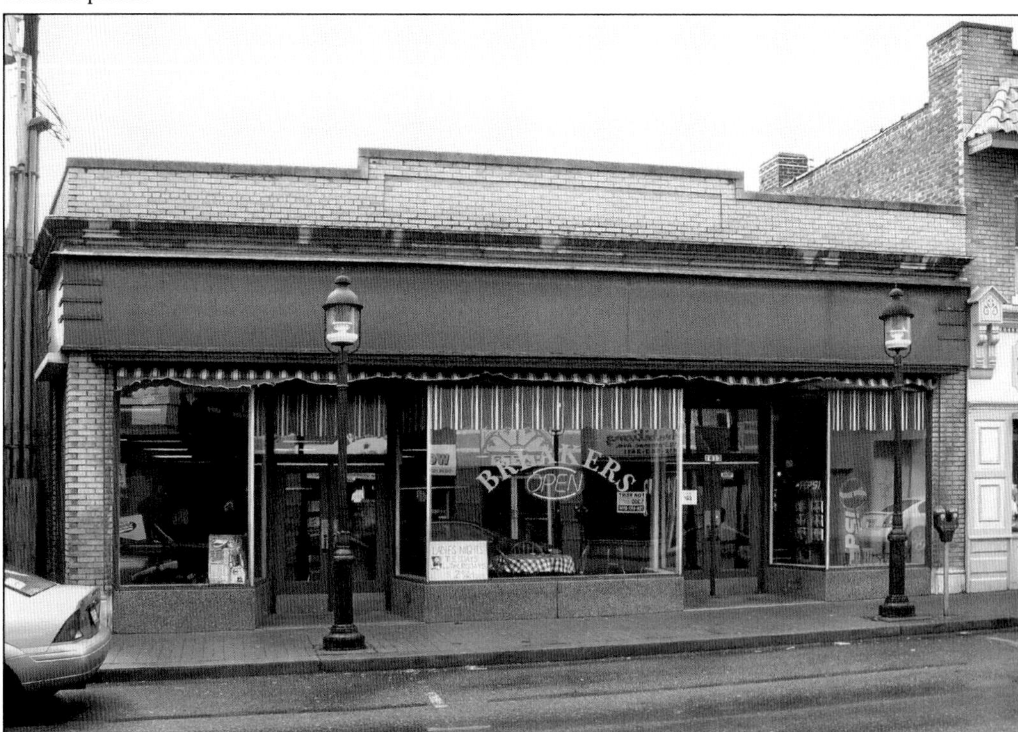

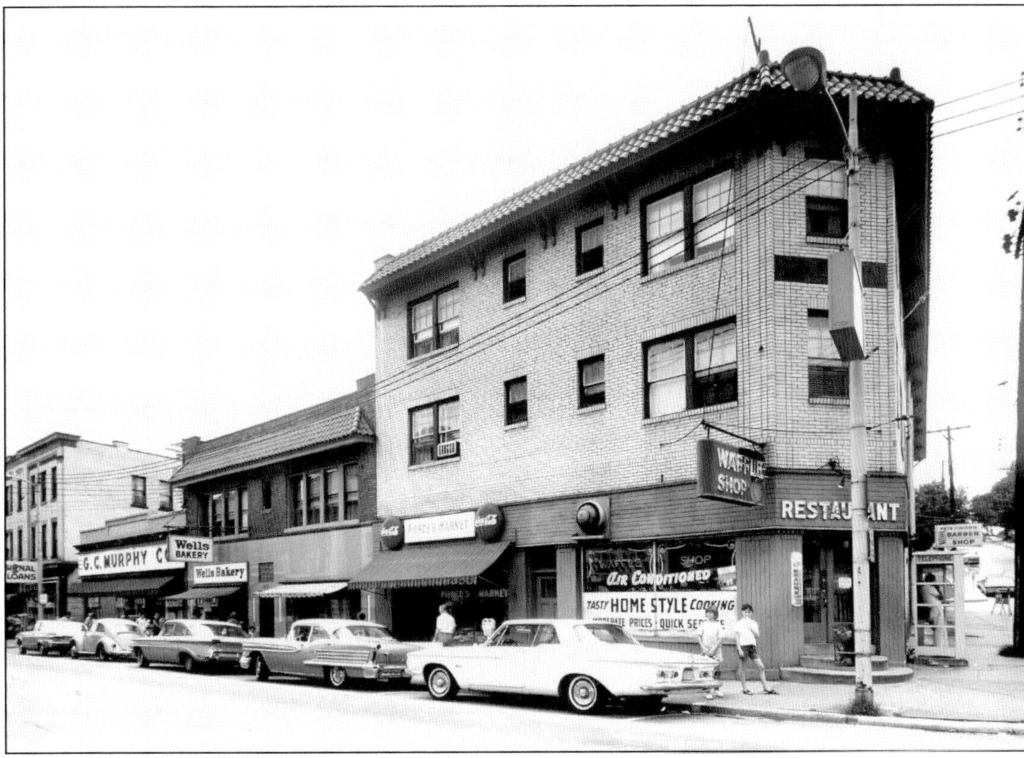

The steps leading into the Wasson Building at the corner of Potomac and Glenmore Avenues make it unique in the borough. The Waffle Shop was located there from 1923 until 1967. The Mekong restaurant serves Hunan cuisine there now.

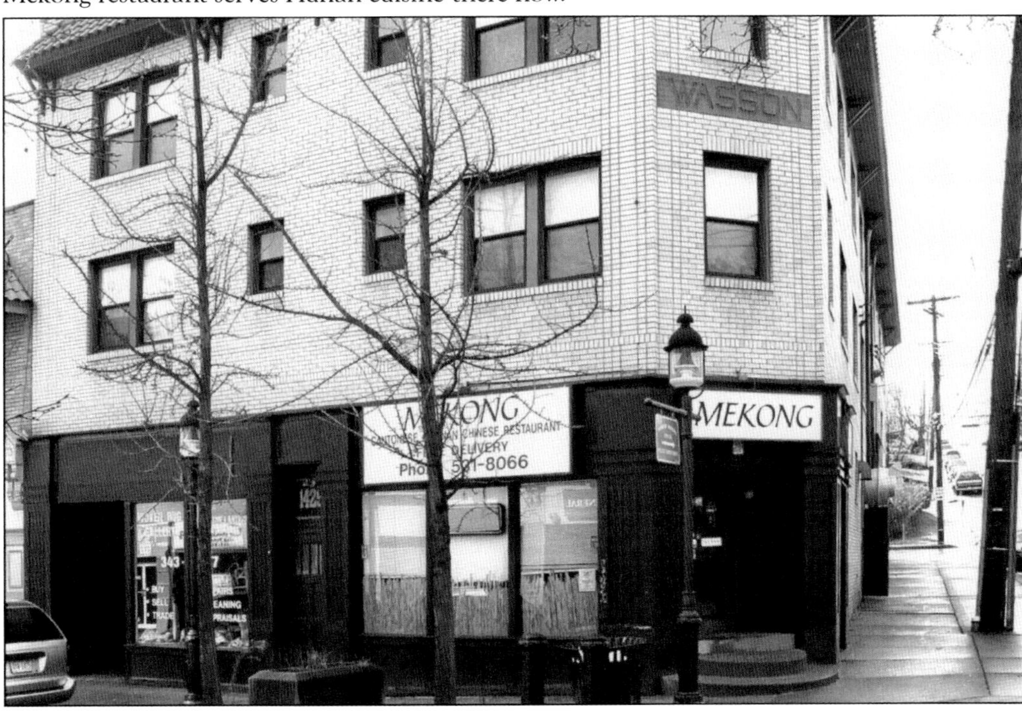

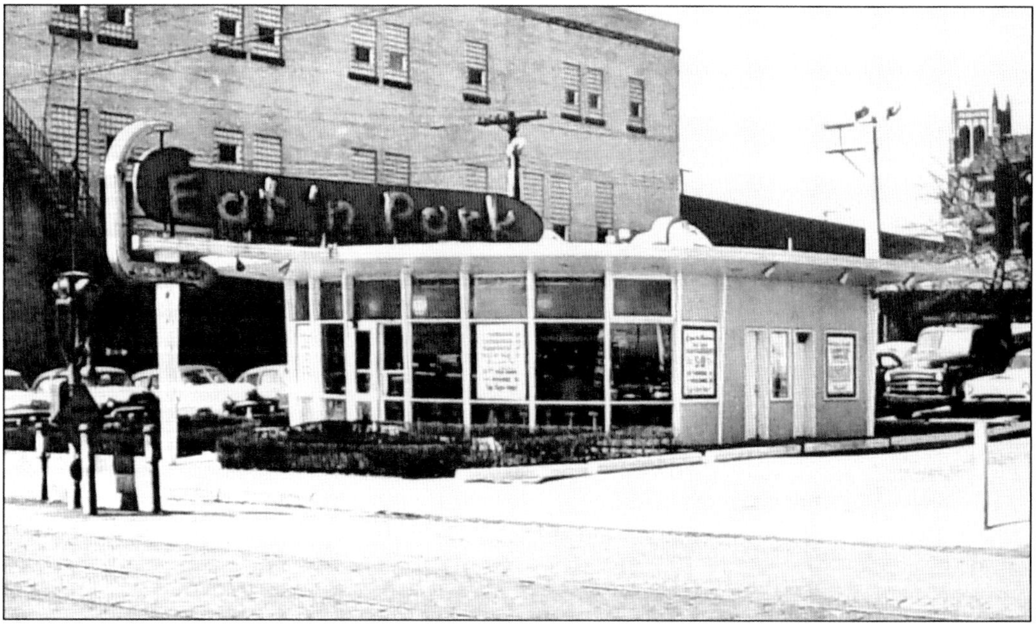

Dormont's Eat 'n Park, at the intersection of West Liberty and Pioneer Avenues, was one of the first in this area. During its early years, patrons could sit in their cars and carhops would bring their orders to them on trays that fit onto the cars' "windowsills." The remodeled and expanded restaurant is still very much a part of the borough's social hub.

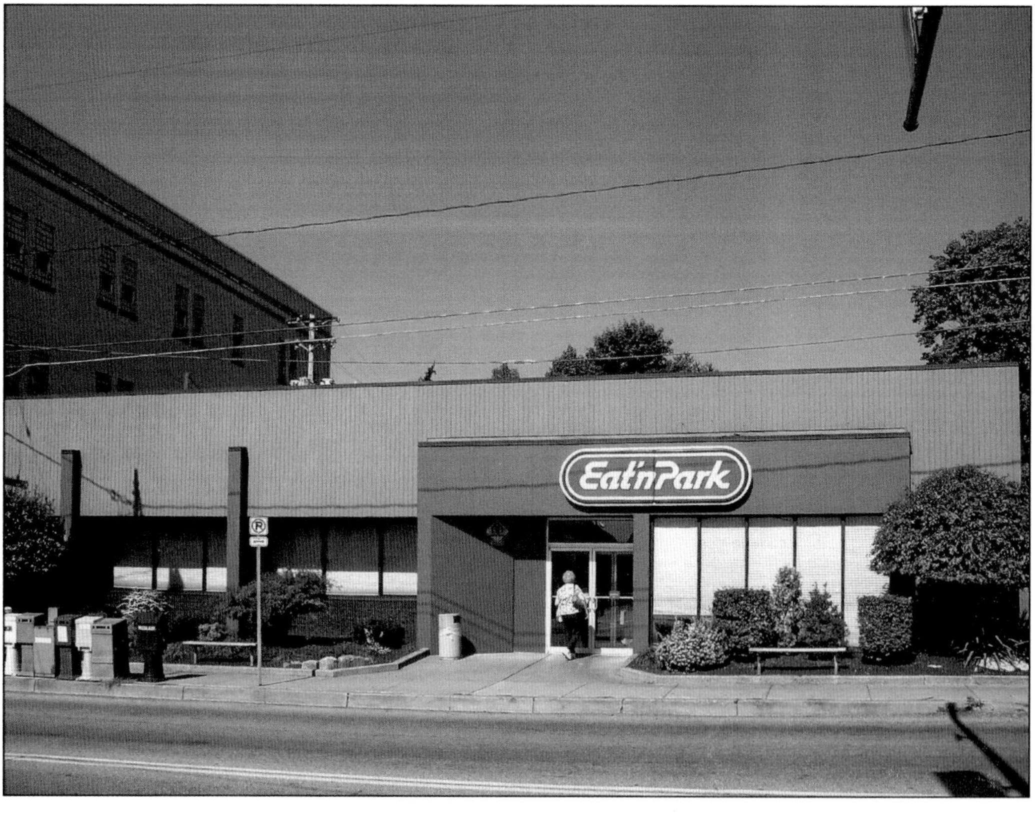

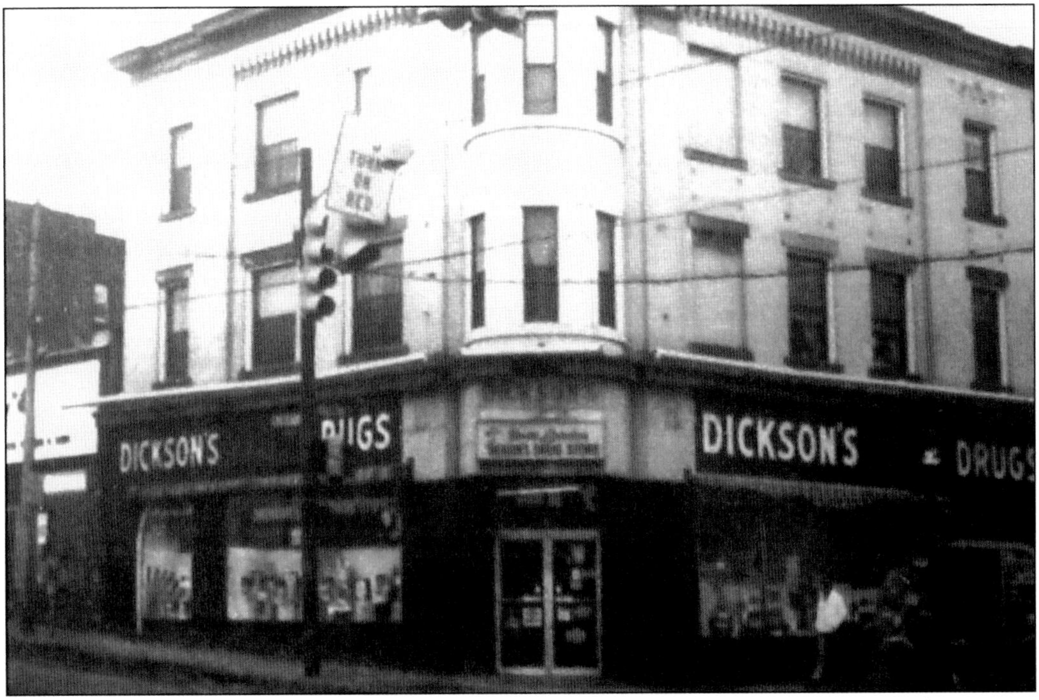

Heinrich's Pharmacy was in this building at the intersection of West Liberty and Potomac Avenues during the 1920s. Dickson's Drug Store was located there from 1936 until 1967. Besides being a place to go for pharmaceuticals, Dickson's had a section with booths where folks could sit while eating sandwiches or ice cream. The building's domed roof was destroyed when a bad fire burned neighboring buildings on Potomac Avenue around 1940. Dormont Florist is now at that site.

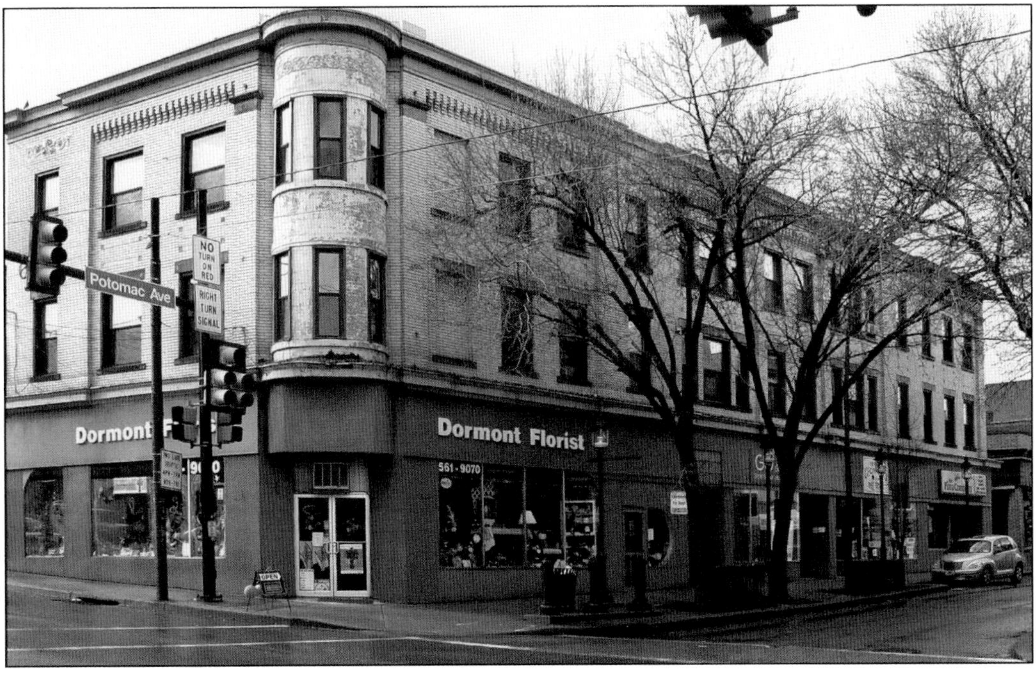

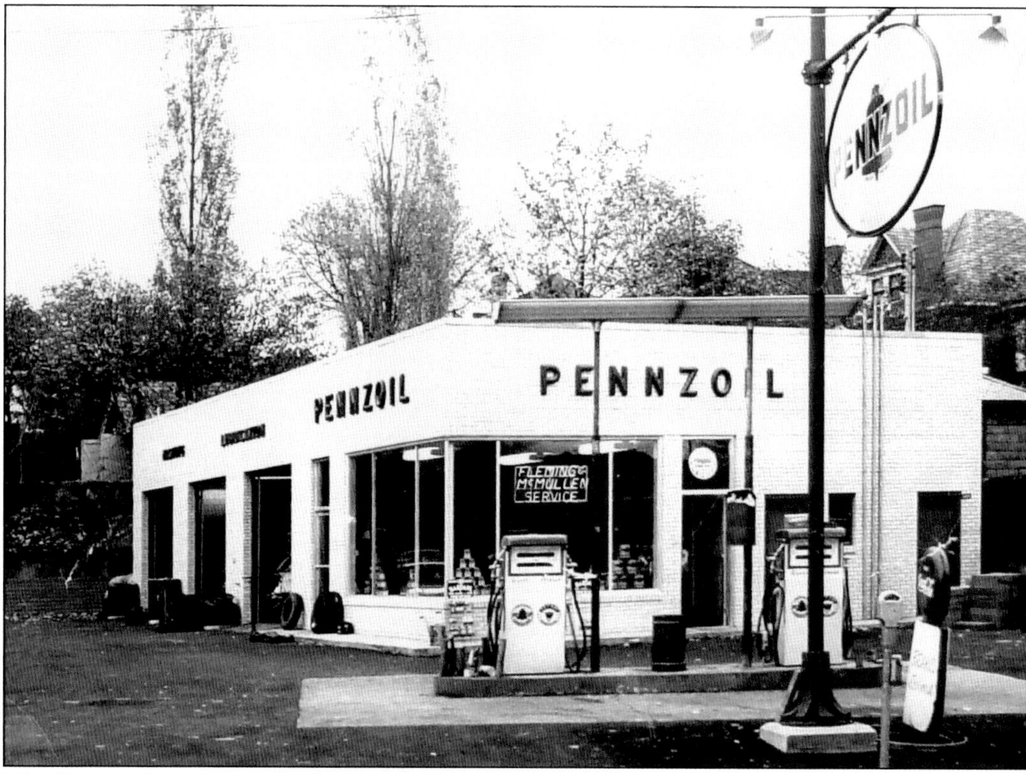

This Pennzoil station was at the corner of Potomac and Broadway Avenues from 1949 until 1978, when its popular owner Tom McMullen retired. Co-Go's has had a combination gas station/convenience store there since.

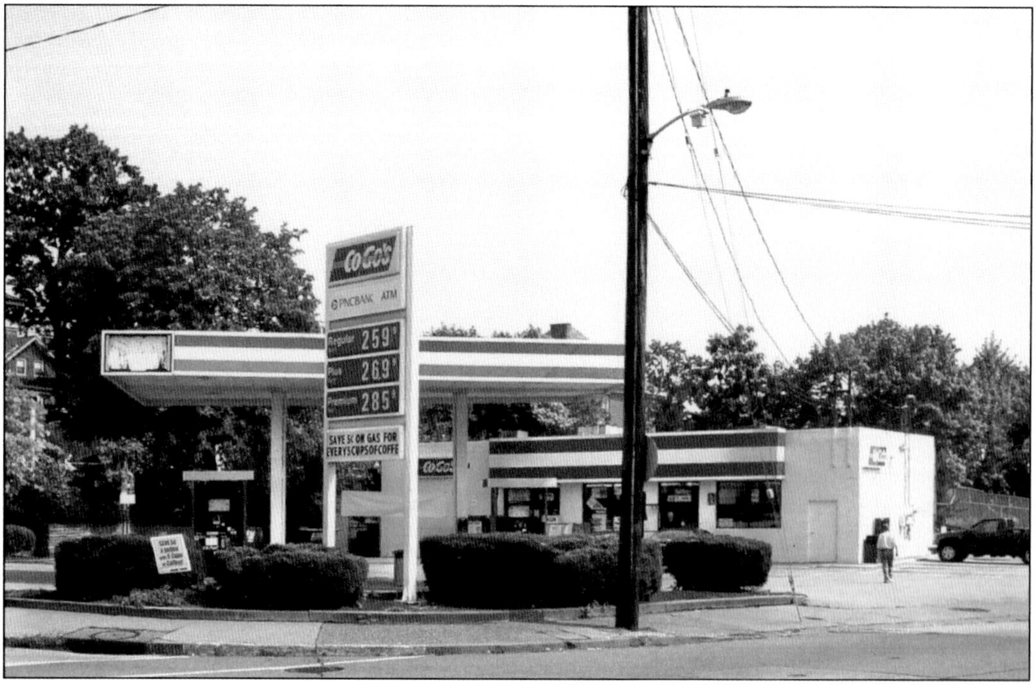

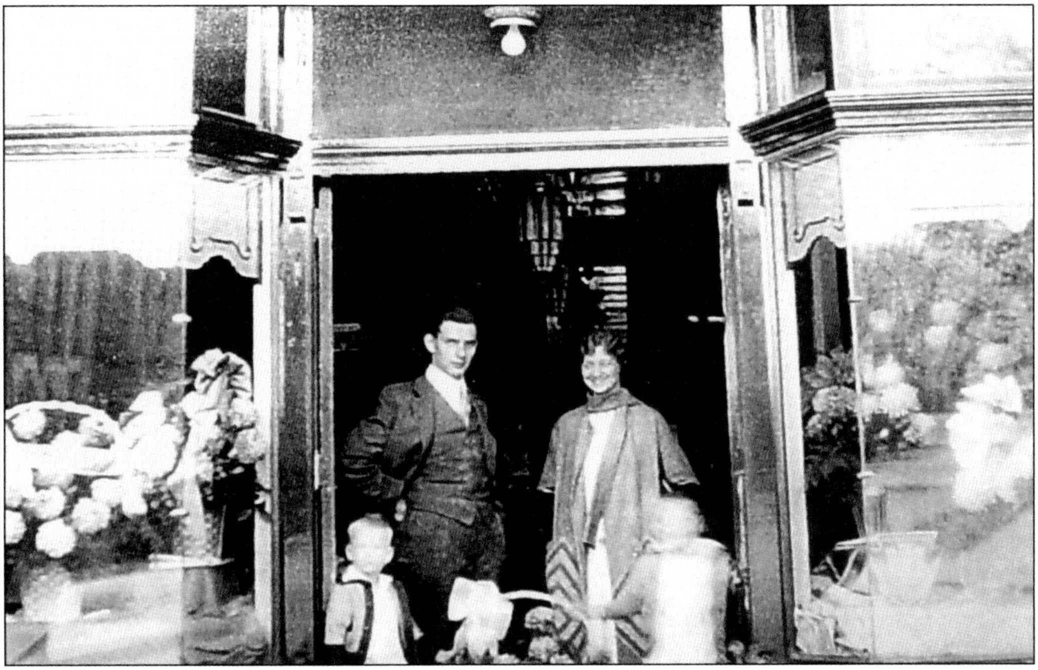

Wendel and Anna Fleckenstein and two of their children stand in the doorway of their first bakery, which they opened at 1503 Potomac Avenue in 1927. The Fleckensteins moved their bakery to 1451 Potomac Avenue, then to its present location at 1419. The store, now in its third generation of family ownership, was expanded in 2007.

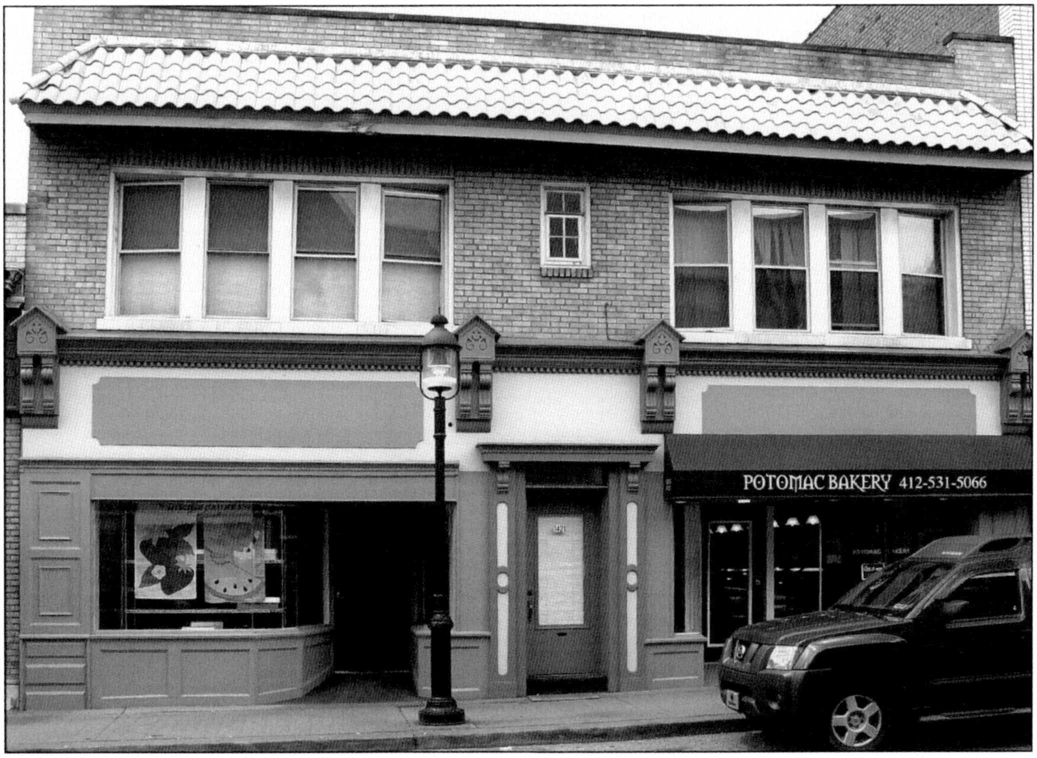

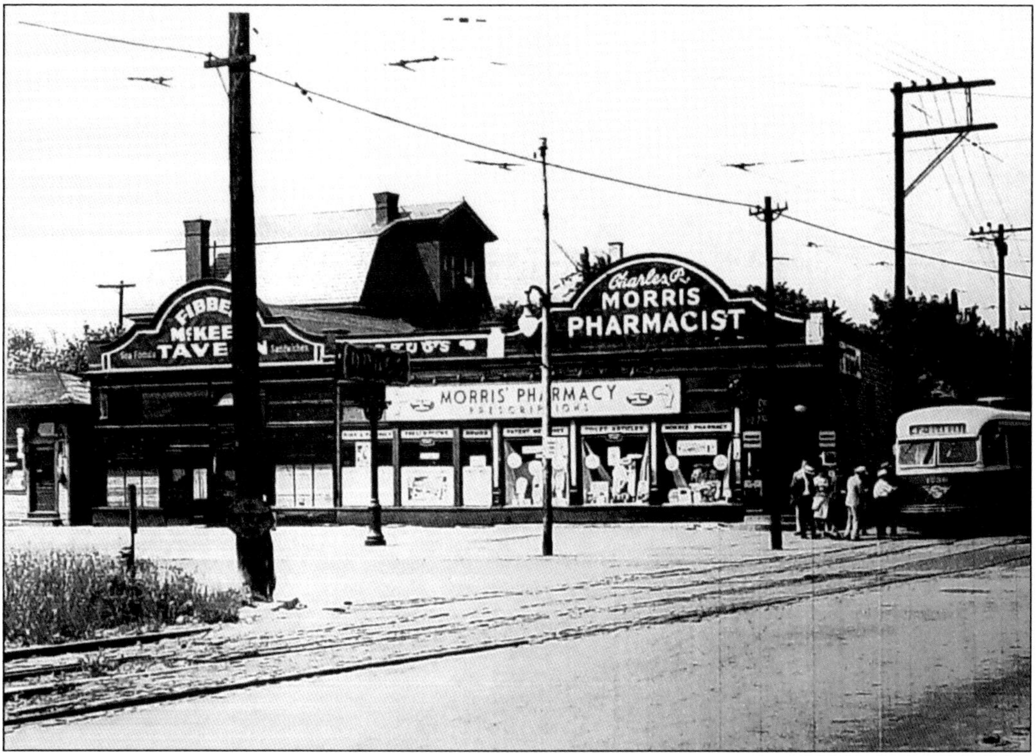

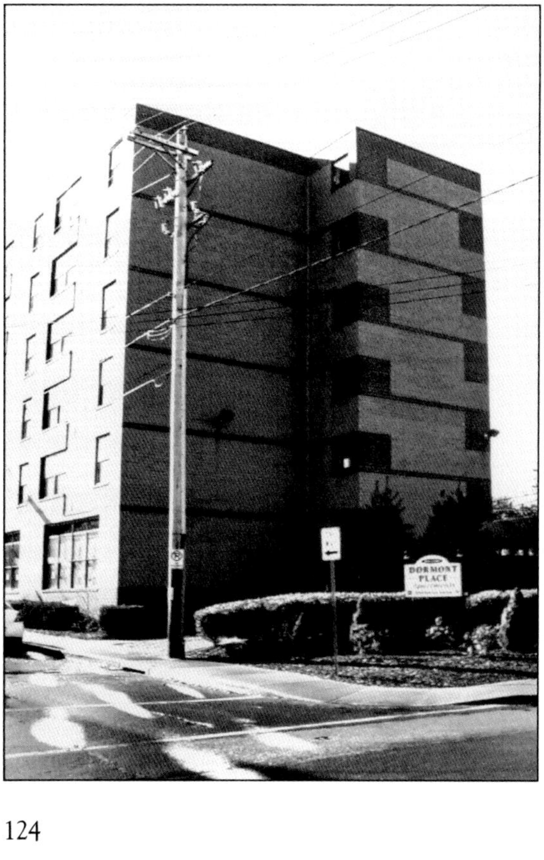

These businesses were razed when their properties were bought by Port Authority Transit. Dormont Place, a senior citizen high-rise, was erected on the left half of the block; the T station is on the right half where the pharmacy had been.

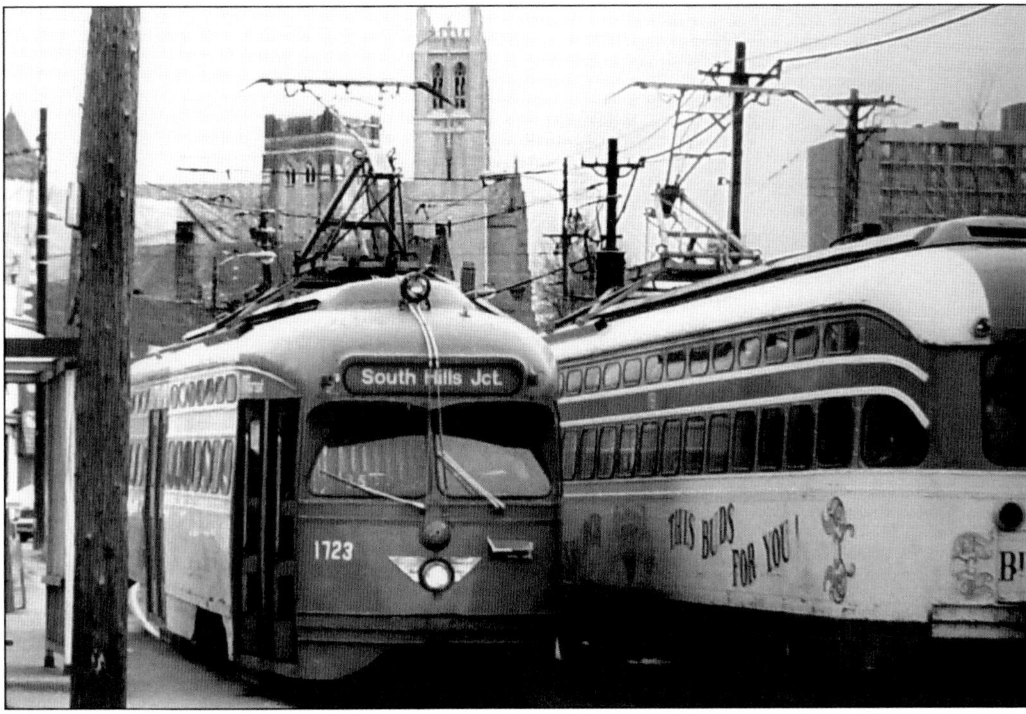

Pictured here are two of the last streetcars to ever run on the Dormont line. They are quite a contrast to the T trains that have been running there since the 1980s.

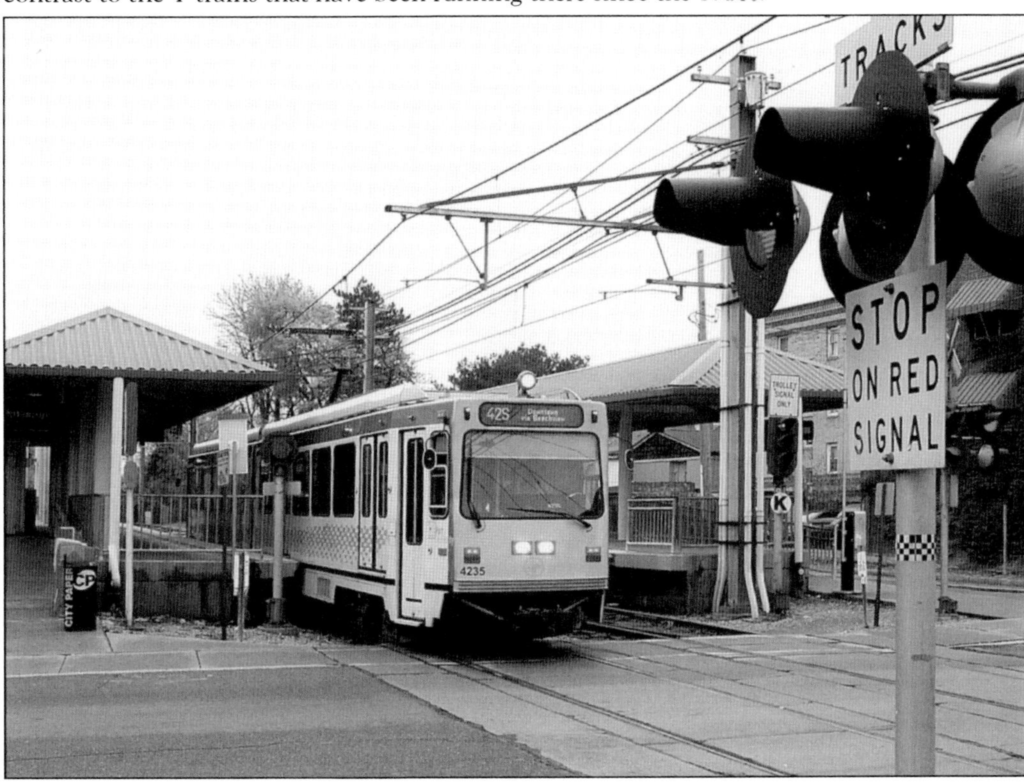

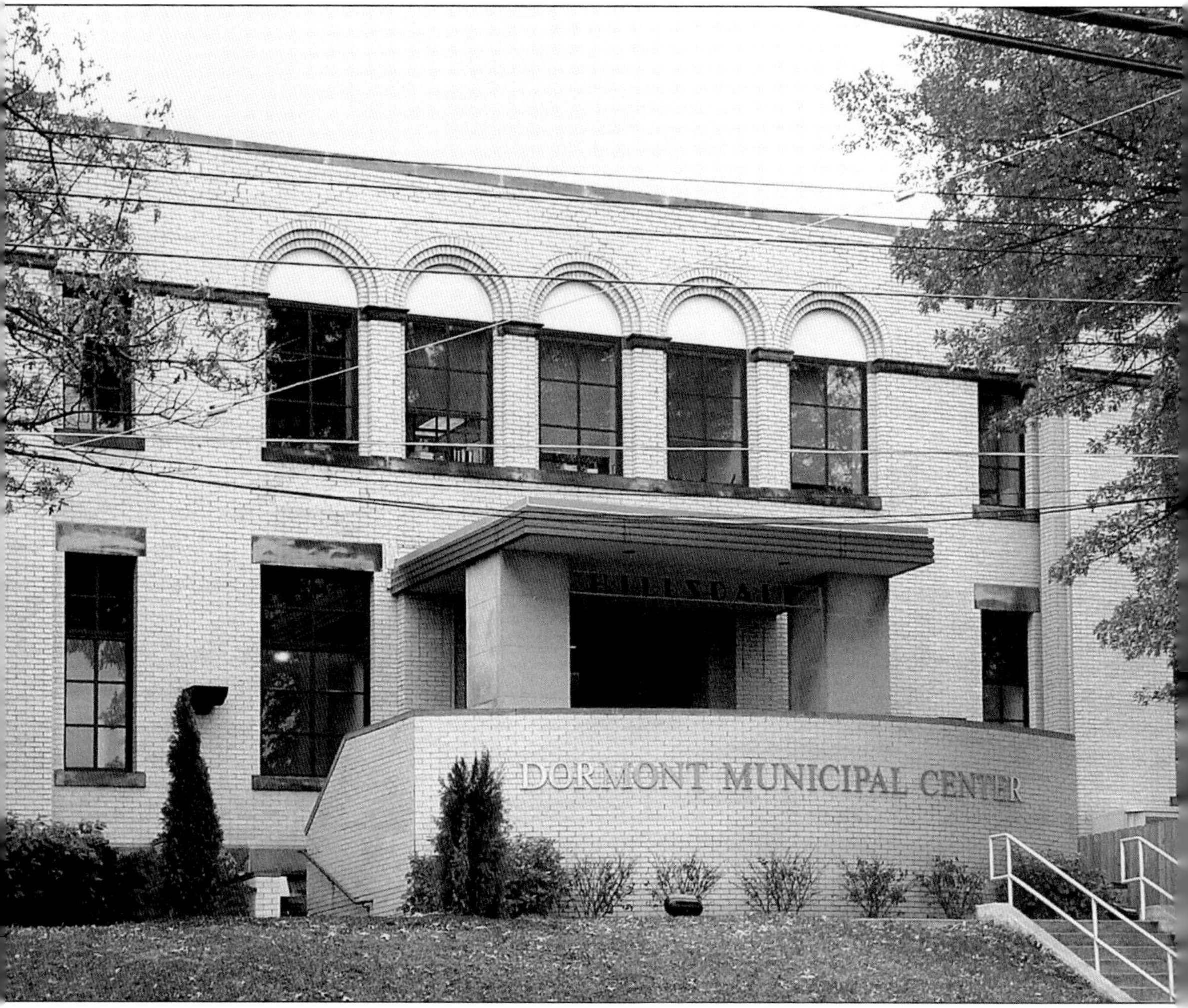

Since 1999, the completely renovated Hillsdale School building has been the Dormont Municipal Center. The beautiful marble center staircase and the lower-level room that once housed a small gymnasium and later the art room are about all that Hillsdale pupils might recognize. While the large gymnasium/auditorium remains, the ramp that connected it to the main part of the school had to be removed so that trucks could be driven into the back parking area, the former primary playground. The borough offices, police department, LifeSpan, and Dormont Historical Society are housed there. Office space, the large community room, and the gymnasium/auditorium are used for borough events or rented for classes and private activities.

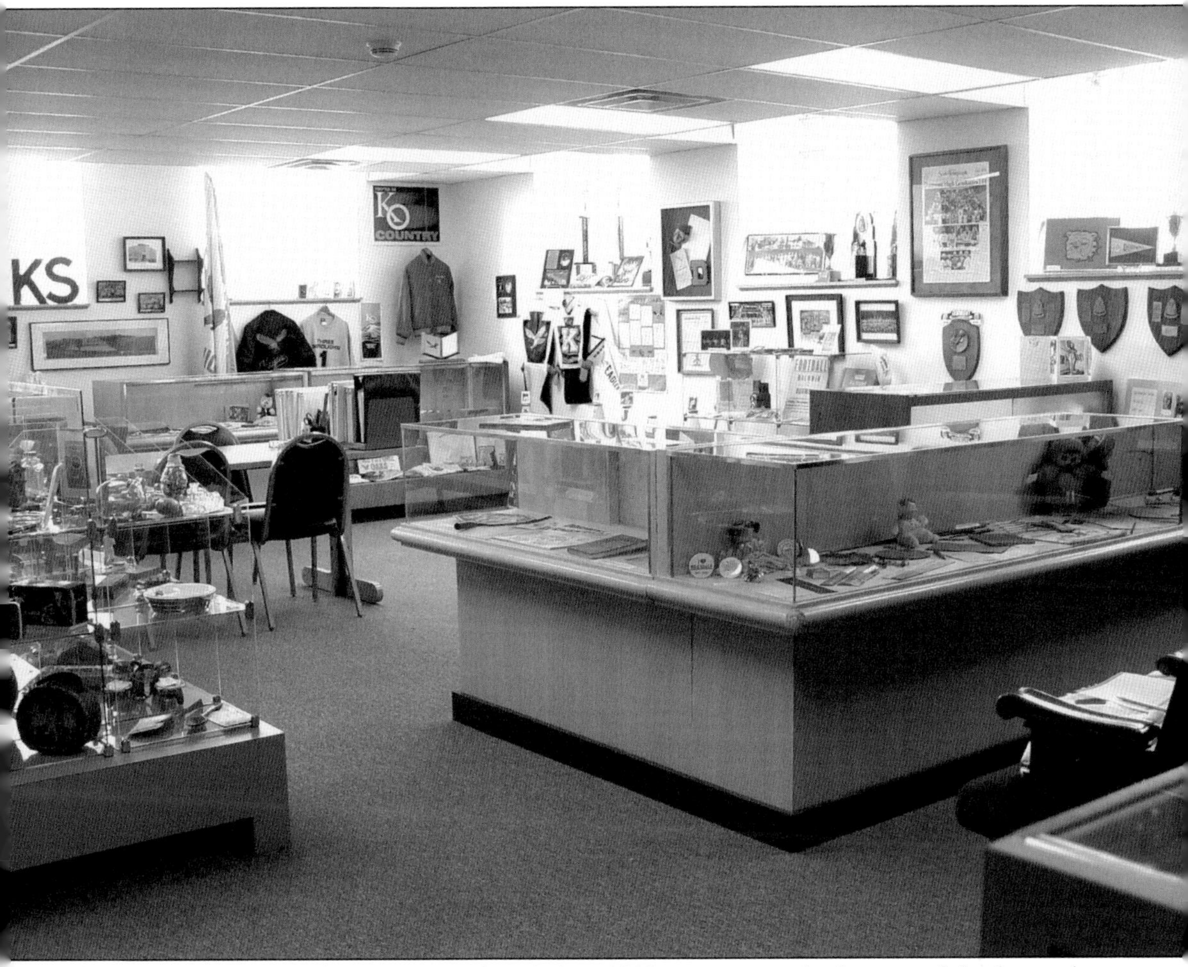

The Dormont Historical Society was founded in 1999 to preserve the history of the borough. After moving a few times, it was granted permission from the borough council to occupy a room in the lower level of the municipal center. Soon the collections were growing so rapidly that more space was needed to preserve and display the items properly. In 2006, the council allowed the society to expand into the room across the hall. In doing so, the members were able to incorporate the hall itself into the display area. The original room is basically a work area where volunteers are kept busy working on informational and picture files and updating the veterans register and residential, school, and business transfers. The rest of the space has been developed into a museum for displaying the vast amount of memorabilia that represents all aspects of Dormont's history. The generosity of past and present residents who have shared their memorabilia and memories and sent monetary donations has made all this possible. Do come to visit the museum, which is free and open to the public at scheduled times or by appointment.